A Will of Her Own

A Will of Her Own

Sarah Towles Reed and the

Pursuit of Democracy in

Southern Public Education

LESLIE GALE PARR

The University of Georgia Press ATHENS & LONDON

The paper © 1998 by the University of Georgia Press

in this Athens, Georgia 30602

book All rights reserved

meets the Designed by Kathi Morgan

guidelines Set in Minion by G & S Typesetters

for Printed and bound by McNaughton & Gunn, Inc.

permanence Printed in the United States of America

and 02 01 00 99 98 C 5 4 3 2 1

durability Library of Congress Cataloging in Publication Data

of the Parr, Leslie Gale.

Committee on A will of her own : Sarah Towles Reed and the pursuit of

democracy in southern public education / Leslie Gale Parr.
Production
p.   cm.
Guidelines
Includes bibliographical references and index.

for Book ISBN 0-8203-1932-5 (alk. paper)

1. Reed, Sarah Towles, b. 1882.   2. Educators—Louisiana—
Longevity
Biography.   3. Feminists—Louisiana—Biography.   I. Title.
of the
LA2317.R44P37   1998

Council on 370'.92—dc21   97-33400

Library [B]

Resources. British Library Cataloging in Publication Data available

For my parents, Jane Gale and Marion Parr

CONTENTS

ACKNOWLEDGMENTS

I cannot imagine having finished this book without the help of many people. My acknowledgments must begin with Clarence L. Mohr, Tulane University history professor, whose intellect, generosity, and friendship have enriched my life immensely. I cannot thank Clarence enough for the many hours he devoted to this study. His confidence in its value persuaded me that it was indeed worth doing, and his encouragement and enthusiasm helped me complete it.

Patrick J. Maney, professor of history at Tulane, also contributed enormously to *A Will of Her Own*. I am indebted to Pat for his perceptive critiques, which helped to guide the research and shape the work. His scholarship, combined with his wonderful sense of humor, made my task both easier and a lot more fun. Pat and his wife, Elaine, kept my spirits up when I was most overwhelmed.

Many other generous colleagues improved this book by offering astute advice and criticism. I want to thank particularly Sylvia R. Frey, Lawrence N. Powell, Elna Green, Pamela Tyler, Cita Cook, Jonie Griffin, and Betty Wood. My readers for the University of Georgia Press, Adam Fairclough and Joseph Logsdon, provided thoughtful and detailed critiques. Veronica Hill, Jacqueline Leonhard, Nora Marsh, and the late Fred J. Cassibry all generously gave their time to tell me about their lives and what they knew of Sarah Reed's.

I am also thankful for Bode Noonan's masterful command of the English language and her discerning editing ability. Bode's involvement in this project extended from its earliest beginnings to the final edit. I thank her for her assistance as well as for her friendship. Kim Wargo also put her talents to work on my behalf. Her computer and editorial contributions, including thinking of the title, were invaluable.

My family has been a constant source of encouragement. I am grateful to my mother, Jane Gale Parr, for unselfishly applying her literary expertise to this book, which I dedicate to my parents with love and thanks.

I would like to single out for sincere thanks Bill C. Malone and Gertrude M. Yeager, whose graduate courses at Tulane made a lasting impression on me. I also thank Bobbie Malone, Mark Cortez, Barbara Scott, Kay DuVernet, Deborah Schell, Richard Macaluso, Linda Martin, John McCusker, Richard Snow, and Christine Marlow. My work and my life would have been much more difficult and much less enjoyable without the kindness and support of Helen Psareas. I am grateful to Loyola University for giving me course release time to complete the manuscript. Special thanks to my colleagues in the Communications Department and the Women's Studies program at Loyola.

Librarians Beatrice Ousley and Marie Windell at the Earl K. Long Library at the University of New Orleans and Susan Tucker at the Newcomb Archives greatly facilitated my research. Al Kennedy at the Orleans Parish School Board provided important assistance on several occasions. I also thank Jennifer Manley Rogers and Sharon Ihnen, editors at the University of Georgia Press, for being so easy to work with and so good at their jobs. To Karen Orchard, director of the Georgia Press, I want to express my deep appreciation for believing in the worth of a book about Sarah Reed.

INTRODUCTION

Time after time, [Sarah Reed has] sought to override the wishes of the electorate of this community by annoying, humiliating and embarrassing the members of the . . . Board, the Superintendent . . . and her principals . . . in an attempt to impose her will, her thoughts, her ideals, her opinions, her doctrines and her methods of teaching on this community.—Orleans Parish School Board

If there is one teacher in the public schools of New Orleans . . . who is known for independence, courage in fighting injustice and oppression, and unwillingness to allow anyone to impose on her or on anyone else, it is, and has been for close on to 40 years, Mrs. Sarah Towles Reed. She has worked and written and spoken and fought for the rights of teachers against arbitrary and unfair action, rulings, decisions of Boards and Superintendents for more than a generation.—Ethel Hutson

Of all the professors and teachers I have ever come in contact with, you had the greatest effect on me. . . . Your impression stuck and left me with the memory of a very courageous, a very interesting, and a very free personality. You gave me a feeling of warmth toward others which I lacked, a feeling of respect for the rights of others, a feeling that all is possible through cooperation and friendliness and effort.—Perry Willis

When it came to longtime New Orleans public school teacher Sarah Towles Reed, no one was ever at a loss for words. To her colleagues, she was a "guardian angel." [1] Members of the Orleans Parish School Board, with whom she did battle for nearly fifty years, considered Reed "disobedient, argumentative, obnoxious, and contrary." [2] But the opinions others voiced about Reed were no stronger than the ones she herself expressed. Driven by an unshakable sense of justice, a passionate commitment to intellectual freedom, and a willingness to fight for her convictions in the face of powerful opposition, Reed embodied the finest qualities of indigenous southern liberalism during the first half of the twentieth century.

From the time she graduated from H. Sophie Newcomb College in 1904 until her retirement in 1951, Reed identified herself with the chief concerns of liberal reformers: women's rights, educational reform, the plight of labor, civil liberty, and racial justice. Her story presents an opportunity to reevaluate the strength of liberalism and the intensity of women's activism in the South—and in New Orleans in particular—during the first half of the twentieth century. Her public life illuminates the challenges that faced southern women, and it sheds light on forces that contradict conventional views about southern traditionalism and parochialism.

At a time when southern women were expected to defer to men, Reed led a largely female army of teachers into battle against an exclusively male educational establishment, fighting for better schools, better working conditions, and better salaries. Reed demanded equal pay for equal work for women in the 1920s, and she helped to overturn the prohibition of marriage for women teachers in the 1930s, when many states were adopting or reinforcing exclusionary regulations. In midst of the Great Depression, when most professionals shied away from unions, Reed organized an aggressive teachers' union that led the fight for educational reform. From the New Deal onward, with the South in the grip of Jim Crow, Reed defiantly worked with black colleagues, joining their struggle to secure racial equality in public school education. Willing to brave the wrath of local conservatives, she responded to attacks on her patriotism by championing civil liberty and academic freedom at a time when Cold War pressures frightened many liberals into silence.

During the years when Reed was most concerned with public activities in New Orleans, the city occupied a unique position in the South. As part of the former Confederacy with a history of slavery and a tradition of white supremacy, New Orleans was definitely southern. But it also was an ethnically diverse and predominantly Catholic port city. Heir to a legacy of sporadic labor militancy and a robust strain of women's civic activism, New Orleans was, in many respects, a very unsouthern city.

The influence of New Orleans and its civic-minded women was central to Sarah Reed's development and the shaping of her philosophy and career. Reed's ability to draw people into her causes and organize them depended, in part, on precedents established by strong New Orleans women who came before her. Although women in the Crescent City lagged behind those of the North in organizing women's clubs and associations, social feminism took root in New Orleans sooner than in most parts of the South. By the late nineteenth century, local women had developed a strong tradition of community involvement, working as volunteers in myriad organizations and as paid employees in business and education.[3]

In some respects Reed's life followed a pattern that had more in common with the experiences of northern women than with those of women elsewhere in the mostly rural South. Like Jane Addams, Julia Lathrop, and Florence Kelley of Hull House, Reed came from a middle-class background, graduated from college, made a commitment to socially useful work, and enthusiastically engaged in politics. The teachers' associations and unions with which Reed worked for most of her adult life provided a base of emotional and political support similar to that provided by Hull House. Florence Kelley, for example, rose to the position of state labor supervisor because her experience at Hull House had given her the self-confidence she needed to take on such a responsibility.[4] Likewise, Reed and other members of teachers' associations advanced to positions of leadership in their own organizations, developed reform strategies, created networks that gave them political influence, and used their collective strength to fight the men who held positions of power over them.

Like women in settlement houses, members of teachers' associations gained power from the encouragement of other like-minded women, who inspired activists such as Sarah Reed to become leaders. Reed's background also contributed to her sense of self-esteem, endowing her with the courage required to confront local authorities when issues of principle were in dispute. Although Reed had no aristocratic pretensions, she possessed the self-confidence that came with membership in a respected family with deep roots in the antebellum South.

At the end of the Civil War, many of the "good" families in the South found themselves either impoverished or reduced to a relatively modest scale of living. Economic necessity following the war was largely responsible for many well-bred young women seeking employment as teachers. Although teaching had long been considered a respectable occupation for "the better sort of southern young womanhood," it was the postbellum daughter's need to support herself or assist a struggling family that swelled the ranks of woman teachers. Economic necessity also fueled a drive for advanced education, resulting in the creation of new teacher training schools. Sarah Reed's parents did not escape financial difficulties, and it was, in part, her desire to help her family financially that drove her decision to enter a teaching career.[5] It was her desire for independence, however, that sustained her.

Independence in a woman was not an attribute that found much favor among the social arbiters of Reed's South. From the southern perspective, Reed, with her attractive appearance, lively personality, and good family name, should have been happy to accept her destiny and enter the ranks of southern ladyhood. Instead, she challenged the convention and its posture of docility throughout her adult life.

Reed also defied custom by assuming a consistently left-leaning political stance. Many New Orleanians considered her a "radical," a label she deserved within the context of her time and place. Her political commitments to women, blacks, and labor were enough to mark her as subversive, unsouthern, even un-American in the minds of conservative antagonists. Indeed, Reed's career illustrates just how radical a liberal might appear to a society joined to the twin idols of patriarchy and white supremacy.

Viewed from a more hopeful perspective, the record of Reed's accomplishments presents a valuable reminder that not all southerners shared the values associated with the "southern way of life." Reed's struggles to secure equal rights for women and blacks, no less than her insistence upon academic freedom, economic justice, and unionization, aroused intense opposition, but they also garnered impressive support at the grassroots level and among civic leaders, academics, and political figures. Allies in the community protected Reed from critics who periodically tried to discredit her. Teachers, members of women's clubs, labor unionists, and other concerned citizens rallied to her side time after time.

Reed emerges from these pages as a southern liberal whose concerns dovetailed with those of the most progressive reformers throughout the United States. She frequently stood in the forefront of social activism, occupying a minority position and seeking to rally others to her cause. While Reed had a plethora of opponents, she also had many supporters, and virtually all of them were southerners. Her story attests to the long tradition of civic activism among New Orleans women and also constitutes an important chapter in the ongoing story of southern liberals' efforts to transform their society from within. What is most surprising about Reed's public life is not that she was so often attacked, but that she was so consistently defended.

Resisting Ladyhood

Sarah Butler Towles was born March 8, 1882, at Ouida plantation, fifteen miles north of St. Francisville, Louisiana, the third of ten children born to Daniel and Sarah Ker Towles. Her mother was the daughter of Captain John Ker Jr., a lawyer from Natchez. The Kers, a prosperous and prominent family in status-conscious Natchez, boasted of an ancient Scottish lineage. The patriarch of the Ker family in America, Judge David Ker, completed his education at Trinity College, Dublin. He and his wife, Mary, came to America about 1790 and settled in North Carolina, where he founded and served as the first chancellor of Chapel Hill College, which later became the University of North Carolina. The Kers moved to Mississippi in 1800 at the request of President Thomas Jefferson, who appointed David Ker judge of the territory's Supreme Court. In 1801 Ker established a school for girls in Natchez. He was buried at Linden plantation, one of the showplaces of Natchez.[1]

Judge Ker's son, John, graduated from the University of Pennsylvania in 1811 and became a noted physician. He settled in Natchez and married Mary Baker, a member of a well-known Kentucky family. The Kers owned two plantation homes in Louisiana, in addition to their home in Natchez. The couple had twelve children, two of whom became distinguished educators: Mary Susan Ker (1838–1923) and William Henry Ker (1841–1902). "Willie" Ker served as principal of the Natchez Institute, superintendent of the Natchez public schools, president of the state Board of Education, and head of Peabody Summer Normal Schools. Willie's sister Mary Susan had a long teaching career in the Natchez public school system. Their brother John Ker Jr., who married Rosaltha Routh, was a lawyer and a cotton planter and Sarah Ker's father. During the Civil War, John Ker Jr. commanded Company D of the 31st Regiment of the Louisiana Infantry. He fought in the Battle of Vicksburg and was taken captive by the Union army.[2]

After the death of their mother in 1865, Sarah Ker and her three sisters went to live with their aunt, Olivia R. Wade, at Ellerslie plantation near St. Francisville. The four Ker girls were well educated according to the standards of their time; all of them attended boarding schools in the South. Sarah went with one of her sisters to the Sacred Heart Convent in Convent, Louisiana, and later transferred to the Millwood Female Institute in Jackson, Louisiana, from which she graduated in 1874. The Kers took education seriously. In 1873 Annie Ker, who boarded at Nazareth Academy, wrote to her sister Sarah, "I am applying myself diligently to my books, hoping to receive at the close of the year a 'Second Literary Honor.'"[3]

In 1878 Sarah Ker married Daniel Turnbull Towles, a member of a family as prominent as her own. Daniel Towles's grandfather, Dr. John Towles, a physician, moved to Louisiana from Virginia in 1804. He established Rickahock plantation in St. Mary's Parish, where he died of yellow fever in 1832. Dr. Towles's son (Daniel Towles's father), John Turnbull Towles, was born at Rickahock in 1815. A planter in West Feliciana Parish and member of the Louisiana legislature, he ranked as one of the largest slaveowners in the state. During the decade preceding the Civil War, the number of slaves he possessed varied between 89 and 118.[4] In 1861 he was a delegate to the state convention at Baton Rouge that passed the Ordinance of Secession, and he served as a major in the Confederate States Army.[5]

John Towles, like many other Louisiana farmers, found himself deeply in debt after the Civil War. In 1867 a plague of worms practically destroyed his cotton crop. By 1870 his fortune, estimated in 1860 to be nearly $200,000, had shrunk to only $5,000 in real estate and personal property.[6] During the war, Towles borrowed money from a Mrs. Groesbeck of Philadelphia, and after a poor harvest he offered her some land to help cover his debt. Land had little value in Louisiana at the time, and he realized that it would not go very far toward paying off what he owed her. However, Towles had no cash to spare, as he explained to Mrs. Groesbeck: "You may know I have no money for I will be obliged to bring my son Robert from Virginia who is now at school there. I have not the money to educate my children." [7]

Education meant as much to the Towleses as it did to the Kers, but their financial resources were scarcer. In the late 1850s the Towles family hired a tutor for their children, but the ravages of the Civil War made education a luxury they could no longer afford. John Towles was still trying to pay off his debt in 1872 when he wrote Mrs. Groesbeck's son, "The good men in the North ought to feel sorry and do all they can for us, for we are having a hard old time of it out here." [8]

After John Towles died in 1878, his son Daniel inherited little except Weyanoke, the family homestead. In the same year, Daniel married Sarah Butler Ker at Grace Episcopal Church in St. Francisville. Like his father, Daniel experienced little success at farming in post–Civil War Louisiana. Cotton prices plummeted during the late 1870s, and the family lost the plantation. [9] Daniel and Sarah and their first two children went to live at Ouida, the home of Sarah Ker's cousin Alice Wade, Olivia Wade's daughter. [10] Daniel never really recovered from the distress of losing Weyanoke and having to depend on his wife's relative. Perhaps to help save his dignity, Alice Wade entered into a legal contract with Daniel in 1886, agreeing to pay him $150 a year plus board and lodging for his growing family in return "for good and efficient services rendered and to be rendered during the present year in managing her affairs," particularly her planting interests at Ouida. [11]

Ouida was not one of the grand plantation houses built in the St. Francisville area before the Civil War. Cotton and sugarcane flourished in West Feliciana Parish in the antebellum years, making the parish one of the richest in the state and giving rise to such showplaces as Rosedown, Oakley, and Greenwood plantations. Instead, Ouida was a modest 320-acre farm with an attractive two-story house sitting on a small hilltop. Alice Wade, with Daniel's help, managed to make Ouida profitable enough to support the three adults and seven children who lived there. Of Daniel and Sarah's ten children, three died in infancy. The others, in order of birth, were Alice, John, Sarah, Daniel, Roberta, Katherine, and Anne.

In keeping with tradition on both sides of the family, the Towleses made sure that their children received an education despite their meager financial resources. They hired a tutor to board at Ouida, set up a classroom in the house, and invited their neighbors' children to join them. The school at Ouida remained the only one in the parish for several years before it was housed in its own building. Sarah remembered being in its primer class and longing to switch her copy of *McGuffey's First Reader* for the bigger and more challenging *Scholar's Home Companion.*[12] The Towleses instilled in their children a respect for education and an ambition to excel. "A high standard of education was a family tradition," one family member observed, "and the children were never allowed to forget this."[13]

The family lived in relative isolation at Ouida. Roads were poor and transportation primitive. One year it rained for ten consecutive days before Christmas. Because there were no bridges and the creeks were flooded, no one could go into town to shop for Christmas gifts. The adults solved this problem by keeping the date secret from the children and celebrating Christmas a week late.

Although Sarah lived only fifteen miles from the Mississippi River, she did not see a steamboat until she was ten years old. She never forgot the exhilarating experience. "As the 'Leathers' rounded a big bend in the river," she recalled on her ninetieth birthday, "she answered our signal with a deep-throated whistle and ringing of landing bells in the pilot house. As the big boat hugged the shore, my eyes, trained to lamp-light, were not prepared for this magnificent creature of light—a flood of light! It was as if I was visioning the Promised Land; as if the swing low of heavenly chariot was at hand!"[14]

Sarah grew up with a strong and joyous sense of family. She loved and respected her parents, adored "Grandma Alice," as the children called Alice Wade, and kept in close contact with other aunts, uncles, and cousins. Domestic servants also played a role in Sarah's youth, despite the family's modest economic circumstances. The dearth of opportunities for the large black population of the parish made domestic and agricultural labor inexpensive and workers easy to find. One of the family's servants, Caroline Webb, who died in 1895, was buried in the family cemetery near the house. "Mammy is Asleep in Jesus," her tombstone read.

The Towles children had their share of chores. Sarah's favorite was to ride the mule that turned the cotton gin. New clothes and shoes were a rarity. Sarah never forgot her mother calling the children to come inside and save their shoes when rain threatened. "And so Sarah grew up associating rain and wind with a feeling of panic and a compulsion to run indoors!" Sarah's niece recalled.[15]

Occasionally, however, the children seem to have been indulged, judging from a description of Sarah written many years later by a childhood friend. "Do you remember a picnic, under the beech trees, north of the Wildwood house?" he asked Sarah. "You were between twelve and fourteen. You came on horseback, across the Sandy Creek woods. You wore little brown shoes, a challenging broad-striped dress, soft tan-leather riding gloves with fringe on the gauntlet. To complete the sketch, wide, very dark eyes, a sensitive mouth and dark hair done in the mode associated with Jeanne d'Etoiles. You carried a slender riding whip." [16]

The family's economic situation grew worse after the panic of 1893, and Daniel realized that he could no longer remain at Ouida, particularly if the children were to receive a decent education. They could not afford the boarding schools that their wealthier neighbors' children attended. Once again, family ties proved invaluable. Sarah Ker Towles's sister Rose Ker had married sugar planter Murphy S. Foster, who in 1892 was elected governor of Louisiana. Through this connection Daniel Towles secured a position at the customs house in New Orleans and moved his family there in 1895.[17]

The child Sarah knew that this move produced in her parents a deep feeling of failure and damaged her father's sense of pride. Several years after moving to New Orleans, Sarah wrote her parents, "To me, Mama and Papa, you have been *successful.* There has been sorrow and sickness and debt and utter grief, but in spite of all . . . your motto has been 'Strive and hold cheap the strain!'" Sarah's devotion to her family was central to her life, though she rarely expressed it as openly and passionately as she did in this letter, written at age twenty-seven. "With perfect frankness and truth," she continued, "I can say that I would point you out as a shining example of courage, loyalty and devotion. I may strive hard but I can never hope to come near the standards always upheld by both of you and Grandma. God knows that these words come from my very heart of hearts dictated by the perfect love and trust there for you all three." [18]

"Grandma Alice" stayed on at Ouida when the family moved to New Orleans, but she remained an important influence on her foster grandchildren. Sarah remembered Alice Wade as the pivotal figure in the family. "Without her help and love and example the struggle would have been without its sunshine," Sarah wrote. "There never was and never will be another like her—beautiful in word and deed, cultured morally, mentally and socially, and the incarnation of the spirit of love and self-sacrifice. . . . I often wonder what our life would have been without her, but I cannot form any idea of it." [19]

The family returned to Ouida every summer to escape the yellow fever plagues that so often threatened New Orleans during the hottest months. At Ouida Grandma Alice reigned. For Sarah Towles these were the happiest of times. She spent the summer months "reading and reading," she remembered.[20] "As children we longed for the hydrangeas to blossom as it meant going back to Grandma and Ouida. How she spoiled us! Cookie jars filled to overflowing, cream cheese waiting in the dairy, ponies ready with shining

saddles and bridles—and all of it against a background of the mingled fra-
grances of old-fashioned roses, high thyme and honeysuckle," Sarah wrote
many years later. "And it seems to me we could always find, even in summer,
sporadic cape jasmine on the great big bushes." [21]

Ouida held happy memories for all the family, especially for Sarah's older
brother, John, who after receiving his Ph.D. from Yale lived in New York for
the rest of his life. "West Feliciana was always the love of his dreams. He, and
his father before him, referred to it always as God's country," Sarah recalled
shortly after John's death. "Conditions made his visits here few and far between, but he felt that he always breathed more freely when he crossed to this
side of Thompson's creek. . . . He felt that he would be young again if he could
drink and rest under the trees by Uncle Wade Bonner's spring, only a stone's
throw from the Ouida house." [22]

Family ties were strong in the South, and for the Ker-Towles clan, no less
than for most southern families, kinship held a transcendent importance;
stories about forebears abounded. Sarah's biological grandmother Rosaltha
Francina Routh, who died in 1865, held a special place in family lore. When
Rosaltha went to visit her captured Confederate husband after the fall of
Vicksburg, Union soldiers discovered that she and other rebel women were
smuggling supplies, tied to the hoops of their skirts, to the captives. When
approaching Yankee troops threatened to invade Natchez, Rosaltha joined a
crowd of citizens who went to the levee and burned hundreds of bales of cotton to keep them from falling into Yankee hands. Olivia Wade, Grandma
Alice's mother and Sarah Ker's aunt, also figured prominently in family history, having built with her own money the first true plantation house in West
Feliciana Parish, a massive Greek Revival structure named Ellerslie. [23]

By almost any standards, the Ker-Towles family produced an abundance of
strong women. The most important to Sarah were her foster grandmother,
her own mother, and her great-aunt, Mary Susan Ker, who lived in Natchez.
Sarah corresponded frequently with her great-aunt, a teacher, who served as
a role model to her niece. "Grandma" Alice Wade exemplified strong self-
confident womanhood. She never married and was proud of her independence. As she wrote Sarah, "[I'm] so glad I'm a free agent, and no one to say
me nay. Don't you wish you could be able to say the same of yourself, all the
days of your life." Alice did not have a high regard for men. "So far as men are
concerned there is very little difference in them," she told her foster grand-
daughter, "some probably a little more selfish than others." [24]

Sarah's mother undoubtedly made the greatest and most lasting impression
on her. She admired her mother's capacity for hard work and her contributions

to the family income. Sarah Ker Towles had no easy life. Of her ten children, three died in infancy. In addition to caring for her children, Sarah Towles, like most rural wives of modest circumstances, spent much of her time in farm labor. She worked long, hard hours during Sarah's childhood, and she later regretted the necessity for having to work so much that she could not give her children more attention. She always intended the best for her children, but she knew she had sometimes failed them along the way.

"For one thing," she wrote her daughter in 1908, "I would have let you go more ragged and dirty and petted you more. You know, when you all were little tots, my life was a mighty busy one. Many a morning, I have slipped out of bed when you were asleep, gone to the gin house, spent the whole day there attending to the ginning, came home at dark and made you a little dress or John a shirt . . . whereas I should have spent those hours before you went to sleep petting and fondling you which I so often longed to do, but thought my duty called me to do the others." Still, she was glad that Sarah seemed to have understood that "all our efforts were for you children's good and now in your young womanhood you see and realize the love and care we have bestowed upon you. It is worth all those years of struggle and toil to have you children's love and gratitude and feel what we have done was for the best—even if we have made mistakes." [25]

Sarah, however, clearly did not consider herself neglected in childhood. She remembered her young life, especially her teenage years, as carefree and happy. "I was eighteen at the turn of the century," she recalled in her old age, "a member of a gay group that considered themselves adept in the ability to shake a wicked foot. Because of parental indulgence, we danced the darkness into dawn." Often these dances took place at the governor's mansion, where her aunt and uncle lived during Sarah's adolescence. [26]

"Parental indulgence," however, was subject to the strictures imposed upon the children of the elite class to which both the Kers and the Towleses belonged by virtue of tradition and background, if not by virtue of wealth. Sarah seemed to have accepted these governances without complaint. She would not have been surprised by the letter written by her aunt Rose Ker Foster to Mary Susan Ker concerning the Fosters' daughter, who, like many of the Ker girls over the years, attended Stanton College in Natchez. "What I wish is that Mary should be thrown [in] with people of refinement and culture—it makes no difference how reduced in means or how humble their surroundings [just] so they have lived as they should and are *good* people," Rose Foster wrote. "Now I know blood usually tells, and I am a great stickler for it, but at the same time, there are *black sheep,* and these I would have Mary avoid." [27]

The Kers and Towleses subscribed to these sentiments completely. The young Sarah Towles described her mother as living in "deadly terror" that the "mixed" society near Ouida might lead the Towles girls to "change our name for one that is not our social equal." Sarah Ker Towles relaxed, young Sarah told Aunt Mary, when the Towles children visited their cousins at Bayou Sara, Louisiana, and attended parties and dances where they could meet "the Butlers, Forts, Lawrasons, and all their circle," whose social prominence no one could question. "Mamma was delighted for she said she always liked to know who our associates were," Sarah wrote. Mrs. Towles had nothing to fear from her daughter, who held similarly disparaging views about socially unacceptable young men. As Sarah told her aunt, "Those boys up here have nothing to support a wife on, unless it is pickled pork and cornbread for life, and, as yet, I think my aspirations seek a more lofty mark!" [28]

While Sarah's early social views were conventional, she had a hard time trying to conform to the standards of dress and behavior expected of her. When her mother insisted upon her wearing long dresses in the summer of 1899, Sarah complained in a letter to her beloved Aunt Mary. Although the dresses were "more becoming," she admitted, "I surely did hate to put them on, for now I cannot be a 'tom-boy,' but have to act as becomes a young lady and I cannot reconcile myself to the idea of being a young lady, although I am almost eighteen, for to save me, I cannot be dignified." [29]

Another problem—one that Sarah never completely overcame—was her temper. The year Sarah entered college, her friend Frank Percy remarked on her tendency to give free expression to her anger: "You are very pretty and exceedingly attractive—unusually bright—and a fine 'kid' generally. But you are troubled with a temper which you unwisely seem to satisfy instead of control." [30] The same year, Frank sent Sarah a letter of introduction in the form of verse that expressed the mixed emotions he felt toward her.

> This will introduce my friend,
> Miss Sarah Towles,
> an elegant lady, of a family old,
> Her manners are not haughty,
> nor her actions bold.
> She is respectfully known
> all over the South
> For her quiet little way
> [and] her big noisy mouth.
> She is quick to her pistol

as she is to her purse
She is not afraid of anything
on the face of the earth
As you see she is most lovely
Comple[x]ion so fair
eyes most exquisite and lovely hair.[31]

Sarah was known for her hot disposition. When she was confirmed in the Episcopal Church in 1899, Sarah told her mother that she was going to try to curb her temper and be a Christian.[32] There is little evidence that she succeeded in achieving her first goal, and organized religion played only a small role in her life.

In New Orleans, the Towles children attended public schools. Sarah enrolled in the Girls High School, as public schools in New Orleans were segregated by sex as well as by race. This separation reflected the educational tradition of New Orleans, a majority-Catholic city which by the late nineteenth century had nearly one hundred parochial schools that had always been sexually segregated. The segregation reflected the conviction that girls did not need the same education, or as good an education, as boys. As one school superintendent tactfully explained this prejudice: "The characteristics of the female mind [are] . . . distinct from those of the other sex."[33]

In high school Sarah discovered a love for English literature, and in her senior year the faculty chose her to deliver the Shakespearean essay at graduation.[34] Her high school years also saw the beginning of what would become a lifelong interest in New Orleans politics. "Our city is in a state of excitement over the coming election," Sarah wrote Aunt Mary in October 1899. "The 'Jacksonians' and the 'Regulars' are simply 'scouring' each other; each party has a big 'rally' every night. Papa is a 'Regular' and I of course follow him. At school we engage in the warmest arguments and sometimes the ringing of the bell saves lots of trouble."[35]

New Orleans was in the midst of fierce political battles when the Towleses arrived in the city in 1895. On one side stood the Regular Democrats, the powerful political machine that controlled city hall, the municipal court system, and municipal government offices. The other side consisted of a loose coalition of Republicans, Reform Democrats, Populists, and blacks. The reformers defeated the Regulars in the 1896 city elections, but they were soon overpowered by a machine organized in 1897 known as the Choctaw Club or the Old Regulars.[36] The Old Regulars supported Governor Murphy Foster's move to disfranchise blacks and backed him in the Constitutional Convention of 1898, which eliminated most blacks from the voting rolls by restricting suffrage to literate property owners. Voters whose fathers or grandfathers had been registered in 1867, however, could vote regardless of their ability to read or their ownership of property, thus assuring most whites of the vote.

The Old Regulars were challenged in the city elections of 1899 by the Jackson Democratic Association, a reform group that had little chance against the New Orleans version of Tammany Hall. The Regulars won the election handily and continued to control New Orleans politics for more than forty years. As a recipient of his brother-in-law's political patronage, Daniel Towles supported the faction that had given him a job. Sarah, who greatly admired her father, echoed his choice. Over the years she changed many of her youthful opinions; certainly her admiration for the Old Regulars diminished considerably.[37]

One conviction that Sarah never changed was her passion for education. To her it was no less vital than it was to her parents, particularly her father, whose own education had suffered because of his parents' economic misfortunes. In 1899 yellow fever again confronted New Orleans. The danger had not passed by the time school was to open in the fall, but Daniel Towles decided to bring the children back from Ouida anyway, for fear they would miss too many classes. "Every time we have a pain or feel the least bit warm, Mama declares we have the fever and nothing will suffice but that our temperature must be taken and we must have a dose of Phosphate of Soda," Sarah Towles wrote her aunt. "We all laugh immoderately at the number of times it is possible for this family to have the fever. Still, I do think we run a great risk."[38]

Public education in New Orleans suffered from a variety of ills by the late 1890s, when Sarah attended high school. The school system had boldly implemented racial and sexual integration during Reconstruction, but these innovations had come to an end with the Redeemers. When the Democrats returned to power, New Orleans began supporting a four-layered school system that separated blacks from whites, girls from boys. Making the situation even worse, lower taxes and assessments designed to keep politicians in power kept the public schools in a state of poverty. By the turn of the century, the state had the highest rate of illiteracy in the nation. New Orleanians who could afford parochial or private schools for their own children paid little attention to the plight of the public schools. The McDonogh fund, the bequest of wealthy slaveowner John McDonogh dedicated to public school education in New Orleans, financed all new school construction from 1862 to 1893 without the help of a single tax dollar. As one historian characterized the situation, "Private charity, not public concern, kept the schools afloat."[39] Public support for education in New Orleans and in the state as a whole suffered from an "antipathy toward public education that bordered on hostility."[40]

In 1900 Sarah won a competitive scholarship to Sophie Newcomb College, which had opened only four years earlier as the women's coordinate college of Tulane University, making Newcomb the first of its kind in the country. Because of its large endowment, Newcomb could keep tuition relatively low, at one hundred dollars a year, and offer about 25 percent of its students scholarships, without which Sarah could not have attended.[41] Like nearly all Newcomb young women at the time, Sarah lived at home. She took the streetcar from Uptown, where her family lived in a modest bungalow, to Newcomb, then located on Washington Avenue, the wealthy, beautiful Garden District of New Orleans.[42] "The beauty of its situation and surroundings is unsurpassed," the Newcomb bulletin assured prospective students. "Its extensive grounds, shaded by numerous live oaks, palms, and other trees and shrubbery, afford ample opportunity for open air recreation."[43]

Sarah was an enthusiastic student who, like the rest of her family and many of her peers, took education seriously. As a student in a private college, Sarah knew that her family had to make sacrifices for her education, even though she had a scholarship. As one of only 2.8 percent of women aged eighteen to twenty-one who went to college in the United States in 1900, and as one of only twenty-two in her class at Newcomb, Sarah could easily see that she was part of an elite group of young women. Recognizing that she was in a privileged position, she worked hard to deserve it.[44]

In one of her undergraduate essays, Sarah wrote with all the earnestness of a college sophomore: "One of the many precious legacies that the nineteenth century has sent down to us is the proof of the fact that if there is to be any real and permanent progress, the race must be educated from the lowest to the highest ranks."[45] She took this ideal to heart, judging from a comment made by one of her young beaux, who wrote that he had heard from her grandmother that Sarah's eagerness to fill her head with knowledge was about to kill her.[46]

In fact, Sarah flourished in college. Her grades were uniformly high, particularly in English; she was a successful member of the debating team and adept at basketball, a popular sport at Newcomb.[47] In her junior year she won a prize endowed by the Reverend Beverley Warner of Trinity Episcopal Church for the best essay on Shakespeare. Sarah served as class poet in her junior year and was a member of the YWCA. She also developed a gift for oratory that she would enjoy all her life. At the "Newcomb feast" of 1902, Sarah, sophomore class secretary, offered a toast to the faculty who, according to the *New Orleans Times-Picayune,* "came in for a share of the pleasantry, a pretty play of words making the toast all the more significant as Miss Sarah B. Towles offered it." [48] The seniors also enjoyed Sarah's tribute to her graduating friends:

> Examples brilliant, noble, fine
> Geniuses all, like stars they shine.
> May their fame extend o'er land and sea
> And quickly may they married be. [49]

For all the gaiety of their Newcomb feasts, these college women generally reflected the seriousness that characterized their generation. Because college education was not available to most women in the South until twenty years or so after colleges had opened for women in the Northeast, southern women of Sarah's age belonged to what historians of eastern women's colleges have labeled the "first generation." [50] First-generation college women were ambitious, conscientious about their work, and driven to succeed. They saw themselves as pioneers but were still very much a part of the "true woman" tradition, accepting their roles as pure, pious women, albeit not necessarily as domestic or as submissive as their mothers had been. [51]

Sarah Towles was even less submissive and less domestic than most of her contemporaries, and she was not particularly pious. Her cousin Albert characterized her most succinctly when he described Sarah as "a fine girl, has plenty of good common sense and not a bit stuck up." [52] At the annual class night play in 1903, Sarah took the role of Sir Hubert Moreton, the "stern parent," in her classmate Fannie Heaslip Lea's production, "A Will of Her Own." The title aptly described the determination of this first generation of southern college women, as well as Sarah's own determined—and sometimes stubborn—character. [53]

The turn of the century was a heady time to be a college woman. The suffrage movement was in full swing and the "new woman" was on the rise. [54] Despite earlier warnings about the dangers of higher education for young women, who might be rendered infertile by engaging in too much mental activity, according to Dr. Edward H. Clarke in *Sex in Education; or, A Fair Chance for Girls* (1873), women emerged from college without any apparent damage to their minds or bodies. [55] In a paper on John McDonogh, Sarah ridiculed the New Orleans public school benefactor's disapproval of allowing girls to study Greek and Latin. In McDonogh's opinion, such an endeavor "often retards their settlement in life, or after marriage is the source of discontent and un-happiness." He would have changed his mind had he lived in the twentieth century, Sarah predicted, "for as to women you have to make up your mind today to surprises."[56]

As early as her sophomore year at Newcomb, Sarah began to address the "woman question." In her paper "The Advantages and Disadvantages of Physical Culture as Illustrated by a Dialogue in the Gym Dressing-Room," she depicted two undergraduates in conversation:

> Mary: "Well, the girls today are trying to put themselves on an equality with the men. Why, actually, the women have gone to fencing. I detest a masculine woman. I prefer, anyway, the fragile style of beauty."

> Rose: "Why Mary, you would be an excellent model for the heroine of a Medieval Romance. Wake up and look around you! See, we are living in the Twentieth Century—woman's century! If you are man's equal in intellect, why shouldn't you be his equal in health[?]"[57]

In making these early feminist avowals, Sarah followed in the footsteps of many strong and assertive New Orleans women dedicated to advancing the position of women in society. In 1881 New Orleans women organized the Woman's Social and Industrial Association to aid working women.[58] Four years later women formed the New Orleans Woman's Club to help women find employment, to support job training, and to advance "the intellectual growth and spiritual ambition of the community."[59] Although southern women were some years behind northern women in organizing such groups, by the 1890s and early 1900s women's clubs had mushroomed throughout the South, in New Orleans in particular. The Woman's Club soon joined the General Federation of Women's Clubs, a move that led its members increasingly into the public realm of politics and reform.[60]

Although it was not until about 1915 that women's suffrage gained a large following at Newcomb and other colleges throughout the nation, the movement was already well organized in New Orleans by the time Sarah Towles entered college.[61] Women organized the first suffrage association in New Orleans, the Portia Club, in 1892, having nine members and Caroline Merrick as president.[62] Four years later, New Orleans women founded a second suffrage organization, the Era (Equal Rights for All) Club under the leadership of Kate Gordon.[63]

Representatives from the Portia and Era Clubs organized the Louisiana Woman Suffrage Association and petitioned the state Constitutional Convention of 1898 for the vote, arguing that until women could cast ballots, they should not have to pay taxes, since they were without representation.[64] The convention relented to the extent that it gave women who paid taxes the right to vote on taxation issues. It was, in the opinion of suffragist leader Caroline Merrick, "a mere crumb—but a prophetic crumb."[65] The next year New Orleans women, under the direction of the Era Club, used their new vote to organize a massive campaign that successfully pushed through a tax hike to fund a sewerage and water board in the city.[66] In 1903, during Sarah's junior year, the National Suffrage Association held its annual convention in New Orleans, featuring such luminaries as Susan B. Anthony, Alice Stone Blackwell, and Carrie Chapman Catt. New Orleans's Kate Gordon served as program chairman.[67]

Newcomb girls eagerly discussed the merits of suffrage during Sarah's undergraduate years. In 1904 Jean Gordon sat on a panel of judges for Newcomb College's Agnostic Club debate on votes for women. Other members of the Era Club were in the audience to hear the nearly unanimous vote in favor of the prosuffrage debaters.[68] While there is no evidence that Sarah took an active role in the suffrage movement, she frequently addressed the issue in her college papers. In one essay, Sarah voiced her faith in the power of voting women to effect change. "This is an epoch unique for the fair ones who already sizzle with a sense of their importance," Sarah wrote, predicting that when a woman was at last elected to office, "she will treat the position as no sinecure. Less obtuse than man she will not prove so docile as men fondly hope." In keeping with the progressive concerns of her day, Sarah predicted that the woman officeholder could "be trusted to register an absolute veto against squalor and disease. . . . She will write a requiem for heinous injustice."[69]

Sarah's comments reflect the progressive spirit of social activists in New Orleans and at Newcomb. Like many of her contemporaries in college at the turn of the century, Sarah believed that educated women could make a contribution to society, and she was impressed by the reform movements taking place outside the college gates. Many suffragists and reformers also worked inside those gates and undoubtedly influenced their young students. The second president of the Era Club, Evelyn Ordway, taught chemistry at Newcomb during Sarah's undergraduate years, and other Newcomb faculty members were also active in women's organizations in the city, actively pursuing urban reform and municipal improvements.

The great majority of Newcomb's faculty was female. With nearly three times as many women as men teaching at Newcomb, undergraduates saw tangible evidence of women's intellectual capabilities and professional success. And while most Newcomb women were destined for lives devoted primarily to marriage and motherhood, historian Pamela Tyler is undoubtedly correct in concluding that the "confidence, vigor, self-esteem" and other qualities fostered by an all-female environment would eventually act as "a powerful acid" to dissolve women's traditional reluctance to enter the male world of politics.[70]

The social justice component of the southern progressive movement was led, in large part, by women. Sophie Bell Wright, who ran a day school for girls, opened a free night school for working boys in New Orleans, organized a fund-raising drive to build a hospital annex for crippled children, and lobbied for public playgrounds.[71] Laura McMain began her thirty-year career as director of Kingsley House, a settlement house in a poor Irish neighborhood in New Orleans, in 1901. Kate and Jean Gordon were active in nearly every reform effort in town, including the Milne Home for Destitute Orphan Girls, the prevention of cruelty to animals, the treatment of tuberculosis, the admission of women to medical school, and myriad other causes.[72]

A New Orleans feminist in 1919 pointed out that Louisiana women had organized for "mother's pensions, better babies, school hygiene, prison reform, care of the feeble-minded, prevention of blindness, laws to give women equal rights and opportunities, more money for schools, more playgrounds, cleaner movies, homes for working girls, better markets, lower living costs, a single standard of morality, and, in short, a higher type of civilization."[73] Nearly all of the leading women reformers had some involvement with Newcomb at one time or another, and it is safe to say that Sarah, always curious and always reading, was well aware of their efforts.

Sarah repeatedly affirmed her strong commitment to progressive reform and the idea of "municipal housekeeping," popular among women activists of the day. "It is not to be thought that our ideals are any better than those of our grandmother's day; not any better perhaps but undoubtedly they are bigger," Sarah wrote. "Our grandmother's vision was bounded by her home; we contemplate not only home but homes—the homes of all people." She cited passage of child labor laws, the work of the Red Cross, the movement for old age pensions and workingmen's insurance, the improvement of hospitals and asylums. "And the good of the present, the past and the future—the greater part of it—is due to women's direct effort and indirectly to her influence," she concluded. "And those women who are doing the greatest good today are women who have left the sweet protection of the home and given themselves to the world. . . . The teacher, the Social Welfare worker, the business woman—these are the types that are opposing the forces of destruction with construction. And with these women, we here and now cast in our lots."[74]

Sarah shared many of the assumptions and goals of the progressive women reformers who would later place their stamp on the New Deal. She was part of the generation that included Molly Dewson, Frances Perkins, Lucy Randolph Mason, and Eleanor Roosevelt, a generation that finally achieved success for the suffrage movement and fought for social reform all of their lives. These women, born in the 1870s and 1880s, carried progressivism into the 1920s and 1930s and contributed significantly to the idea and image of women taking an active role in public affairs.[75]

Soon after graduating from Newcomb, Sarah entered the public world of reform as a volunteer teacher in the Newcomb College Alumnae Association's Night School. Eleanor McMain of Kingsley House gave Newcomb the names of more than a hundred young women who were employed during the day and who might want to continue their education. The school opened in January 1905 and met three times a week from 7:00 to 9:00 P.M., with Newcomb alumnae contributing their time to teach "poor servant girls and factory workers."[76] This yearlong experiment in the classroom may well have decided Sarah's future career. Certainly, teaching had not been her lifelong ambition. While in high school Sarah had dismissed the idea of following in her Aunt Mary's footsteps. "I could never teach," she explained, "for I have not patience enough."[77]

That Sarah would take some kind of job after graduation, however, was never in doubt. While some middle-class parents assumed that their daughters would marry immediately and let their husbands support them, Sarah's family seems to have encouraged her to find a career; her father at one point suggested that she go into pharmacy.[78] Her family's shaky economic situation undoubtedly influenced Sarah's decision to work. Four siblings still lived at home, and her parents needed the extra income. What Jane Addams referred to as the "family claim," the tradition of a single daughter's obligation to her parents, shaped Sarah's choice after graduation.[79]

Sarah also shared Addams's desire to find a satisfying life outside traditional domestic concerns. Like many women college graduates of the first and second generations, Sarah wanted to use her education to the fullest extent, and she placed a high priority on achieving economic independence.[80] In fact, Sarah's commitment to independence proved to be one of the overriding concerns of her life. In some ways, Sarah's attitudes resembled those of educator Emma Willard, whom Anne Firor Scott described as holding both new and old values in a seemingly contradictory combination. Willard was part independent "new woman," part traditional "true woman." As paradoxical as this mixture of attitudes might seem, Scott argued that it was exactly what made Willard so effective. She combined elements of new and old values in a way that people could accept. Willard, Scott said, believed in a domestic role for women and in separate spheres, as well as in women's education and women's rights.[81]

Sarah's was also a transitional generation, linking the Victorian and the modern eras in the South. Like other young women who attended college during the years from 1890 to 1920, Sarah held beliefs that were common to both ages. She was both dutiful daughter and independent woman. This duality formed an inevitable aspect of her years at Newcomb. As one of its earliest graduates, she must have been struck by the uniqueness of her experience there. College was still a rarity for young women, and the example of so many competent women faculty would have made a strong impression on someone who already loved learning, books, and discussion.

The decision to work outside the home was not an uncommon one for a woman college graduate to make in 1904. A significant number of Sarah's twenty-six classmates either went on to graduate school or began earning a paycheck immediately after graduation.[82] The first two generations of women college graduates generally delayed marriage and childbirth much longer than their contemporaries who lacked college degrees.[83] Although the majority of women college graduates did eventually marry, a sizable minority did not. While 90 percent of the general population married, a survey of the alumnae of the eight major women's colleges and Cornell showed that only 39 percent of them had married as of 1915.[84]

Sarah exhibited no inclination to marry during her college years. She had a number of male admirers, but she did not seem to take any of them very seriously. One of the most persistent of her suitors, Frank Percy of St. Francisville, spoke highly of the importance of being a "True Woman," and he reminded Sarah of her promise to "never kiss another boy."[85] Sarah was a bad choice for a man who wanted a "true" Victorian woman. If the true woman was to be "virtuous, compliant, passive, dependent, and childlike," as one historian characterized her, Sarah would never have measured up to Frank's ideal. Perhaps that is why their relationship fizzled.[86]

Sarah did not conform her behavior to suit her beaux's expectations, and she was particular in her choice of company. Discussing one of her current crop of admirers, she once confided to a friend, "Yes, he is a nice boy, but un-lettered in more ways than the alphabet. By the way," she added, "several of the 'long agos' have come to the center of the stage lately, and the age that has happened to one in the meantime turns up its nose with an almost audible sniff at some of these outgrown illusions." Sarah also had a mischievous streak that sometimes showed itself in her courtships. One of her young men, she told her friend, would soon be coming home from Cornell "arrayed in all the splendor of his highly respectable Prebyterianism. . . . Do you know I sometimes feel tempted to take him for better or worse, just to see if I could convert him into a sure-enough devil. . . . There's no unburying anything wicked in him. . . . I ought to be saying 'Bravo!' but instead—pshaw, I'm a villain!"[87]

While Sarah obviously enjoyed a good flirtation, she had more interest in school than in marriage. In addition to teaching in the Free Night School for the first year after graduating from Newcomb, Sarah enrolled in graduate school at Tulane, where she received an M.A. in 1906, concentrating on English and Latin.[88] Sarah enjoyed school and, given her enthusiasm for the liberal arts, perhaps teaching seemed the most compatible career choice. In the early 1900s, moreover, not many choices were available to women college graduates, most of whom settled on teaching.[89]

In 1906 Sarah accepted a teaching position at Belhaven College in Jackson, Mississippi. She taught English and Latin and sent money home regularly. She was, however, very homesick, particularly when her grandmother died in 1907, and she suffered from debilitating headaches. After two years at Belhaven, Sarah returned permanently to New Orleans to begin her long teaching career there.[90] She spent a year working as a substitute teacher before receiving an assignment to the Esplanade Girls High School, where she taught during 1909–11. For the next six years, she worked at another girls' high school, Sophie B. Wright. From 1917 to 1919 she taught at the boys' high school, Warren Easton, before transferring back to Wright.

Although Sarah sometimes conducted summer school classes in New Orleans, in the summer of 1918 she traveled to Washington, D.C., to work for the Red Cross. Sarah joined thousands of other young women who flocked to the nation's capital to contribute to the war effort, many discovering new career opportunities by taking government jobs vacated by draftees.[91] For the most part, Sarah enjoyed her interlude in the capital. Always fascinated by politics, she visited Congress frequently to observe government in action, an experience that contributed to her growing interest in legislative proceedings. Still, she found it difficult being away from her family and, as in Jackson, she longed for Louisiana. "There are so many things here like West Feliciana that I do get powerfully homesick," Sarah wrote her sister Roberta. "Somehow I resent the similarities."[92]

Her Red Cross colleagues, however, seemed to consider Sarah more different from than similar to themselves. For the first time, Sarah found it necessary to defend herself and her region against criticism. "As for pronouncing their r's you've never heard the like of these people," she wrote home. "They are never tired of correcting me. And I hope if I come home pronouncing a single r you'll hang me to the nearest tree."[93]

One "Yankee upstart" who worked in her office particularly irked Sarah, as he forced her "to ward off blows about the South constantly." One day he told her, "Up in Massachusetts, Miss Towles, we think of you people in the South as foreigners." Sarah replied, "We people down in the South, Mr. Allen, never think of you people in Massachusetts at all." This would not be the last time that Sarah would use her quick wit and sharp tongue to defend herself and the things she valued.[94]

Sarah's southern background shaped many of her opinions. During this period of her life, she shared with other natives of her region a common belief in white supremacy and a commitment to the southern way of life. Her experiences had not prepared her for anything except prejudice in racial matters. She grew up in a segregated white world where the fears of "mixed" marriages referred only to a mingling of social classes; racial mixture was beyond the pale of possibility. She had never attended schools with black children and had no black friends. The only African Americans she had ever known were agricultural workers and servants. The year after Sarah and her family moved to New Orleans, the Supreme Court handed down its decision in *Plessy v. Ferguson,* which established segregation on a legal basis. She lived in a city controlled by a racist political machine, in a state that disfranchised and segregated African Americans under the leadership of her uncle, Gov. Murphy Foster.

It took a long time for Sarah to overcome her racial prejudice. In 1912 she wrote her brother John about their sister Roberta's plans to attend summer school at Columbia University, expressing reservations about the presence of African Americans in the classroom. John, who lived in New York City, reassured Sarah, advising her, "Tell Babs that I think if she can possibly go to Columbia she should do so. Negroes do not 'cut any ice' in northern universities; they are just as distinct socially as they are in the South. They are so very, very few that one scarcely knows that any are in the school." Lots of southern girls went north to school, John continued. If Roberta should, "by the merest chance, get a laboratory desk near a student of the dusky shade, all Babs would have to do would be to tactfully ask the instructor to change her desk and that would be that."[95]

The idea of attending school with blacks—or teaching blacks—repelled Sarah at this time in her life. In August of 1919, when Sarah traveled to Seattle to visit relatives and possibly to relocate there, she was upset to find that the schools were integrated. As she wrote her parents, "The salaries here are almost *double* those in New Orleans but then again *negroes* attend the white schools."[96]

Any departure from the racial status quo was hard for Sarah's family to accept, particularly if it inconvenienced them. When the family moved from West Feliciana Parish, with its large underemployed black population, they lived for a while in Kenner. At that time, Kenner was a small agricultural community near New Orleans with a large population of self-employed black farmers. John Towles worried that their parents would not like living there, primarily because they could not find a cook. "I am afraid that the Towles family will find it does not like an industrious, farm-owning, self-made community where to vary Mr. Wilson's slogan, the negroes are all 'too proud to cook.'"[97]

The family still considered West Feliciana Parish home, and since they spent most of their vacation time there, it was not surprising that when Sarah did form a serious romantic relationship, it was with a young man from St. Francisville. Elkanah Reed, an attractive, quiet man, came from an established family and worked in a relative's general store. Eck deeply loved Sarah, and she secretly married him sometime before 1921, when he was killed in an automobile accident.[98] The couple never lived together, and when or where the marriage took place, no one knows. It was a secret that Sarah Towles Reed never disclosed, and the fact of the marriage became known only when she became a widow. She omitted the marriage date from all family records, at the same time carefully noting the dates of her siblings' weddings. According to family lore, the only person who had known of the marriage at the time was Sarah's mother. Some family members have speculated that perhaps Sarah and Eck married while she was in Washington in 1918; others think the marriage took place some years earlier. Even her beloved brother did not know how long Sarah and Eck had been married. When he wrote her following Eck's death, he speculated, "I had thought back in April 1913 . . . that you might be married but I was by no means sure."[99]

One compelling practical reason helps to explain why Sarah kept her marriage a secret, at least as long as Eck was alive—married women were not allowed to teach in Orleans Parish public schools. Had she made her marriage public, she would have been fired automatically from Sophie B. Wright High School, where she taught English and Latin, and her family still depended on her financial contribution. She also loved her job and would not have wanted to lose it. She had to choose between her marriage and her job as well as between Eck and her family. The family claim and the job took precedence.

Still, Eck was enthralled by Sarah. "As you know you have always been the dearest girl to me in all the world," Eck wrote Sarah in 1909, "and I'll never be happy until I can say that you are mine. . . . Sarah, I do now and all ways [*sic*] did love you. . . . You know I all ways [*sic*] did do anything you asked me to do except quit smoking cigarettes. I am yours forever."[100] The only two surviving letters from Eck after their marriage, addressing Sarah as "My very own precious darling little sweet baby girl wife," are filled with protestations of love as well as loneliness. "My own baby how I do miss you," Eck wrote Sarah. "Have just wished and wished for my own little wife ever since I left town. Darling life I'm foolish when I get away from my own little girl." In the other letter, he admits, "It just simply crushes my life out to think that I can't see all that I live for in this world . . . it gives me the blues so very bad when I can't be with the sweetest thing in all the world."[101]

Eck remained in West Feliciana Parish while Sarah lived in New Orleans. Sarah had compelling reasons to keep her marriage secret, particularly if she did not want to give up her career, but it is harder to understand why Eck would have endured a long-distance relationship, separate living arrangements, and a secret marriage. Eck loved Sarah very much, and presumably she returned his affection; that, perhaps, is all the explanation there is. Perhaps the long-distance nature of the relationship suited Sarah better than a more conventional arrangement. Perhaps Eck simply had to be satisfied with what little Sarah would give him. But none of these considerations accounts for Sarah's lifelong silence about her marriage or her determination to keep the marriage date a secret long after the reasons for doing so had passed.

The marriage remains shrouded in mystery. For reasons that are still unclear, it was made public only after Eck's fatal car accident on August 20, 1921. A brief announcement in the *New Orleans Item* on August 26, 1921, stated that Sarah and Eck had been married in June. The place and exact date of the marriage were not given and have never been revealed. After Eck's death, Sarah spent hours alone, sitting on the porch, hardly eating and speaking little.[102] When school authorities learned of Sarah's marriage, they immediately fired her. As Sarah's principal, Alice Lusher of Sophie B. Wright High School, explained to her, Sarah's position had been automatically vacated by her marriage, even though news of it did not reach authorities until she had become a widow. Lusher asked the president of the Orleans Parish School Board to reinstate her, and he in turn requested a letter from Sarah explaining the circumstances.[103] In September the board allowed Sarah to return to her teaching position at Sophie Wright.[104]

In the fall of 1921, Sarah enrolled in night classes at Loyola law school, perhaps motivated by her arbitrary dismissal and looking for a way to fight school authorities in the future. Or, as her brother John suggested, she may have been looking for "difficult subjects" to help her get over her grief.[105] In any case, she plunged into her studies with such a fervor that Eck's mother became worried about her. "Sarah is attempting the impossible, it seems to me," she wrote Sarah's mother. "Teach all day and study all night. I do not see how her health can stand the strain." [106]

Sarah, always a hard worker and determined to accomplish her goal, graduated in 1924 and passed her bar exams. But she never practiced law; nor did she ever profess any ambition to become an attorney. As she put it many years later, "I never practiced law because for me it looks backward too much." [107] Her lack of interest at least shielded her from the prejudice women faced in the legal profession. In 1920 women made up only 1.4 percent of the practicing lawyers in the United States.[108] Sarah did, however, put her legal education to good use. Like many other women lawyers of the time, including Florence Kelley, Crystal Eastman, and Alice Paul, Reed used her knowledge of the law informally to advance women's causes—in her case, the rights of the predominantly female teaching force in New Orleans.

2 Equal Pay for Equal Work

After Eck's death Sarah did not remarry. She lived the rest of her life with her sister Roberta Towles, also a teacher in the Orleans Parish public schools. Although Sarah was the more politically active and publicly outspoken of the two, both sisters became heavily involved in the movement to secure economic justice for New Orleans teachers. Sarah and Roberta spent their evenings together telephoning other teachers, organizing meetings, and maintaining friendships with other women who shared similar concerns.

To a large extent, Sarah's ability to devote so much of her time to teachers' causes depended on Roberta's willingness to take care of the household responsibilities. Roberta did all the cooking, cleaning, shopping, and, since Sarah refused to learn how to operate a car, all of the driving as well. On most weekends Roberta drove the two of them to Weyanoke, their house outside St. Francisville. It had come back into family possession in 1916, when Sarah and her sister Kate bought the house and one hundred acres for a thousand dollars.[1] Sarah and Roberta restored the dilapidated house, where Sarah, who was not very handy around the house, somehow figured out how to do all of the work on the plumbing.[2]

Roberta, who loved the country, spent most of her weekends and summers tending the cattle she raised and tramping over the hills of the plantation. Sarah also loved the trees and plants of the countryside, but the society, which she once described as "feudalism in full flower," bored her, and she had no particular interest in cows.[3] To keep herself entertained in West Feliciana Parish, she pored over historical records and family genealogies in the St. Francisville courthouse, accumulating huge piles of notes for a parish history that she never got around to writing.[4] Roberta dutifully dropped Sarah off in St. Francisville in the morning, then returned in the afternoon and drove her the fifteen miles home.[5]

Sarah and Roberta lived in a largely female world.[6] They were self-supporting women who managed their own finances and two households without the help of husbands or brothers. After the deaths of their father in 1924 and their mother in 1928, they relied mainly on each other, while keeping in close contact with their five brothers and sisters, as well as helping to raise their brother Dan's daughter, Nora. Sarah did not like Roberta's trips to Weyanoke or elsewhere without her. As she once wrote to her niece, "Lands alive, I'd run off if I had to live by myself."[7] The sisters were also part of the larger female world of teachers' associations and the community of women who formed the bulk of the membership. The teachers' organizations provided a base for their political activism and the mechanism to help secure the economic and intellectual independence that both sisters felt was their right.

The economic dimension of Reed's activities on behalf of teachers linked her incipient feminism with her later dedication to the labor movement. Reed believed that all workers had the right to economic security and that women were the most vulnerable workers in this respect. Like many early twentieth-century feminists, Reed assumed that political rights were intrinsically bound up with economic rights.[8]

The linking of economic and political rights predated organized feminism by many decades. It extended as far back as the founding of the nation, when eighteenth-century republican men claimed that female economic dependence prevented women from thinking and acting entirely on their own. This dependency, men argued, rendered women incapable of making free, independent choices; thus the rationale for excluding women from the franchise. Of course, not all women were economically dependent upon men, but even single women who owned property were denied political rights.[9] The American Revolution, one scholar has concluded, strengthened an already widespread misogyny. Women's status deteriorated because of the triumph of republican ideology, which considered all women — most of whom relied on men economically—in the same light as slaves, children, and other dependents who lacked the moral virtue that only economic independence could bestow.[10]

Independence thus assumed both political and economic dimensions that were inextricably intertwined. Nineteenth-century Americans widely accepted the assumption that freedom and independence depended on ownership of productive property.[11] The acquisition of such property, in turn, depended upon "free labor," the right to choose one's own form of work toward the ultimate goal of economic independence.[12] Women leaders and writers had long called for women's "right to labor," their right to participate in the marketplace and to receive equal wages for their work. At the end of the nineteenth century, writers such as Charlotte Perkins Gilman and Olive Schreiner argued against a purely domestic role for women and called for women's economic independence from men. Gainful employment, they thought, would help equalize relations between men and women.[13] In *Women and Economics* (1898), Gilman wrote that women had an inherent need for satisfying work, for their own wages, and for personal relationships founded on love rather than on economic necessity.[14] Some feminists believed that earning their own money would not only bring economic independence but would also make them as powerful as men.[15]

Women understood only too well the relationship between power and money. Their lack of power enabled men to discriminate routinely against them in matters of employment and salaries, and there was little they could do about it. When the Women's Bureau was incorporated into the United States Department of Labor in 1918, its attempts to guarantee wage equality in federal contracts met with failure. Over and over, managers argued that men's "family responsibilities" required their higher wage scales. Mary Anderson, first director of the Women's Bureau, reminded one manager that widows also had family responsibilities. "If I paid them the same," he protested, "there would be a revolution. There is a tacit understanding that women should not make over 25 cents an hour," compared with men's 45 cents.[16] In a 1928 study, the Department of Labor found that women workers routinely earned only one-fourth to one-half the salaries earned by men.[17] During the 1920s, the Women's Bureau, the Women's Trade Union League, and the National Consumers' League all agitated without success for wage equality.[18]

Critics of women workers frequently justified women's unequal salaries by invoking the "pin money" myth—the idea that women, unlike men, did not need money for essentials; these, critics claimed, were taken care of by a husband or father. Women's wages went to pay for frivolous luxury items. Consequently, women could reasonably be paid less than the men who were supporting them. Moreover, since a woman's true vocation was marriage and motherhood, she should not stay long in the workplace in any case. Critics of working women accused them of contributing to the downfall of the family, divorce, and other societal ills.[19]

By stigmatizing women as less than serious workers, the "pin money" argument provided a convenient rationale not only for low pay but also for the feminizing of unskilled occupations that offered few opportunities for training and advancement. Unless they could destroy the pin money myth, women's demands for equal pay and opportunity would never be met. "I resented this theory more than any of the other misstatements that were so often made about women in industry," Mary Anderson said.[20]

The Women's Bureau worked hard to dispel these erroneous ideas about women's employment. As director, Anderson initiated at least six studies of women's labor needs between 1919 and 1929, but the myth proved more powerful than the facts. In reality, no study ever validated the pin money perception. A 1908 Department of Commerce and Labor report concluded that "the girl or woman living at home and working only for pin money was scarcely found in this investigation." Unexpectedly, the study found that women who lived at home kept even less money for themselves than those who lived independently. Some 70 to 90 percent of women who lived at home contributed all of their wages to the family finances. Less than 5 percent of these women kept all of their earnings. Even women who lived on their own often gave a portion of their earnings to their families.[21] All evidence pointed to the conclusion that most women worked because they had to, for one reason or another.[22] Anderson reminded proponents of the pin money theory that working ten-hour shifts in a factory was not what most people considered fun. Women would not work under such conditions if they did not have to.[23]

Sarah Reed knew all of this and more from firsthand experience. Her teaching income had always helped support her family and herself; that was why she had kept her marriage secret. Reed also knew that other women found themselves in similar circumstances. She once told her colleagues in the teaching profession that her early involvement in the fight for equal pay for women stemmed from her experience with a young woman to whom she had given some financial help to attend the Louisiana State Normal School. The woman, Reed told her audience, was "spirited, clever, but frail—very frail." She had three younger brothers, whom her family expected her to help through school. She took a teaching position she did not really want, in a rural area where no extensive wardrobe was needed and boarding with a family was inexpensive. "She did without the bare necessities to send money home—

washed, ironed and really starved, as the only people in that place who would board the teacher were a rough rude couple who breakfasted this teacher numerous times on cold mustard-greens and coarseness." One day, Reed continued, the woman "went crazy in her own schoolroom. . . . Today that girl is in Jackson, Louisiana. She has been there for years in the asylum." Her brothers became financially successful and influential, "but the sister is a part of the big scrap heap of life." From this woman's experience, Reed became convinced of the "viciousness" of paying women teachers less than men. "This girl didn't have to marry to get dependents—she had a ready-made family handed out to her. Men teachers create their family responsibilities—women teachers usually inherit theirs." [24]

When Sarah Reed assumed a leadership role in the New Orleans teachers' fight for equal pay for equal work in the 1920s, she encountered a salary disparity between men and women at least as great as that found in the nonacademic labor market. This inequality had deep roots that seemed impervious to all efforts of amelioration. Paying women teachers less than men had long been common practice in academia. As women began to take over the teaching field, it became routine to justify their lower pay under the theory that only higher salaries would keep men in the field, where not only their scholarship was needed but also their example as role models for adolescent boys. [25]

In the article "The Vanishing Schoolmaster," a professor of psychology at Louisiana State University wrote that not even the best woman teacher could serve as a role model for an adolescent boy. "She might teach him history but she could not show him how to be a man," the academic claimed. He also dismissed what he called the "old cliché, 'Equal work for equal pay.'" Adolescent boys needed good men teachers; at least half of their teachers should be men, he asserted, while also questioning the effects of "an economic and social system which tends to make school teaching the profession of celibate women." [26]

Women in Memphis in 1872 made one of the earliest attempts to rectify salary discrimination after the school board slashed women's wages while raising men's. Debates on the "woman question" filled the city's daily newspapers. One school board member called women who worked outside the home "interlopers who usurped the place and function of men." Women were inherently inferior to men, he claimed, as "the only thing the women beat the men at was . . . suckling and nursing babies." Women picked up the gauntlet, arguing that they were better teachers than men by nature; that men were "by virtue of their sex not competent to preside over children." [27]

Men frequently invoked the "woman peril" to assure more pay for themselves. In 1904 the Male Teachers Association of New York City justified their higher salaries by asserting that boys needed men teachers "as ideals." Female teachers actually harmed a boy's education, the association claimed. Women preferred "the softer and more showy arts at the expense of the hard essentials." They were too sentimental in discipline, whereas a man would more likely impress upon the boys "notions of right and justice." Male teachers were "less mechanical in instruction than women," the men said, arguing that "women prefer to follow, and are willing to do so without knowing any reason for such action." In short, men should be paid more because they were not doing the same work as women—they were doing better work. The woman teacher "works as a woman and after all cannot quite undo her true, womanly self." Woman's true nature lent itself better to marriage and motherhood than to teaching. Was it not evident, the Male Teachers Association asked, that "the differentiation of the sexes indicates a differentiation of vocation?" [28]

In 1906 the women teachers of New York responded to this question by forming their own organization, the Interborough Women Teachers' Association, dedicated to equal pay for equal work. Its president, Grace Strachan, wrote the *New York Times* in 1909 protesting women's unequal wages, motivated by a proposal that would have raised female teachers' salaries but not to a level equal to men's.[29] Strachan was just as unimpressed as Reed with the "family-to-support" justification for men's higher pay. In 1908 her association compiled statistics that showed that 377 women teachers supported 707 other people—mothers, fathers, brothers, sisters, nieces, and nephews.[30] The "family wage" argument, said Strachan, was absurd. It was "a sad commentary" on teaching that the men in the profession objected to equal pay for women. "Is it not sad to see men, American men, shoving aside, trampling down, and snatching the life preservers from their sisters?" Strachan wrote. "I say life preservers seriously and mean it literally. For to a woman obliged to support herself, is not her wage earning ability truly a life preserver[?]" she asked. "How can any man . . . take from a woman any part of the wages she has earned and remain worthy even in his own eyes?"[31] After intense lobbying in the New York state legislature, the female teachers secured a law in 1911 that mandated equal pay for equal work.[32]

Despite continuing disagreements over the merits of the "feminization" of the teaching profession, the percentage of women teachers continued to climb during the first twenty years of the twentieth century. By 1920 women accounted for fully 86 percent of all public school teachers. Because women teachers were cheaper, school boards generally ignored arguments that more men teachers were necessary. On the whole, women received about two-thirds the salaries paid to men even though they had equal experience and often more education.[33] School administrators preferred to hire women not only because they cost less but also because women were viewed as "unambitious, frugal and filial." Administrators thought that they had little to fear from compliant, undemanding women stuck in low-paying, unprestigious teaching jobs. When it came to filling better-paid, more respected administrative posts, however, they seldom chose women. Despite all of the hand wringing over the feminization of the teaching profession, one woman observed in 1914, nearly all authorities in public school systems were male.[34]

The new associations that teachers organized in many American cities in the early twentieth century exhibited what one recent writer has described as "a decided air of attack on the male dominance of the profession."[35] As the worst paid of all "professionals," women teachers organized themselves in hope of gaining the power to improve their economic circumstance and to eradicate sexual discrimination in matters of salaries. In New Orleans, female teachers angrily challenged salary inequities in 1913 when a so-called merit plan resulted in a salary schedule that clearly discriminated against women.[36] Moreover, a general salary cut in the same year reduced all teachers' salaries. When the board announced the pay cut at a meeting in the fall, the teachers' reaction "was like a subdued and feminized edition of a mob's roar in revolution a la Carlyle," a New Orleans newspaper reported. "Time after time the room resounded with stamping of feet, clapping of hands and cries at some particularly daring and plain spoken words, voiced by an indignant teacher."[37]

In 1913 teachers in the predominantly female New Orleans teaching force organized the Associate Teachers League to fight pay cuts. When women continued to complain about their automatically lower salaries, the school board president told them that school officials had to pay men more than women in order to attract more men into the profession. Besides, he added, "many of the women in our schools could not earn as much in any other kind of work."[38] The school board retained the differential between male and female salaries. Under the budget adopted in 1914, white male teachers in the high schools (the only male teachers in the New Orleans public school system) received at least $30 a month more than female high school teachers: $100 a month in the first year, compared with the women's $70, and rising to $165 a month after ten years, compared with $115 for women. All black teachers automatically received $10 less than any white teacher.[39]

During World War I New Orleans schools faced a teacher shortage for the first time, when new jobs for women opened as men left to join the military. With their bargaining position strengthened by the crisis, women stepped up their campaign for higher salaries. In 1919 the Associate Teachers League joined the Central Trades and Labor Council, AFL, making it the first teachers' union in New Orleans and in the Deep South as a whole. Teachers hoped that allies in the labor community might strengthen their fight for higher, more equitable salaries. "Our teachers are shamefully underpaid," Teachers League president Augustine Aurianne admonished the school board.[40]

Although protests succeeded in securing a raise for all teachers in January 1920, school board president Sol Wexler continued to support higher salaries for male teachers. Wexler told the women that the principle of equal pay for equal work would be taken into consideration "only when woman suffrage has been established."[41] Women's suffrage activists and educational reformers worked closely with each other in New Orleans, primarily through the activities of progressive women's organizations such as the Era Club, the suffrage association founded by Jean and Kate Gordon. Another was the Portia Club, which even before women had won the vote had convinced Governor Murphy Foster to appoint four women to school boards in northern Louisiana.[42] The Era Club called for a constitutional amendment allowing women to become members of parish school boards throughout the state.[43]

Members of women's clubs and suffrage associations consistently supported educational reforms and teachers' demands for better salaries. Women teachers, in turn, joined the fight for the vote. In the Associate Teachers League journal, *The Teacher's Forum*, one militant woman teacher argued that joining organized labor might counteract the "work of the insidious disease, which is sucking the lifeblood and sapping the energies of the army of women teachers; but the ballot in the hands of teachers, would be a powerful weapon for its gradual but certain annihilation."[44]

With the passage of the Nineteenth Amendment, New Orleans women took up Wexler's challenge, forcing authorities to consider women's demands by electing a woman, Fannie C. Baumgartner, progressive reformer and member of the Era Club, to the Orleans Parish School Board. Baumgartner was the first woman to win elective office in Louisiana and the first female member of the school board in New Orleans. Considering that Louisiana was the only state in the union in the 1920s that did not have at least one female legislator, Baumgartner's election ranks as a major accomplishment for women activists.[45] But the presence of a single woman on the Orleans Parish School Board, committed as she was to women's interests, could not change the rest of the board's ongoing commitment to male supremacy.[46]

The continuing discrimination against women, regardless of their newly won right to vote, convinced some women to keep suffragist Alice Paul's National

Woman's Party alive after passage of the Nineteenth Amendment in order, said Alva Belmont, to "obtain for women full equality with men in all phases of life and make them a power in the life of the state."[47] The National Woman's Party called for an Equal Rights Amendment, first introduced in Congress in 1923, which stipulated, "Men and women shall have equal rights throughout the United States and every place subject to its jurisdiction." Feminists divided over the ERA. One influential contingent, including the League of Women Voters, the National Consumers' League, and the Women's Trade Union League, lobbied against its passage on the grounds that the amendment would make protective legislation for women unconstitutional.[48]

The National Woman's Party countered that "the removal of all forms of the subjection of women" could be accomplished only by eliminating all legal discrimination, and they pointed out that discriminatory laws remained on the books throughout the United States. In some states a husband still had power over his wife's and children's earnings, and women could not serve on juries, hold public office, or sign contracts. Laws made divorce harder to obtain for women than for men, and a married woman's nationality was determined by her husband's. In some cases, a woman could inherit only one-third of her husband's property if he died without a will, whereas a husband in the same position would receive his wife's entire estate.[49] A survey conducted by the National Woman's Party confirmed all of these legal disabilities and concluded that, in 1921, all states with the exception of Wisconsin had an average of six significant discriminatory laws against women.[50] The Louisiana legislature did not abolish its "head and master" law, which gave the husband complete control over community property, until 1980.[51]

In the early 1920s, women's organizations, such as the National Woman's Party, the League of Women Voters, the National Consumers' League, the Women's Trade Union League, and the General Federation of Women's Clubs, had enough influence to help push through some legislation favoring women. Although the ERA failed to pass, partly because of the divisions among women's groups, women presented a united front in favor of the 1921 Sheppard-Towner Act, which provided federal funds for public health programs, including visiting nurses and prenatal care classes.[52]

In the same year, representatives of the National Woman's Party (NWP) lobbied the Louisiana legislature in favor of amendments to the state's civil code that would give women full civil and political rights. As in the rest of the country, Louisiana women split on the issue of legal equality. Supporters of the National Woman's Party, which included the Louisiana and the New Orleans Federations of Women's Clubs, opposed a more conservative faction led by Anna Pleasant, president of the Southern Conservative League of Louisiana and wife of former governor Ruffin Pleasant. Both groups appeared before a legislative judiciary committee. "I object to being classed with idiots and insane," Florence Huberwald, former president of the Portia Club, told the legislators. "We do not plead, we demand our equal rights." In her rebuttal Anna Pleasant confided to the all-male committee, "I am tired of this crusade against men."[53]

The female crusaders had limited success in their campaign to repeal discriminatory laws in Louisiana. Legislators voted to remove from the civil code thirteen areas of discrimination against women, including the right to be consulted before a family home was sold or mortgaged. But many inequalities remained, including limitations on women's property rights and stipulations that husbands were legal heads of the family and that married women could not choose their legal residence.[54]

Leaders of the National Woman's Party were disappointed with their failure to secure full citizenship for women in Louisiana. Elsie Hill, chair of the executive committee of the NWP, told the press, "The woman's rights movement seems to have met its Waterloo at Baton Rouge. I regret very much that the Legislature has failed to take advantage of the opportunity to make Louisiana the second state to grant equal political and civil rights with men to its women citizens." Lavinia Egan of Shreveport, president of the Louisiana State Federation of Women's Clubs, believed that Louisiana laws were particularly discriminatory against women. "The legislators at Baton Rouge know this," Egan said, "and I am wondering if they are standing pat on their masculine superiority of position because they are afraid to have women meet them on equal ground in the home, in business and at the polls."[55]

Both Hill and Egan happened to be in New Orleans during the continuing campaign waged by women teachers for equal pay, and the two leaders eagerly lent their support to their sisters, who faced a new setback. The Orleans Parish School Board in 1920 had voted to decrease the differential between men's and women's salaries by one hundred dollars a year. As a result, a delegation of male teachers from Warren Easton, the boys' high school, went before the school board requesting a salary increase for men. They complained that the board had not increased their salaries in the same proportion as those of women teachers at the two girls' high schools. Wartime inflation had decreased the purchasing power of the dollar, they argued, and their salaries did not now match those paid before the war. Although the board at first declined their request for a raise as impractical, it reconsidered the men's request the following year and recommended that male teachers receive a retroactive raise. Fannie Baumgartner voted in favor of the raise, but recommended, unsuccessfully, that the board raise female teachers' salaries as well.[56]

The school board's action prompted a meeting in September 1921 of representatives of various women's organizations, who gathered to write a protest resolution. Delegates from the New Orleans Federation of Women's Clubs, the Newcomb Alumnae, the Girls High School Alumnae and the Parents and Teachers Club agreed to present the protest to the school board at its next meeting. Women teachers, who had been assured by the board in 1920 that the one-hundred-dollar reduction in the differential between male and female salaries was the first step toward full equalization of pay, were outraged by the quick return to business as usual.

Teacher representatives met with the National Woman's Party leaders and outlined their plans for a joint appearance before the board to present their protest petition.[57] The *New Orleans Item* sided with the women teachers' argument for equal salary. "It seems a heavy penalty to impose upon a capable teacher because she was born a woman," the paper editorialized, noting that the petition had the support of several women's clubs. "As a permanent policy the salaries should be exactly equal," the *Item* concluded, unless it could be shown "that men were doing school work beyond women's efforts to accomplish, which we suspect would be a task of some difficulty."[58]

Representatives from Newcomb Alumnae, the Louisiana League of Women Voters, the New Orleans Woman's Club, the New Orleans Business and Professional Women, Normal School Alumnae, Parents' Clubs, the Daughters of 1912, the National Woman's Party, the Consumers' League, the Louisiana Equal Rights Party, the Public School Alliance, as well as Kate and Jean Gordon, Elsie Hill, and Lavinia Egan, all attended the school board meeting to publicly endorse the demands of the women teachers. Women, a newspaper reported, "jammed the room, hung over the windows from the hall and crowded into the open door of the School Board office."[59]

Several organizational representatives spoke on behalf of the female teachers, including one from the Women's Equal Rights Party who tried to invoke the regional heritage of the school board men in her appeal for the salary raise. According to one newspaper report, she "concluded a spirited talk by declaring: 'If the members of this Board deny women the same pay received by men for the same work, where is your sense of Southern chivalry?'" The Louisiana branch of the National Woman's Party presented a letter to the board that incorporated phrases of a more feminist nature: "Believing as we do not only in equal pay for equal work, but in full equality for men and women in the exercise of political, legal, and civil rights, we protest for the sake of justice and of equity and in the name of all women in whose interest and advancement is our sincerest concern against the unjust treatment of the women teachers in the public schools of New Orleans."[60]

When one woman from the City Federation of Women's Clubs asked why the board saw fit to raise the salaries of men teachers if it was "financially embarrassed," board president Daniel L. Murphy replied that the raise was necessary because male teachers were more difficult to find than female teachers. As proof, he pointed to the school board's teacher waiting list, which contained the names of fifty-two women but only two men.[61] Murphy persisted in arguing against the women's petition, claiming that if women's salaries were raised, schoolchildren would suffer, for salaries of principals and supervisors would also have to be raised, at the expense of the building fund. "It does not appear advisable to me, at the present time," Murphy said, "to put the requested changes in effect for it means that the children now improperly housed in some school buildings would have to wait for some future date to be relieved of the present unsatisfactory conditions."

Taking the floor, Sarah Reed publicly dismissed this specious argument by pointing out that men and women teachers had to meet the same qualifications, covered the same amount of work, and worked the same hours. A salary scale based on sex alone, she contended, discriminated against both women teachers and girl students since it obviously placed a higher value on the education of boys, whose teachers, more likely to be men in New Orleans's sexually segregated high schools, were paid more.[62] Former suffrage leader Ethel Hutson reminded the board that teachers' salaries had been cut 5 percent in 1913 because the schools were short of money; the same cut had been made in 1914. "If you had asked businessmen to contribute 5 percent of their earnings for any such need, there would have been a howl of protest," she said. "You can teach without buildings, you can teach without grounds, but you cannot teach without good teachers."[63]

Baumgartner moved that the school board go on record in support of equal pay for equal work "to take effect at once," but no one seconded her motion.[64] Instead, school board member Percy Moise "came forward and melodramatically declared that the Board had 'no intention of cutting a single salary!'" the Item reported. President Murphy accompanied his vote with a warning that, while the board favored equalization, it was impossible to put it into effect without reducing salaries. In the end, the board endorsed only the principle, not the practice, of "equal pay for equal work, no salaries to be reduced."[65]

Apparently forgetting that the board had just raised men's salaries, Murphy claimed that the board simply did not have the money to raise women's wages. In response, one woman demanded to know why the board president had voted for a principle that might have sounded all right "but meant nothing?" The board made no further comment on the subject and, as the Item reported, "went on record as being in favor of the 'sentiment.'"[66] The *New Orleans Times-Picayune* also noted the emptiness of the board's action. "The victory," the paper observed, "turned out to have a distinctly hollow ring."[67]

The school board publicly defended its actions, arguing that if it were to meet the women's demands, the cost to the taxpayers would be "close to a million dollars." It presented a scenario in which all supervisors, principals, and elementary school teachers would also demand raises, leaving no money for construction, building maintenance, or supplies. The board remained unalterably opposed to decreasing men's salaries. The fight continued, however, with New Orleans clubwomen rallying around the women teachers. The president of the Civics Department of the City Federation of Clubs said that her organization unanimously favored equal pay for equal work. The president of the Consumers' League of New Orleans strongly criticized the board's resolution, alleging that it did "not ring true. One might say it was not passed in good faith."[68]

Sarah Reed and other women high school teachers responded to their defeat by organizing the High School Teachers' Association (HSTA), dedicated to achieving equal pay for women. Even after it achieved its goal, President Alice Malony announced optimistically, the teachers would not disband but remain organized to tackle other issues later.[69] "The Board certainly must have foreseen that the women would demand justice when they raised the men's salaries last April," she pointed out. "That was the time for the Board to think. The women feel that they are justified in their demand for fair play."[70]

Again the women found an ally in the *New Orleans Item*. "We confess to our incapacity to follow the lines of thought—and assertion—attributed to School Trustee Moise," the *Item* editor wrote, suggesting that the board raise women's salaries and lower men's "to a point somewhere between the present higher scale for men and the lower scale of the women." The editor reminded the board that this issue was not likely to just go away, especially now that "the new position of women as political factors makes this a subject requiring more serious discussion than it has formerly received."[71] Representatives from the High School Teachers' Association kept the issue alive, repeatedly going before the school board with petitions for equal pay for equal work, but the board consistently put them off. The only victory the group registered came when Baumgartner succeeded in her motion to raise the pay of women teachers in the evening high school from $4.25 a night to $4.50, the same amount paid to men.[72]

In the midst of the controversy over sexual discrimination in the salaries in New Orleans public schools, the Women's Bureau of the U.S. Department of

Labor announced that it intended to destroy once and for all the idea that women worked for "pin money." The bureau said it intended to show that women had the same kinds of responsibilities as men and therefore should not suffer wage discrimination.[73] The publicity had no effect on the Orleans Parish School Board in the fight for equal wages; the High School Teachers' Association continued to demand action, and the board kept postponing further discussion.[74]

Alice Malony went before the board's Committee of the Whole in April of 1923 to point out that the disparity in pay between men and women ranged from $900 to $1,050 a year and that men obtained maximum salaries after ten years' service, as opposed to fifteen years for women. School board president James Fortier responded by suggesting that the money needed to raise women's salaries could be generated by decreasing the size of the faculty at the girls' high schools. Or, he added, perhaps the men could be paid less. The committee voted for a new resolution, eliminating the provision that no salaries be reduced and promising to devise a new salary schedule.[75]

At the general meeting of the school board, Percy Moise introduced the new resolution to effect equalization of men's and women's salaries, but he omitted the stipulation that no salaries be reduced. The large delegation of male teachers who attended the meeting announced their intention to fight any reduction in their salaries.[76] The threat of diminished salaries worried another group of teachers as well. Elementary school teachers opposed the women high school teachers' salary demands, fearing that their own salaries would be adversely affected. Nevertheless, the board rescinded its earlier policy and voted for one that would allow "absolutely no sex discrimination" in determining salaries.[77]

If the school board intended for the new policy to further divide the teaching corps, it succeeded. Teachers split into separate factions: the male high school teachers and female elementary school teachers on one side, and the High School Teachers' Association on the other.[78] In May the men went before the board again to request that it continue paying them "a living wage." A faculty spokesman from Warren Easton High School suggested that while the men's salaries were higher, the high schools were in fact already operating on the principle of equal pay for equal work. Even with higher teacher salaries, it cost less to run the boys' high school, he claimed, because fewer substitutes had to be hired. President Fortier stoked the flames of acrimony when he replied that, since the principle of equal pay had to be implemented, men's salaries would have to be reduced.[79]

Finally, in August 1924, the school board announced a new salary schedule that reduced men's salaries by one-fifth of the salary differential between men and women. The 20 percent reduction would be continued for five years, the board promised, until the salaries of men and women were equalized. The school officials also announced that, because of a shortage of funds, those employees on a ten-month pay schedule would from then on be paid for only nine months, and those on a twelve-month schedule would receive pay for only eleven months.[80]

The compromise—which meant lower salaries for everyone—did not please anyone, particularly the men. In September, teachers from Warren Easton complained that, in addition to receiving paychecks for only nine months instead of the customary ten, money would be deducted from the nine checks they would receive. The men requested a delay in implementing the new plan.[81] School board president Fortier agreed to postpone the new salary schedule because the reduction had not been announced before the beginning of the school session. Fortier and the board hoped that an amendment permitting them to levy the full rate of taxation permissible under law for school purposes would be passed by voters in an upcoming election, thus allowing the board to pay ten months' salary and to start deducting the differential after November. One board member, Fred Zengel, objected to Fortier's plan, stating that he wanted to go on record as voting against the motion because he thought that it meant an "indefinite postponing" of the issue. He was right.[82]

The tax levy amendment failed to pass. After the election, male faculty members of the Warren Easton school petitioned school officials once again in an effort to safeguard their economic advantage, arguing that their higher salaries were "no more than commensurate" with services rendered. Their pupils needed male influence during their adolescent years, they claimed, and "the question of supply and demand necessitates the payment of a higher salary to men than women in the teaching corps." The men asked the board to defer its equalization plan until it had enough money to equalize salaries by raising women's salaries to the level of men's.[83] The Parents' Club of the Warren Easton High School supported the men in their fight for higher salaries, petitioning the board to defer equalization and arguing before the Committee of the Whole that men deserved more pay because they had greater responsibilities, as most were married and had families to support. Men might leave their teaching posts for more lucrative positions elsewhere if their pay was cut, the parents argued, and the schools would be left with only female teachers. The parents asked the board not to place women in charge of their sons during adolescence.[84]

The High School Teachers' Association was back before the board in January and again in February, protesting the indefinite postponement of salary equalization.[85] Finally President Fortier admitted that the board was divided on the issue and could not reach a consensus. In March the board reverted to its original resolution, which included the provision that equalization was fine in principle but that no salaries could be reduced to achieve it.[86] The women were back to square one.

The women teachers' defeat came not long after Sarah Reed's graduation from law school. Before 1924 her teaching and law school schedules left her little time to participate in extracurricular activities. But when she was ready to join the fray and become involved, she never gave up. Gradually, Reed assumed a leading position in the teachers' associations with which she would be associated for more than fifty years. Over the course of her career, she helped transform these organizations into vehicles for protecting the economic and intellectual independence that she considered essential for everyone, men and women. And she furthered the cause of sexual equality, to which the women's movement had long been dedicated but had not yet achieved.

3 "I Belong in the Ranks"

At the point when salary equalization seemed as far away as ever, when women were "worn out with protests, promises and pledges," Sarah Reed became the most visible and vocal activist in the women teachers' fight. In 1925 Reed and her colleagues founded the New Orleans Public School Teachers Association (NOPSTA), which expanded its membership beyond high school teachers to include all white New Orleans teachers and principals (maintaining the strict racial segregation that characterized the New Orleans school system). Before it could accomplish anything, NOPSTA first had to reunify the splintered, angry white teaching corps. Consequently it postponed further agitation for salary equalization. Instead, the organization concentrated on assuring that teachers would be paid consistently, if not fairly.

NOPSTA advertised itself as an organization of professionals, trying to avert the stigma associated with working-class unions. In its founding document, the association pledged to work for teacher unity, protection of the best interests of teachers, and recognition of teaching as a profession. Colleagues urged Reed to accept the presidency of NOPSTA, but she declined, choosing instead to head the salary committee, to edit the organization's magazine, and to serve as chairman of the legislative committee, a position she continued to hold for nearly fifty years.[1]

Reed realized that teachers could achieve nothing if they continued in the divisiveness that had arisen over the issue of salary equalization. Addressing her peers in the first issue of the NOPSTA's new organ, *Quartee,* Reed emphasized the importance of unity among the teachers. "If teaching ever becomes a profession—and it must—it will be because teachers will learn that they must 'get together,'" she declared. Reed mailed issues of *Quartee* to teachers throughout the United States, forming a nationwide network of teachers, many of whom thanked her for a publication that addressed their own problems as well as those of New Orleans teachers.[2]

NOPSTA followed in the tradition established by other teachers' organizations. As a historian of the Chicago teachers' association has written, these groups embodied "the growing sense that self-supporting women were the exemplars of independent womanhood." Women had begun to realize that they deserved higher wages than they were getting, as well as adequate pensions. They were no longer swayed by appeals to the self-sacrificing nature of women. "The gimmick of reminding teachers that the enterprise of education was ultimately for the children would no longer hold these inspired women back."[3]

When NOPSTA president Augustine Aurianne announced the formation of the group in February of 1926, she informed the Orleans Parish School Board that the newcomer boasted more than 1,040 members and would henceforth be the only organization with the authority to represent the city's teachers. Reed explained that her salary committee had decided to concentrate on salary stabilization rather than equalization. For the time being, teachers were more interested in receiving full pay than in receiving equal pay.[4]

Customarily, teachers had received their salaries in the form of ten equal monthly paychecks, but in 1924 the board started notifying them, after school had already begun, that they would be paid full salaries for only nine months. The amount of their tenth-month salary would depend on the school system's financial situation at that time. Teachers never knew just how much that sum might be. Teachers' salaries had been reduced by 3 percent in 1924 and 8 percent in 1925, and in 1926 the board announced a 10 percent reduction.[5] The board managed to find money in its budget for new buildings, but at the same time it informed teachers that it had to reduce their salaries because of a shortage of funds. Despite lower educational revenues, a consequence of lower property tax assessments in 1923, the board remained committed to an extensive school construction program.[6] Repeatedly, it sacrificed teachers' salaries for new buildings. The board recognized that it would not have much trouble keeping women teachers, even at lower salaries, since the job market for women had shrunk after its World War I expansion, as men returned to their old jobs.[7]

In addition to the money taken from salaries, the board found more revenue for its building program in the maintenance fund. Until 1924 it paid janitors' salaries out of the school building fund, but in that year the board decided that it was illegal to pay salaries from this account. A friendly test case—*School Board v. Murphy*—followed, and in July of 1924 the Louisiana Supreme Court ruled that janitors' wages could not be considered maintenance and thus were not payable from the maintenance fund. Henceforth, the board paid janitors from the operating budget, the same account from which it paid teachers. As a result, teachers experienced a salary cut. In 1925 the board decreased teacher salaries again to pay for physical equipment for the new schools.

By that time, Reed pointed out to NOPSTA colleagues, the school officials were charging every item, except for land and the actual construction of the schools, to the operating fund, resulting in a continual reduction of faculty wages. "This was grossly unfair to the teachers," Reed noted, "inasmuch as every brick in a new building meant a cut in teachers' salaries." Given the board's plans to build more schools, "the outlook for the teachers was gloomy indeed." Reed reported that a member of the board, speaking unofficially to a group of teachers, had informed them that "teachers' salaries would go down, down, down."[8]

In her blunt, straightforward manner of speaking, Reed told the school administrators that they should explain to the public why they could afford to build new schools but could not pay teachers full salaries. Furthermore, new buildings required additional equipment, janitors, and teachers. In accordance with the law, all of these expenditures had to be paid out of the operating fund, which meant that the salaries of the present teaching corps would have to be cut. To remedy the situation, Reed suggested that the board pay for its bonds out of the building fund rather than the operating fund, and she recommended that the board consider a change in the school law that would allow a reallocation of the school tax to earmark more money for the operating fund to cover teacher salaries. President Fortier assured Reed that he agreed with her suggestions but that he could do little to implement them. In fact, he said, it was up to the teachers to convince the state legislature to change the school law regarding apportionment of school taxes.[9] As the Orleans Parish School Board was a state, not a city, agency, state law governed it. Since 1916 the school board had been separate from city government, operating with funds from its own dedicated property tax. The city government was, in fact, legally bound not to pay for any aspect of public education.[10] The only other money that went to the Orleans Parish School Board came from the state government in the form of an allotment for each student enrolled in the public schools.

Fortier also hinted that, for the second consecutive year, teachers would not receive full salaries. Nearly six hundred teachers, overflowing into adjacent rooms and corridors at the board meeting, did not like what they heard. At the conclusion of Fortier's remarks, some teachers hissed, leaving the meeting disappointed and angry.[11] They knew that nothing had changed. The next day's newspaper reported that the board had opened bids for the construction of the new McDonogh No. 9 school.[12] As Reed aptly characterized the situation, "The horns of the teachers' dilemma are an elastic building fund and an inelastic operating fund." [13]

Despite repeated attempts on the part of NOPSTA, the board refused to grant a hearing to teachers to discuss the salary issue. Stymied on the local level, the association wrote a bill that would reapportion school funds and found a legislator to take it to Baton Rouge.[14] Although the teachers did not receive any help from the board, several women's organizations, including the New Orleans Federation of Clubs, the Presidents' Cooperative Club, the Normal Alumnae, the League of Women Voters, and the High School Alumnae, worked with the teachers to help get the bill passed.[15] Other educational organizations also backed NOPSTA, with a major endorsement coming from the New Orleans Public School Alliance, a twenty-year-old civic organization devoted to educational improvement. The alliance thought that something should be done to "eliminate the permanent unrest which exists among teachers." [16]

The teachers wanted a constitutional amendment that would authorize the redistribution of the seven-mill tax levied by the school board. The amendment would require the board to reallocate one-half mill from the building fund to the operating fund, making possible a restoration of teachers' salaries to the levels in place before the cuts began. As the current law stood, a minimum of one and three-quarter mills had to be set aside for the building fund and not more than five and one-quarter mills could be used for operations, which by then included teachers' and janitors' salaries, supplies, books, and all other expenditures for operating the schools. A lawyer hired by NOPSTA to make sure that its bill was constitutionally "hole-proof" pointed out, "As the operating expenses of the school system increase faster than the assessments and as supplies and books must be bought, it necessarily follows that the teachers' salaries must be cut."[17] The proposed amendment required all expenses for maintenance, equipment, and upkeep of the schools to be paid from the building fund, where, NOPSTA maintained, "they rightly belong."[18]

NOPSTA mounted an extensive publicity campaign under the slogan "New Orleans is on the increase. Shall its teachers decrease?" The teachers reminded the public that they were not asking for raises in pay; they wanted only salary restoration. The amendment would not require any increase in taxation, and the building program would not be affected. Teachers argued that "to lower wages lowers standards," and they pointed out that minimum teachers' salaries in New Orleans were lower than those in any of twenty-two comparable cities. The *Times-Picayune* reported that NOPSTA had the support of "virtually the entire teaching force," which was making "an effort as concerted as the charge of the 'six hundred' and with the objective of 'half a mill onward.'"[19] Although the majority of the school board supported the bill, President Fortier opposed it, declaring that diverting one-half mill would mean the "veritable assassination" of the building program. The board would never be able to catch up with its construction plans, and some schools would never be built, Fortier predicted.[20]

At a meeting of the New Orleans Federation of Clubs on May 24 to organize a delegation to lobby in Baton Rouge for the "teachers' rights" bill, club women warmly applauded Sarah Reed when she reported on the program that teachers planned to present to the legislature. Teachers were fighting not only to restore salaries for the present, Reed told her audience, but to prevent further cuts in the future, as teachers had in fact been told that they faced cuts as high as one-third of their salaries. It did not make sense, she asserted, "to have worse teachers for better buildings."[21]

In September 1926, the board announced that a new tobacco tax would increase revenues enough to pay teachers for a full ten months for the 1926–27 session. The announcement alleviated the teachers' immediate problems but offered no long-term guarantee or solution.[22] As late as October 22 the teachers felt confident about the chances for the success of their amendment in the November general election. Both houses of the legislature had passed the teachers' bill unanimously. It had the endorsement of the school board, which told the press that it would work to have the amendment ratified at the polls.[23]

On October 17, however, less than a month before the election, the *Item* quoted board member Fred Zengel at length regarding his opposition to the amendment. Zengel alleged that Amendment 8 would destroy the building fund. A few days later, the *Times-Picayune* came out with an editorial against the amendment.[24] The *Times-Picayune* agreed that teachers should be paid for a full ten months. It supported the plan to charge janitors' salaries to the building fund and regretted that the court had declared the move unconstitutional. Although it had originally supported the teachers' amendment, the editor said, a closer look at its wording had caused the paper to change its mind.

Specifically, the *Times-Picayune* objected to the amendment because the board would not be required to reserve any part of the seven-mill levy for the building fund. The building fund, which had been protected by a mandatory provision, could now be wiped out. The editor went on to say that representatives of the teachers' organizations had assured him that they had no intention of abolishing the building fund. When he had asked them to promise that they would support another amendment to restore constitutional protection for the building fund, the teachers refused, he reported, "on the ground that the teachers' organization must reserve full liberty of action against the uncertainties of the future." The *Times-Picayune* concluded that "a wiser and safer amendment" should be considered later and that the one proposed should be defeated.[25]

The teachers were angry about the results of their meeting with the editor. They had no intention of promising to "change the law to suit the dictates of the *Times-Picayune*," Reed wrote. "We do not buy victory. We may go down to defeat, but we'll go with our colors flying."[26] On the afternoon the editorial appeared, the teachers held "an indignation meeting," during which Reed received a phone call from the editor of the *New Orleans States,* who said he would also withdraw the paper's support for the amendment unless the teachers signed the *Times-Picayune*'s pledge. The teachers rejected the ultimatum "in a fresh burst of indignation." Not one teacher dissented. Reed, along with her legislative committee, went to the *States* offices that night to give the editor their decision. He told the committee the paper would fight them in New Orleans as well as in Shreveport. The Baton Rouge press soon joined the opposition.

The teachers were dismayed by the suddenness of the late-breaking attack and by what they considered unfair use of the news page for editorial opinions.[27] In a broadside published in New Orleans newspapers, the teachers assured opponents of Amendment 8 that teachers had always supported building programs and "can always be depended upon to support legislation for the good of the public schools." The allegation that the building fund would be retarded by passage of Amendment 8, the teachers said, "is the result either of baseless fear on the part of the uninformed or biased minds or of the morbid imagination which prejudice fosters."[28] NOPSTA continued its intense politicking for the passage of the amendment, conducting a telephone campaign, running ads in seven out-of-town newspapers, handing out circulars, hand-bills, and automobile stickers, putting up signs and billboards, and making badges for workers at the polls.[29]

Despite the weight of press opinion, the amendment passed. The teachers gave Sarah Reed and her committee most of the credit for their victory. In a letter to members of NOPSTA, outgoing president Augustine Aurianne wrote, "We cannot be too profuse in our thanks to Mrs. Reed and her immediate as-sistants for the work done under stress at a time when the outlook was very uncertain."[30]

The victory was indeed impressive. Even former school board president James A. Fortier, who had fought Reed and the teachers' organizations throughout his tenure, wrote the president of NOPSTA that her organization had good cause to celebrate. Its success "in passing the Constitutional Amend-ment of 1926 was epoch-making and absolutely necessary," Fortier said. "The more I think it over the more I wonder how that was done, and I think it was entirely due to the unflinching bravery of the leaders of that movement."[31]

After the passage of Amendment 8, Reed set her sights on a new campaign—back pay. She immediately began soliciting information from other cities that had won salary restoration after successive reductions. With her law school training, she understood the value of assembling facts and details of court de-cisions that affected teachers' legal status. She also met on a regular basis with school board members, attempting to work out a compromise that would bene-fit both contingents.[32]

In February 1927 NOPSTA and the High School Teachers' Association jointly applied to the school board for reimbursement for losses teachers had suffered in 1924, 1925, and 1926 because of salary cuts. The board agreed to pay them the money asked in three installments. Delighted with the decision, Reed told the board that "she was sure that all past misunderstandings be-tween the Board and the teachers would be put aside and [that] this was the beginning of a new era of good feeling and cooperation for teachers and for the Board."[33]

Her prediction proved overly optimistic. By April board members were fighting among themselves whether to repay the teachers or repay the building fund, which some claimed had been illegally depleted.[34] Finally, in May, the board voted to split any surplus that existed at the end of the academic year between the teachers and the building fund. Sixty-five percent of the surplus would go to teachers and thirty-five percent to buildings.[35] "The decision is final," Reed wrote her NOPSTA colleagues, "and I think the Association may congratulate itself on its victory." [36]

Public school teachers praised Reed's contributions to their success. The association president pointed to Reed's "able leadership and tireless effort" in her work for the legislative committee. Her efforts had resulted, by November of 1928, in teachers receiving 60 percent of the amount owed them, with the remaining 40 percent "a reasonable certainty" by June 1929.[37] Classroom teachers joined in the general appreciation of Reed's work. Upon receiving her first check for salary restoration, one teacher wrote Reed that she and her colleagues "feel that we in the public schools owe a debt of gratitude to you who so energetically and courageously led the movement in our behalf. Will you accept my very sincere thanks and appreciation of your very successful campaign?" [38]

The president of the Louisiana Teachers Association (LTA), impressed with Reed's achievement on the amendment issue, asked her to join him on the state ticket of LTA officers. Reed was "flattered" that he thought enough of her work for the New Orleans teachers to include her on the slate, and she briefly considered the idea but felt she had to decline his offer. "I belong in the ranks," she told him. "I'm happiest there and more useful there." Members of NOPSTA had already "demanded unanimously and insisted" that she become their president, but, she said, "I refused in no uncertain terms. It was my pleasure to work in the ranks; and I was right for I could not have 'put across' back pay for our teachers had I been president of the organization here. There are fine workers, you know, who work best in the limelight—but 'the play's the thing' and the play couldn't go on without workers behind the scenes." [39]

From the beginning of her career as a teacher-activist, Reed worked to achieve economic justice for teachers. Her success with the passage of Amendment 8 showed her what could be gained by aggressive lobbying and the support of a unified group. Already Reed was beginning to think in terms of labor organization. Her reluctance to assume the presidency of NOPSTA or an executive position with the LTA underscores Reed's conviction that she could work more efficiently without the burden and visibility of higher office. The higher her position, the more restricted she might become and the less time she would have for lobbying, which she clearly loved. With her independent spirit and her natural inclination to argue and persuade, Reed had truly found her calling as NOPSTA's legislative chair.

The New Orleans Public School Teachers Association continued to consolidate its influence. Although the group was nonpartisan and did not endorse candidates, NOPSTA recognized, particularly after the fight for Amendment 8, the importance of political involvement. Reed and her legislative committee interviewed 75 of the 105 candidates for the legislature in the November 1928 election, and Reed prevailed upon the Orleans Parish School Board to allow NOPSTA representatives to attend meetings of the board's Committee of the Whole. By June 1928 the association had 1,271 paid-up members.[40]

With salary stabilization accomplished and back pay beginning to be restored, NOPSTA and the High School Teachers' Association, to which Reed continued to belong, renewed the campaign for salary equalization. Finally, the school board announced that beginning in September 1926 new male appointees would be paid on the same basis as female teachers. However, the problem of unequal salaries remained for the teachers already in the corps.[41] Reed pointed out that although female high school teachers had petitioned the board many times for salary equalization, for the past two years they had "been silent on the subject of 'equal pay'—not because we loved equalization less, but we have loved stabilization more." Reed also brought to the board's attention that its own rules and regulations made no distinction in the qualifications for high school teachers. All high school teachers worked equal amounts of time and covered the same amount of work. Nonetheless, the board paid men significantly more than women. The family wage argument, Reed wrote, was "paternalistic." In any case, she argued, "economic necessity does not dictate salary."[42]

Reed rallied the women behind her. It was time, she told the teachers, for them to take up once again their own fight. Reed praised the women teachers who had "unselfishly pushed aside their own cause to join the efforts of the whole corps." Discrimination, however, had to be defeated. Sexual discrimination was not only contrary to the progressive principles to which the school system supposedly subscribed, Reed told her colleagues, it was "un-American," since "America is the country in which women come nearest to getting a square deal." Discrimination could not be justified even on the basis of supply and demand "because cities that have equalization have a larger percentage of male teachers than cities that make a difference on the basis of sex," Reed pointed out. Moreover, a study by the Schoolmasters Club of Cincinnati had found that, contrary to popular belief, men were no more likely to remain in the teaching profession than were women. "If women have used teaching as a waiting station to matrimony, men also have used teaching as a waiting station for law or medicine," Reed observed. "Someone has said teaching is steadily becoming a procession not a profession. The great need is not only to try to keep good men but to keep the whole corps."[43]

The school board replied to Reed's demand for equalization by repeating its claim that it could not afford raises for women, saying it was sure that "the women teachers did not want to disturb the salaries of the men." The board then asked the parish school superintendent to draw up a single salary schedule for the purpose of equalizing salaries eventually. Reed requested that the superintendent "be instructed not to regard the men as a separate entity, but that a single salary schedule be considered that would be applicable to all teachers."[44]

Frustrated by the board's delaying tactics, the teachers of NOPSTA and the HSTA decided to take their problem directly to the state legislature in Baton Rouge. The resulting bill would require the removal of sex discrimination in teachers' salaries. Facing strong opposition in the legislature, Reed and her colleagues undertook an aggressive lobbying campaign. One committee remained in Baton Rouge for three weeks while delegations of teachers appeared before a House committee and lobbied individual lawmakers. A larger delegation of fifty teachers traveled from New Orleans to Baton Rouge to attend a Senate committee meeting. Other teachers solicited prominent members of the New Orleans community to send letters and telegrams to state legislators.[45] Reed actively participated in all of the lobbying efforts.

Despite its avowed commitment to a single salary, the Orleans Parish School Board sent superintendent Nicholas Bauer to the Louisiana Senate Committee on Public Education to help defeat the bill. The superintendent made what had become the standard argument, that because the board lacked sufficient funds, the salaries of men teachers would have to be lowered if women's salaries were raised. The superintendent made it clear that he did not intend to lower any man's salary. He also claimed that if women's salaries were increased, raises would have to be given all the way up the line—to principals and supervisors—to bring them into line with the new salary schedule.[46]

The legislature passed Act 110, prohibiting sex discrimination in salaries, but the superintendent's lobbying efforts had some success. An amendment to the bill extended the equalization process over four years, eliminating 25 percent of the salary disparity each year. Equalization had to be accomplished by 1932. The bill also explicitly prohibited reduction of any salaries already in place.[47]

After the passage of Amendment 8 and Act 110, teachers across New Orleans recognized Reed's vital contribution to their cause. The teachers "as one person wished to express their appreciation of the outstanding service of Mrs. Sarah Towles Reed," according to the *New Orleans Teacher*, NOPSTA's new publication.[48] A group of teachers from NOPSTA decided to thank Reed by donating enough money to enroll her in the school system's retirement program, which she had not yet joined. "The teachers of New Orleans know that they owe primarily to your indefatigable effort and intelligent zeal the victories that they have gained in the last few years," Amy Hinrichs wrote Reed, recalling the many times when teachers had wanted to recognize her accomplishments publicly and to show how much they appreciated what she had done. Finally, after hearing that Reed was not in the retirement program, the teachers had decided to pay the initial sum required for membership.

"If you had been in my place in the last weeks, you would have been deeply impressed again and again as this older teacher or that one dwelt on how you did something for her that she could never have done for herself, or as a younger teacher, not so long out of normal school, expressed unbounded admiration for your courage and ability," Hinrichs wrote her friend. "I have found that united gratitude is as powerful as we, you and I and our fellow teachers, have found that united action is. . . . The amount deposited is the sum of individual expressions of heartfelt gratitude, not at all commensurate with the service you have rendered, but endowed, we hope, with a sort of magic power to symbolize esteem, admiration, appreciation, love."[49] Reed answered that she appreciated the offer, but that it was "impossible . . . to accept any gift whatsoever for services which it was my good fortune to be able to give."[50] The secretary-treasurer of the Teachers' Retirement Fund, with whom the teachers had deposited the check for $678, returned the money to NOPSTA after Reed declined to accept it.[51]

The Orleans Parish School Board did not rush to implement Act 110. Although by law the board was required to achieve full salary equalization by October 1932, it asked for and received from the state attorney general permission to begin the process toward equalization in 1929 instead of 1928.[52] The board justified this delay by arguing that it did not have enough money to cover salary increases in 1928. Reed denied the accuracy of this assertion, claiming that superintendent Nicholas Bauer had admitted to commissioner of finance T. Semmes Walmsley that the board had enough money for this purpose. "The women teachers delayed the passage of Act 110 until they had this statement in writing from Mr. Walmsley," Reed explained.[53] As further evidence that the board could afford to implement the act, she pointed out that the board had raised all the administrators' salaries for the session 1928–29; the superintendent alone had received an increase of two thousand dollars a year. The board had been able to raise the salaries of male teachers and male administrators, Reed maintained, all the while claiming it lacked the money to keep its promise to women teachers. She charged that the board was simply "determined not to put the act into effect."[54]

At the start of the 1929–30 school year, the school board announced that elimination of sex discrimination in salaries in the four years required by Act 110 was economically impossible. "An increase in the salary of practically every member of the teaching corps should be made if the high school teachers are raised," the board said. "To do otherwise, would be inequitable and grossly unjust." The board did not have the funding to raise all the women's salaries or to raise the salaries of all principals, supervisors, and grade school teachers. And of course the board did not intend to lower anyone's salary, making salary equalization impossible. Therefore, deciding to comply "strictly" with the requirement of Act 110 that it eliminate sex differences in salary schedules, the board devised a new schedule based not on gender but on the high school in which a teacher worked. All teachers in each high school would henceforth be paid the same amount, but differences in salaries between schools would be allowed.[55] The men teachers all worked in the boys' high school, none at the two girls' high schools, making it easy to pinpoint which schools might receive higher salaries.[56] As Reed later pointed out, "'Twas thus that buildings came to have the male and female sex."[57]

The ploy did not fool anyone, least of all Reed, who called it "a joke, a farce, a jest." Women, Reed told *Quartee* readers, were once again the school board's target; it had happened so often, she said, "that the idea of being shot at has lost its novelty; it no longer brings a thrill." Reed suggested that the woman teacher "should turn the attack from herself by the militant methods of her British sister, or by the use of British publicity parades." A street demonstration, Reed said, "featuring Teachers' Salaries according to schools would be a project in which all seventy schools could participate."[58]

Reed immediately wrote to prominent members of the community, asking them to join a citizen's committee to help the women in their fight for equality; she and NOPSTA believed that the board never intended to put Act 110 into effect. "Sex discrimination is more flagrant than ever," she told them. "This is an evasion . . . a misconception of [the] statute . . . an arbitrary, egregious injustice." After securing a year's delay from the attorney general, Reed wrote, the board evidently intended to postpone equalization forever with its gendered building scheme. "The whole maneuver is a subterfuge unworthy of the Body controlling the educational destiny of this great city; it is an evasion of the law. . . . It is a misconstruction of the statute and a gross injustice to the women high school teachers who have given untiring service and unswerving loyalty to the schools of this city." Male and female high school teachers had "equal qualifications, experience, success; the same course of study, textbooks, school hours, number of pupils," Reed wrote. "These men and women teachers give the public equal service. The public should give them equal pay! Service—not sex—should determine salary."[59] A NOPSTA flier exclaimed, "Sex discrimination in fixing teachers' salaries is unwarranted, unscientific, undemocratic and un-American!"[60]

Reed, working with NOPSTA's salary committee, had already devised a single salary schedule based solely on years of teaching and academic preparation, with no discrimination according to sex or to grade taught. In fact, the school board's new salary scheme had inspired NOPSTA to change its focus from the high schools to the entire school system, proposing a true single-salary pay scale with no differential between elementary and high school salaries.[61]

The board's salary schedule called for higher salaries for high school teachers than for elementary teachers and higher pay for men appointed prior to 1924. Although women high school teachers were paid a beginning salary of $140 a month, men hired before 1924 were paid $170 month; wages for women and men hired after 1924 increased to a maximum of $240 a month after ten years, compared with $330 for men hired before 1924.[62] Despite what the board said about the necessity for principals to receive larger paychecks than teachers, NOPSTA observed that many male high school teachers earned higher salaries than any female elementary school principal.[63]

At the end of the 1929–30 academic year, representatives of several civic organizations, called together by the League of Women Voters, went before the board to protest its failure to equalize pay. Both the president of the Louisiana League of Women Voters and the mayor of New Orleans asked why the board had refused to comply with the law. Now mayor, T. Semmes Walmsley said that he realized that the board was experiencing financial difficulties, but the legislature had obviously intended that men and women be paid equal salaries.[64] The state tax collector also joined the women's delegation and expressed his opinion that "the board's alleged shortage of funds was only an excuse, not the real reason for refusing to equalize salaries."[65]

In *Quartee,* Reed reviewed in verse the school board's delaying techniques, treating her readers to one of her many light-hearted compositions, a poem entitled "Rime and Reason of Act 110." It read in part:

> It is true we live in modern times, but it smacks of the Middle Ages
> When men and women do equal work and get unequal wages.
> It is hard to believe in '28 that what a teacher got
> Was more if the teacher were trousered,
> And less if the teacher were not.

> We know this has been a man-run world, Louisiana a man-run state,
> For practices antediluvian are not yet out of date.
> And though the schools have made great strides, one unprogressive
>   feature
> Is the flagrant lack of recognition accorded the woman teacher.
> Before the Board the women proved, not once but again and again,
> The justice of their protest, but the Board proved MEN FOR MEN!
> A resolution in '22, the Orleans Board produced,
> 'Twas 'Equal pay for equal work, no salary to be reduced'
> *Reductio ad absurdum* this — a joke, a farce, a jest.[66]

In addition to the lack of progress on salary equalization, matters of back pay arose again at the end of the 1929 academic year when the board failed to make payments for previously lost salaries as it had promised. Although it had reimbursed teachers for 60 percent of the back salary due them, the board owed them the remaining 40 percent.[67] In May 1929 NOPSTA sent petitions to the school board, demanding that it eliminate all additions to buildings, supplies, equipment, and furnishings "until the teachers have received their just dues." The president of the board took offense at NOPSTA's attitude and retorted that the board had never promised that it would have a financial surplus with which to pay back lost salaries. He reminded the teachers that school authorities had pledged to pay as much as they could of the "back pay" only if a surplus existed.[68] NOPSTA urged the board to include the 40 percent back pay in the budget for the following year since, according to the board's own argument, a financial surplus could never be guaranteed. The school board ignored NOPSTA's demand that it meet the 40 percent obligation by July 1929. The issue of back pay and whether it should be budgeted into the board's ordinary expenses continued to divide teachers and the board. Despite the efforts of NOPSTA to keep the issue before the board, teachers received no more of their promised back pay in 1929.

Although NOPSTA had accomplished a great deal in a short time, much remained to be done by the end of the 1920s. Salary equalization was still only an empty promise, and pay cuts had not been fully restored. With the coming of the Depression, teachers' economic circumstances were placed in even greater jeopardy. Reed had always understood that organization was essential to achieving teachers' goals. "Teamwork only will give results," Reed wrote in the inaugural issue of *Quartee*. Later, when the Depression stimulated a resurgence of interest in labor organizations, she started to see the advantages of affiliation with a national organization.

Professionalism, one of NOPSTA's original goals, was beginning to seem less important than political alliances that could achieve greater results. What difference did it make whether people viewed teachers as professionals if they were underpaid anyway? True, professionalism benefited women to some extent. Women teachers had always been held back by their socially prescribed roles; they were expected to act unselfishly, to devote themselves to children, to ask little for themselves. Professional standards would put all teachers on common ground and establish scholarly—instead of gendered—measurements for advancement. However, women teachers had already seen how merit plans could be rigged against them and how laws designed to assure them justice could be circumvented. While women teachers had made some progress in the 1920s, led and inspired by Reed and women like her, by the close of the decade they were still far from achieving their goals.

4 Depression Years

The Great Depression marked a turning point in Reed's public life. She moved beyond NOPSTA's almost exclusive emphasis on professional recognition for teachers and began to identify them as members of the American working class. The economic crisis seems also to have triggered in Reed the realization that the inequality of women was tied to larger societal injustices suffered by workers in general. As the Depression dragged on, Reed concluded that unionization was the key to correcting these inequities.

Like other workers everywhere in the country, teachers experienced a sharp decline in their standard of living as the Depression wore on. Once again, teachers faced pay cuts. Already overworked and underpaid, New Orleans teachers saw their class sizes swell and their salaries shrink in the early years of the financial disaster. Rapidly falling property taxes, the main source of school revenue, cut into the amount of money available to the school board, while enrollments climbed by some twenty-five thousand in the decade after 1925. At the beginning of the school year 1932–33, the Orleans Parish School Board suffered a loss of some $859,000 in revenue. At the end of the fiscal year, it owed $3,789,295.[1]

Financial conditions in New Orleans were so bad that journalist Lorena Hickok, writing to Harry Hopkins at the Federal Emergency Relief Administration, described the South's largest city as a commercial "corpse."[2] Before the worst of the Depression hit, New Orleans was already in debt by some $3.5 million. In the mid-1930s the city's financial situation grew desperate when Senator Huey P. Long, angered by the Old Regular political machine's refusal to back his candidates and his bills in the Louisiana legislature, forced the city into financial and political bankruptcy. Although the school board was not dependent on city revenues, having its own dedicated property tax as well as grants from the state, the board was also in debt to local banks.[3] In 1932 banks demanded that the school board pay its overdue loans and redeem its bonded debt. The board raised the money by again cutting teachers' pay.

Reed tried to bolster the morale of her troubled colleagues. "The light of 1932 needs to be the light of confidence; and, for teachers, confidence in themselves," Reed wrote in the New Year's first edition of *Quartee*. "Too frequently in 1931 was heard the expression: 'Thank heaven, we have our jobs!' Why should not the jobs thank the heavens for having us? We are qualified and competent." The public, she reminded her friends, should be grateful to have its children educated by experienced, trained teachers. "Let us not cheapen ourselves and our calling by an imaginary sense of obligation."[4]

The uncertainty of the times further strained relations between the school board and teachers. Teachers understood that their salaries might have to be reduced on account of the Depression, but they were frustrated with the tendency of school authorities to cut their salaries before making other reductions in the school budget. They were also irritated by the board's total unwillingness to consult them on salary issues. When the Orleans Parish School Board in March 1932 announced salary reductions of 8 percent for the following school year, Reed objected. The announcement was premature, she argued in a *Quartee* editorial, since the board could not yet know what its revenues would be for the next year. "Surely any statement relative to a cut should have been withheld from the public until the board is in a position to be perfectly definite," she wrote. The only advantage to the board of this early decision might be to make it "popular with short-sighted citizens who have joined the hue and cry of cut everything and anything."

In particular, Reed objected to the decision of school officials to adopt such a policy "without any consultation whatever with the people most vitally concerned—the teachers themselves." Perhaps, she speculated, the board had realized that teachers would be the least sympathetic of anyone to its financial difficulties. In light of the newly constructed Alcee Fortier High School for boys (where she was transferred in April 1932), it was apparent, Reed said, that the school system could afford to build expensive buildings. "Surely there should be enough money to pay teachers when there is money to build a school with an auditorium of theater proportions. The public can't appreciate the Board's financial emergency in the presence of such buildings. It seems a wrong system that exalts buildings and cuts teachers."[5]

Reed reminded *Quartee* readers that President Hoover had asked school boards not to reduce teachers' salaries despite the national economic crisis, and that the recent national Superintendents' Conference in Washington, D.C., had reiterated the president's request. "Whatever cuts teachers, cuts the children," Reed argued. "A salary-cut lowers morale and reacts upon the teacher's work and upon the teacher's classes. . . . Now is the time for the Board to accept the teachers as partners in the big business of schools."[6] Teachers had no way of knowing what their salary would be during any given year. The "continual shadow" of a pay cut, NOPSTA argued, seriously undermined teachers' morale.[7]

Depression conditions worsened. In August 1932 a thousand teachers and other concerned citizens attended a meeting at which the Orleans Parish School Board announced its decision to reduce the salaries of all its employees—with the exception of the lowest-paid instructors—by 14 to 26 percent. Employees on a ten-month pay schedule would receive a salary for only nine and a half months with the remaining half-month's salary to be paid as soon as the board could borrow that amount. Furthermore, the board announced, it would deduct in full a substitute teacher's salary from the salary of the absent teacher and reduce increments for B.A. and M.A. degrees from $15 to $7.50 a month. The board curtailed all new building activities and reduced funds for supplies and janitors.[8]

Reed argued that teachers' salaries should be the last items cut during the Depression. The new salary for beginning teachers of $90 a month for ten months, she pointed out to the board, was less than the annual salary paid to assistant janitors (or "women sweepers," as she called them), who during the last session had received $70 a month for twelve months. She also objected to the discrimination against teachers who held degrees. Even if salaries had to be reduced, she wanted teachers with degrees to receive an additional $15 a month.[9]

The board adhered to its original plan for reductions without salary increments for degrees. In Reed's contract for 1932–33, A. J. Tete, school board secretary, notified her that she would be paid $199.50 per month for nine and one-half months. "This amount includes all allowances to which you may be entitled for degrees, college hours, special classes, etc." He hedged the promise of the remaining half-month's pay, saying "It is the sense of some individual members of the Board that the remaining one-half month's salary will be paid as soon as it is possible to borrow and disburse the necessary amount." Tete warned, however, that the stated salary "is not to be considered final for the year, for the Board may find it necessary to make further adjustments should the estimated revenues happen not to be realizable. The Board intends to live strictly within its revenues and will not close the year with a deficit." [10]

In August 1932 NOPSTA hired a firm of public accountants to study the auditor's report on the school board's accounts for the fiscal year ending June 30, 1932. After their examination of the board's books, the auditors suggested that any money remaining in reserves be dedicated to the restoration of teachers' salaries and that the board issue certificates of indebtedness to each teacher. The board refused. [11] Once again, NOPSTA and Reed lost patience with the board's inclination to put the burden of its debt on the teachers. [12]

Teacher morale took another beating in March of 1933 when bank closings prevented more than half of New Orleans teachers from cashing their February paychecks. They had still not received their February salaries at the end of March. On March 30, the school board informed its employees that it could obtain funds to pay only 39 percent of their March salaries and that a bank had arranged to cash this portion of their checks at the school board offices. Separate times were set up for whites and blacks. At 3:30 on the appointed day, more than a thousand teachers, many of whom had not received a paycheck for two months, lined up to wait for the single teller on the third floor to conduct the transactions. As time passed, *Quartee* reported, "the anxiety of those who had not yet been paid was constantly increasing and the crowded conditions within the building were more and more intolerable. To make matters worse, the rough handling of some of the ladies by a policeman still further increased the discomfort of the situation." Finally, by 7:00 that evening all of the teachers had cashed their partial salary checks.

Teachers did not receive their February salaries or the unpaid 61 percent of their March salaries until May. April, May, and June paychecks were also delayed. The *Item* reported that the sporadic salary payments were causing severe financial distress for teachers, many of whom were forced to walk long distances to work because they could not afford streetcar fare. Emery Lively, chair of NOPSTA's salary committee, told the school board in May 1933 that "although the teachers appreciated the board's difficulties in obtaining funds," many of them were "feeling the pinch of poverty and had had their possessions seized."

At the same school board meeting, Reed told board members that teachers had "reached a point of intense anxiety" because of the continuing questions about their salaries. If the board had to cut teacher salaries during the next year, Reed suggested, it should consider instead the possibility of closing the schools, since New Orleans teachers wanted to avoid the kind of financial disaster Chicago teachers were experiencing.[13]

Teachers in Chicago had suffered through three years of sporadic paychecks, and when they finally started receiving steady pay their salaries were cut by 10 percent.[14] Teachers across the country feared that their situations would deteriorate to the level of their counterparts in Chicago, many of whom had lost their homes. "Their life insurance cashed in, their savings gone, some teachers have been driven to panhandling after school hours to get food," the *Nation* reported. Schools everywhere were slashing salaries, increasing class sizes, and eliminating services and programs in an effort to cope with the economic crisis.[15] Teachers lived in a state of nerve-wracking uncertainty about their futures. Hiring had virtually ceased; substitutes were used instead of full-time teachers, resulting in long waiting lists of eligible normal school graduates.[16] Teachers in some cities received their pay in scrip.[17] Sarah's sister Anne, a teacher in Auburn, Alabama, wrote in December 1932 that the public schools there had been closed for three weeks, and the teachers had been paid only in scrip for eighteen months. "The merchants here . . . have been 'carrying' the teachers for months, but they say they can't keep it up much longer as their creditors are pressing them."[18]

Like their sister, Sarah and Roberta faced financial setbacks during the Depression. They had a hard time keeping up payments on their small house in Uptown New Orleans, and their mortgage company informed them regularly from 1933 to 1935 that their account was delinquent. Even with their limited resources, however, the sisters somehow managed to keep their house and Weyanoke, as well as to send their niece Nora to college.

In September of 1933 the Orleans Parish School Board announced several significant cost-cutting measures, including its intention to abolish the salary scale for male high school teachers appointed before 1924, thus putting all men on the lower-paying schedule of their female counterparts. It also reported that it was suspending automatic increases in salaries, as well as the monetary increments for degrees and college hours. Additionally, teachers would be paid for only nine months during the 1933–34 session.[19] The next month the board equalized the pay of male and female teachers in the "colored" high schools by abolishing the separate pay scale for men. In effect, this substantially decreased men's salaries. Ironically, when long-sought salary equalization finally arrived, it came not as a capitulation to women's rights but as a money-saving effort in response to the economic crisis.[20]

Male teachers reacted to this unwelcome development by forming their own organization, the Schoolmasters Club of New Orleans, organized in September of 1933 with a membership that included the parish superintendent of schools, assistant superintendents, directors, teachers, and other male employees holding a teacher's license. "It being understood that only the male sex shall be eligible," the Schoolmasters' rules read. It was also understood, evidently, that administrators would always be male, since all administrators were automatically included in the membership.[21] The organization proposed to work for a salary schedule "more satisfactory to the members of the club." Over the next few years, the Schoolmasters drew up various sets of recommendations in favor of male teachers: one attempting to remedy the scarcity of men teachers in the public school system, another recommending male principals, others advocating the repeal of the single salary scale. The Schoolmasters agreed that "men in the school system should get more pay than women." Consequently, the club members were not generally fond of Sarah Reed, her sister Roberta Towles, or the female-dominated teachers' organizations. On one occasion a Schoolmaster reminded the club that "the teaching corps is top heavy with old women who regard the Towles-Reed outfit as divine."[22]

In August 1934 the school board passed a resolution endorsing "the principle that teachers be paid according to years of experience and scholastic preparation rather than according to years of experience and grade taught." After the implementation of this schedule, the board said, teachers who were transferred between grade levels and between subjects, or from elementary to high schools, would no longer experience a change in their salaries. The board also put forward a pay schedule that listed increased salaries for all teachers, but it included a caveat. Financial conditions made it impossible at that time to pay the salaries listed on the scale, school officials explained, but as a proof of their intention eventually to meet the salaries indicated, they would give all teachers a 2 percent increase in pay. The board also promised that teachers who were not at that time receiving any compensation for their degrees would be paid an additional seventy-five dollars per year for a B.A. and a further seventy-five dollars for an M.A. Salaries would be disbursed over ten months. There was a lower scale for African American teachers.[23]

This bone thrown to teachers in the form of a statement of principle and a 2 percent raise did not satisfy NOPSTA, which unsuccessfully requested an open meeting with school officials. One board member complained that he could see no reason for a public meeting "where anyone so disposed—Communists, socialists and the laity—could embarrass the Board by a barrage of questions that could not be answered." Reed pointed out that because of all the publicity given to the new salary schedule, most of the public believed that teachers were already receiving the higher salaries when in fact they were not. She argued in vain that a meeting would help set the record straight.[24]

Finally, in October 1934, the board appropriated $80,351.23 for some of the "back pay" that it had owed teachers since 1928. The aggregate one-third of monthly salaries, totaling nearly $80,000, had become available from taxes collected during the past year, the press reported.[25] Bolstered by its success in freeing up some of the money owed teachers, NOPSTA continued to press for restoration of the tenth-month salary. In June the school board announced that because the state Department of Education had issued an additional fifty cents per educable person to local boards, it could now pay teachers 75 percent of their tenth-month salary instead of the 50 percent it had anticipated paying. This arrangement did not satisfy the teachers, who over the course of the next year and a half continued to request both a full tenth-month salary and a resumption of increments.[26] At a meeting in October of 1935, board member Isaac Heller, generally sympathetic to teachers' interests, grew impatient when Reed asked him to take some action to restore salary increments. "There are many inequities in the salary scale," Reed said, "and we feel it is imperative that the increments be re-established. It is the thing closest to the heart of the teachers to have these increment payments resumed." Heller responded, "It is the thing closest to the heart of the School Board to pay the teacher salaries in cash and to be sure that we have the cash to pay them."[27]

Teachers' concern over salaries was perennial. A more immediate threat to their jobs arose in September 1931, when school board president Henry Schaumburg announced that the board would not necessarily grant a public trial to teachers, principals, or supervisors who had been dismissed. The city attorney supported this ruling, offering his legal opinion that the act under which the school board operated (Act 100 of 1922) was "very clear and unambiguous on the subject. It says specifically (a) that there must be written charges; (b) that the charges must be of the kind outlined in the act, namely of immorality, neglect of duty, incompetency, malfeasance or non-feasance; (c) that the teacher must be found guilty after investigation and report." The attorney pointed out that "nowhere is the word 'trial' used."[28]

Sarah Reed, as legislative chair of both NOPSTA and the High School Teachers' Association, was alarmed by this new development. She asked the board to reconsider its new policy and to reenact section 202 of the 1930 Rules and Regulations of the Orleans Parish School Board, which had assured teachers the right to a public trial. The board defended its new ruling, which conformed to the current law. Reed requested that the board revert to its previous rule until such time as the teachers could persuade the legislature to change the law.[29]

In a communication to the board published in *Quartee,* Reed expressed the teachers' "genuine astonishment" at the board's new ruling and pointed to the insecurity on the part of teachers, principals, and supervisors that surely would result. "The Board's new policy," she claimed, "will lower the morale and impair the efficiency of the entire system. A sense of insecurity on the part of the corps must inevitably react unfavorably upon the seventy thousand children of the New Orleans Public Schools."[30] NOPSTA initiated a campaign to have the board rewrite its rule and urged the legislature to change the law to guarantee teachers the right to a public trial.[31] The move soon became part of a larger effort to secure permanent tenure laws for teachers. The board suggested that teachers take the matter to the legislature, since in the absence of a state law, future boards could easily overturn any agreement that might be reached.[32]

In the midst of the campaign to secure public trials for dismissed New Orleans teachers, A. P. Harvey, head of the American Federation of Labor's Central Trades and Labor Council of New Orleans, wrote American Federation of Teachers vice-president Allie Mann, suggesting that the AFT might be able to establish a local in New Orleans. He advised her to get in touch with Sarah Reed.[33] Mann did so immediately. The AFT, under the direction of the AFL, had recently initiated a special organizing campaign in the South, with Mann in charge of recruitment.[34] Mann's letter to Reed suggested that "this critical time" was a propitious one for teachers to organize "so that they can express themselves and use their influence to bring about better conditions for the teachers and for education," and Mann reminded Reed that the American Federation of Labor had a long record of defending teachers' rights. Local teachers' organizations that affiliated with labor unions had the most success in achieving increased salaries, tenure, pension plans, and better curriculum, Mann claimed. "Indeed," she commented, "it seems to me that unless a teacher affiliates herself with some such organization she is hardly living up to her obligations."[35]

The AFT was a true teachers' union. Unlike the administrator-dominated National Education Association, the AFT eschewed administrators in its membership and concentrated on the "bread-and-butter" issues that the NEA ignored. The NEA was more concerned with what one historian has called "traditional professional mystique" than with the material needs of classroom teachers. The AFT, on the other hand, dedicated itself to the interests of the educational rank and file and fought the NEA's bias against the labor movement.[36]

Margaret Haley, leader of the Chicago Teachers' Federation and a founding member of the AFT, was a strong labor supporter. "We realized," Haley said of labor affiliation, that teachers had to "fight the devil with fire and, if we were to preserve not only our own self-respect but the basic independence of the public schools, we must make [a] powerful political alliance."[37] In a 1916 article, "Why Teachers Should Organize," Haley maintained that there was "no possible conflict between the good of society and the good of its members, of which the industrial workers are the vast majority." She reminded her readers that teachers and labor had a "common cause."[38]

In 1904, before the organization of the AFT, Haley, en route to a meeting of the National Education Association in Boston, stopped to visit Susan B. Anthony. The suffrage leader encouraged Haley to press for women's equality within the NEA and to demand female participation in its convention program. Anthony also urged Haley to fight for equal pay for equal work and equal opportunity for appointment to administrative positions,[39] educational goals that suffragists had sought since Reconstruction. When Haley looked at the NEA program in Boston, she noticed that men were 8 to 1 on the program, while women were 12 to 1 in the audience. This disparity angered Haley and other women teachers who based their earliest organizing efforts on eradicating sexual discrimination, a fundamental feminist ambition.[40]

Unlike the NEA, the AFT placed women in positions of authority. Many women, effectively barred from leadership positions in the NEA because of the dominance of male administrators, gained their first opportunity to assume significant positions in a national organization through the AFT. By 1919, just three years after organization of the AFT, women accounted for more than half of the union's membership. The AFT was committed to equal pay for all teachers regardless of sex, race, or grade taught. It also supported teacher tenure, sabbaticals, increased salaries, an end to discrimination against married women and blacks, and academic freedom.[41]

The AFT had chosen the right person to help organize a labor union for teachers in New Orleans. In the 1930s Reed enlarged her concerns and her political philosophy by actively participating in several organizations dedicated to promoting social and economic justice. She held memberships in the Southern Conference for Human Welfare, the Louisiana League for the Preservation of Constitutional Rights, the League for Industrial Democracy, and the Contributors for Loyalist Spain. She was also a devotee of John Dewey, whose belief in democratic teaching practices moved the AFT to present him with its first membership card. Moreover, as Reed once told a reporter, she had always been a "firm believer in the labor movement."[42] Reed, realizing that teachers needed an organization stronger than NOPSTA to protect their interests during the economic crisis, eagerly accepted the suggestion that New Orleans teachers organize a local of the American Federation of Teachers.

While NOPSTA and the High School Teachers' Association had been fairly effective in accomplishing their goals, the teachers confronted problems during the Depression that went beyond the powers of these teachers' organizations to solve. Faced with the continual threat of salary reductions and with teachers' rights in jeopardy, Reed and other teachers understood that they needed more political clout than they could muster among themselves. Allies in the local labor council as well as the national trade union movement might mean the difference between success and failure for teachers when pressing their claims before the school board and the state legislature.[43] In 1934 Reed, Towles, and eight colleagues applied for a charter to create the Classroom Teachers' Federation, Local 353 of the American Federation of Teachers, AFL.

In the early days of the Depression, roughly 1930–33, labor activity declined in Louisiana. The only strike during these years took place on the docks in New Orleans; otherwise, workers, anxious about keeping their jobs, were quiet. Union membership rolls also dwindled; the national AFL membership dropped by more than 1 million workers, and the number of locals in New Orleans fell from 113 in 1928 to 70 in 1933.[44] In 1933, with the passage of the National Industrial Recovery Act (NIRA), unionization began to pick up. Workers interpreted article 7(a) of the NIRA, which declared that workers had the right to organize and bargain collectively, to mean that the federal government would protect their right to unionize. Unions gained a new lease on life. Most people incorrectly assumed that the government was urging workers to unionize; article 7(a) was in fact a concession to the AFL to persuade it to quit agitating for a thirty-hour work week.[45] Nonetheless, workers readily seized on the only support for unionization they had ever heard from the federal government and joined unions in the greatest numbers since World War I. They also participated in a rash of strikes that erupted throughout the country in the mid-1930s.[46]

In New Orleans, workers struck at Lane Cotton Mills and at a bridge construction site; in nearby Marrero, workers went on strike at a Celotex plant.[47] An important boost to unionization came in 1935 with the passage of the National Labor Relations Act—the Wagner Act—which guaranteed workers the right to organize and bargain collectively with their employers.[48] The establishment of the National Labor Relations Board further bolstered labor's self-confidence.

The AFT came to New Orleans at a propitious time. By 1935, when Local 353 began recruiting members, the nation viewed labor unions more sympathetically than ever before, and the passage of the Wagner Act made labor more confident. The feelings of despair and hopelessness that had characterized the early days of the Depression began to disappear when there were signs of recovery by the mid-1930s, a development that helped labor's organizing efforts.[49]

Still, many obstacles to teacher unionization remained, and it was testimony to Reed's enormous popularity among her peers that she persuaded some of them to join her in a movement that most professionals scorned. Teachers saw themselves as professionals, and they were just as dedicated to establishing that image as they had been in the 1920s when they formed NOPSTA. Even after the Classroom Teachers' Federation had secured a number of gains for the teachers, it still had to fight the prejudice against white-collar workers joining a labor union. Most teachers resisted the union's organizing efforts despite its frequent assurances that professionals in many fields were beginning to appreciate the power of organization.[50]

In addition to the negative perception of unions that the AFT faced throughout the country, AFT organizing efforts in the South were complicated by the race issue. When the 1928 AFT convention advocated history textbooks that would "call attention to the achievements of the Negro in the past in order that our histories may develop a more tolerant attitude toward the races that constitute our nation," many southern delegates objected. Another resolution condemned the Ku Klux Klan and the Daughters of the American Revolution and urged teachers "to help restore social sanity so that tolerance and brotherhood may play their part in winning for America a place of leadership in the struggle to bring about an international brotherhood of nations." This kind of talk convinced many southerners that the AFT was a radical organization.[51]

A few AFT locals, such as the ones in Chicago and Atlanta, represented a majority of their city's teachers, but most, including the New Orleans Classroom Teachers' Federation, represented only a minority. Like other small AFT locals, the New Orleans group often succeeded in exerting influence far out of proportion to its actual size.[52] Until the late 1940s fewer than 10 percent of the city's white teachers belonged to Local 353. Because of its small size, the Orleans Parish School Board could avoid recognizing the union as an official bargaining agent for classroom personnel.[53] As one school board president told the CTF, the union had the right, as did any other group, to come before the board with its requests, but the board "did not intend to relinquish one particle of its constitutional rights in the management of the schools."[54]

Part of the reason for the board's antagonism toward the CTF can be explained by the organization's affiliation with organized labor. Most administrators scorned trade unions, associating them with working-class power, integration, and left-wing subversion. Even the AFL, conservative as it was compared with the CIO, seemed threatening to the status quo. In Memphis, the hostility toward unions was so great that when teachers organized an AFT local, the school board demanded that they disavow in writing any labor union affiliation.[55]

Portents of change in Louisiana during the 1930s exacerbated union phobia: the presence of the Congress of Industrial Organizations (CIO) in the state, Communists in New Orleans municipal elections, workers on strike, the first stirrings of a civil rights movement. All of these developments threatened to undermine traditional economic, racial, and political relationships. With the Depression disrupting business as usual in all aspects of society, the idea of teachers—the guardians of society's youth—joining a union, even the moderate AFL, was disturbing.

Many teachers shared these concerns with their superiors, and it was not easy to persuade them to join the ranks of the working class by affiliating with a union. Although Local 353 took pride in its labor associations, it sought to reassure members and potential members that it would not take any radical actions. "The New Orleans Classroom Teachers' Federation is dedicated to the principle of collective action," Roberta Towles, membership chair, wrote in a recruitment flier, listing the local's affiliation with the American Federation of Teachers, the American Federation of Labor, the Louisiana State Federation of Labor, and the New Orleans Central Trades and Labor Council. Because many teachers opposed the idea of walking off their jobs in a labor dispute, Towles made a special point of telling prospective members that despite strong ties to labor, the national AFT had a nonstriking policy. "We feel that teachers do not need to use such drastic action as the strike," Towles assured her colleagues.[56]

The charter of the New Orleans Classroom Teachers' Federation, Local 353 of the AFL, clearly affirmed the union's close identification with labor as well as its commitment to democratic procedures and principles. "We believe in democracy and in the schools as the chief agency of democracy," the CTF charter read. The union expressed its opposition to "undemocratic administration, adherence to tradition, and lack of responsiveness to the needs of the community," and declared that teachers had to find a solution to these problems. "We believe that servility breeds servility," the teachers proclaimed, announcing their intention "to democratize the schools by encouraging and promoting teacher and pupil participation." Teachers should cooperate with other workers in the community, "upon whom the future of democracy must depend."

The CTF limited its membership to classroom teachers, excluding principals and other administrators, and pledged its permanent affiliation with the
AFT and the Central Trades and Labor Council. The union intended to protect and advance teacher interests, to raise the standard of the teaching profession by securing good working conditions, to protect the best interests of
the taxpayers, and to ensure the children's welfare. The CTF also affiliated with
the National Education Association and the Louisiana Teachers' Association.
Most CTF members, including Reed, also retained their previous memberships in NOPSTA and the HSTA. In fact, Reed retained her position on the
High School Teachers' Association executive board and on the legislative
committee of NOPSTA and represented all three organizations in petitioning
the school board and lobbying the legislature.[57]

If Reed could coordinate the efforts of various teachers' organizations on
major issues, she knew that they would have a greater chance for success. By
force of personality, perseverance, and intelligence, Reed secured the cooperation of teachers who belonged to associations with divergent and sometimes
conflicting goals and philosophies. Reed used her rhetorical talents to persuade her colleagues to stand together in their fight for better schools and better working conditions. Teachers would stand up and cheer when Reed ex-
horted them in public meetings. "Organization! More organization! And more
organization!" Reed proclaimed. "Talk in corridors—in cloakrooms—at
bridge tables won't get teachers anywhere. But action will—organized action!
And teachers are finding that they must organize or get lost in the shuffle."[58]

With the organization of the CTF, Reed and her colleagues entered a period
of substantial progress for educational reform. Part of this success resulted
from the support of the state government, notably from Governor Richard
Leche and Lieutenant Governor Earl K. Long. Politicians could not ignore
voting blocs as large as that of the state's teachers and their labor allies. Reed's
political acumen and skillful lobbying of state legislators helped account for
the teachers' success in Baton Rouge. When the state legislature in June 1936
passed a bill restoring life tenure to New Orleans teachers, Reed and her allies
experienced one of their greatest accomplishments.

Reed, working with both NOPSTA and the Classroom Teachers' Federation, had engaged in an intensive lobbying campaign in Baton Rouge to secure a strong tenure law for teachers. Tenure provisions had been part of Act
100 of 1922, and a revised tenure bill had been passed in 1934. Then, in 1935,
the Louisiana legislature created the State Budget Committee, which had authority to approve or disapprove of every public school teacher in the state.
The committee, consisting of the governor, the state superintendent of educa-

tion, and the state treasurer, could discharge a teacher at any time for any reason. The budget law, designed primarily to eliminate Huey Long's opponents from the public schools, left teachers exposed to political control.[59] In response, teachers demanded a new tenure law "to make certain that there should be no question of its status," as Emery Lively, CTF president, explained. The Orleans Parish School Board supported the teachers' campaign. Composed primarily of Old Regulars, the board still resented Huey Long's success in breaking the political hegemony the Old Regulars held in New Orleans and the state as a whole. A new tenure law would not only protect teachers from political interference but would also help the board regain control over the employment of its teachers.

Under Reed's leadership, teachers drew up a tenure bill, lobbied legislators and candidates for election in 1936, and secured the support of Governor Leche, Earl Long, and Superintendent of Education T. H. Harris.[60] Long's lobbying efforts were particularly effective, stimulated in part by the threat of the Southern Association for Colleges and Schools to withdraw accreditation from the state's public schools if the legislature failed to enact a new tenure law.[61]

In June 1936 the state legislature amended section 66 of Act 100 of 1922 to grant teachers a public trial before dismissal and to clarify the requirements for tenure. The law, which covered only New Orleans, gave teachers tenure after a probationary period of three years; after that time, teachers would be certified for life.[62] Less than three weeks later, the legislature passed a similar bill that gave teachers throughout the state lifetime tenure, based on the same requirements established for New Orleans teachers. The bill also set up a teachers' retirement system and restored control over the employment of teachers to the parish school boards, giving back to the parishes many of the powers regarding the educational system that Long's state budget committee had taken away.[63] Like the New Orleans law, the state tenure act stipulated that beyond a three-year probationary period, a teacher could be fired only if found guilty of willful neglect of duty, incompetency, or dishonesty after a hearing before the parish school board. The teacher could choose either a private or a public hearing.[64] "We've taken the teachers out of politics," Governor Leche proclaimed with the passage of the law.[65]

The teachers' organizations were jubilant. "NOPSTA feels that the committee . . . who worked for the passage of this law and the State laws gained more for New Orleans than they realized," NOPSTA president Myrtle H. Rey said. "With Tenure a teacher stands in no fear of unjust persecution, and should be able to concentrate on her work." Rey also congratulated the committee on its success in having "undesirable features" removed from the bill, in particular a provision that made "disloyalty" cause for dismissal.[66] Even the Schoolmasters, usually on the opposite end of the political spectrum from Reed, NOPSTA, and the CTF, were grateful to Reed and CTF president Emery Lively "for killing disloyalty as a cause for dismissal in the State Tenure Bill."[67] A friend wrote Reed at the conclusion of the battle, acknowledging her accomplishment. "It sounds like you had hard going towards the end," she noted. "Do you realize what a debt the teachers of Louisiana owe you? Certainly you realize that it was your good sense and courage that put through the right kind of tenure law. I can tell you now I was pretty scared at times but was ashamed to show it."[68]

Reed and the Teachers' Federation became the tenure law's fiercest protectors after a serious threat to the law developed. A state senator introduced a bill that would require all teachers, not only new hires, to serve a probationary period of three years beginning in 1938.[69] During the three-year probation period, the parish superintendent could fire any teacher for any reason. The tenure law enacted in 1936 provided that teachers who had then been in the school system for more than three years would be permanently employed at the close of the first year of the tenure law unless they had been notified in writing that they were no longer needed.[70] To preserve this clause, the Teachers' Federation immediately sent letters to "All Labor Bodies" to rally support for the newly introduced bill's defeat. "Obviously this bill would destroy all the protection which the teachers in our state now have. It would cause teachers to become subject to the whims of partisan politics," the CTF warned. "It would result in the politicization of our educational system. It would create fear among the teachers of our state and would inevitably impair the efficiency of our schools." Although the governor had promised to veto the bill if it should pass, the CTF wanted teachers and organized labor to demonstrate their strength by defeating the bill.[71]

The CTF vehemently opposed any changes to the tenure law and commended Governor Leche for his opposition to any changes.[72] The union initiated a massive publicity campaign designed to protect the 1936 law, writing influential citizens, newspapers, radio stations, and legislators to ask their continued support for teachers tenure. In a letter to the editor of the *New Orleans States,* CTF executive secretary Manfred Willmer took issue with an accusation that the tenure law made it difficult to remove incompetent teachers. "Since there have been no formal charges of incompetence made against a New Orleans teacher within the last several years," Willmer pointed out, "this charge must be based on imagination and not on fact."[73] He also wrote to the governor to protest a proposal that would permit teachers to be fired for "in-subordination," a word that was so vague that it would undermine the whole concept of tenure, he said. "Any argument or criticism could be termed insubordination by a Board that wanted to fire a teacher," Willmer concluded.[74]

In April 1938 Reed attended the Louisiana State Federation of Labor convention in Bogalusa. The delegates passed a resolution in support of the Louisiana Teacher Tenure Law and the Orleans Parish Tenure Law and opposed any change in either statute.[75] The CTF hoped that its strong stand on behalf of tenure might attract more members into the teachers' union.[76]

In addition to the support of labor in campaigning to protect tenure, the CTF secured the backing of the Louisiana Teachers' Association and of many civic and women's organizations in the city, including the President's Cooperative Club, the PTA, the Women's Independent Voters Club, the Federation of Clubs, the New Orleans High School Alumnae, and the 13th Ward Civic League.[77] In a statement to the press, Myrtle Rey claimed that the opposition of the New Orleans Federation of Clubs to modifications of the tenure law proved that "the parents of New Orleans want their children's teachers to be secure in their positions and free from any political or personal influence."[78] The CTF prevailed and the tenure law survived unchanged.

In October 1936 the Orleans Parish School Board announced a partial restoration of salaries and increments.[79] Once again teachers singled out Sarah Reed as the moving force behind their victory. "May I, an obscure primary instructor, express appreciation to you for your unceasing efforts in behalf of the younger teacher?" asked one colleague. "The restoration of increments is only one of your many accomplishments for which I am grateful," she added.[80] Reed and her colleagues in NOPSTA and the Classroom Teachers' Federation were not content with this partial victory, however. They wanted complete salary restoration and a full resumption of the tenth-month's salary. *NOPSTA News* reported that although the teachers had talked to the school board about a tenth-month salary at the March 1937 meeting, the press had made no mention of "this very pleasant little conversation." Teachers asked the board to inform the public through the press that they did not at present receive a salary for the full ten months. "What they do receive is Nine Months salary in Ten Payments," NOPSTA pointed out, "and even the Nine Months salary is still being paid on a Cut Basis!"[81]

As in the past when the board remained recalcitrant on an issue, the teachers made the fight public. In May 1937 the teachers organized a delegation of approximately five hundred to make a plea for ten months' pay before the school board. Myrtle Rey, NOPSTA president, introduced the speakers, who represented the Louisiana Teachers' Association, the President's Cooperative Club, the New Orleans Central Trades and Labor Council, and the New Orleans Federation of Clubs. The International Hod Carriers' Federation of America and the Twelfth Ward Civic League sent letters and telegrams. State Senator Nicholas Carbajal presented a petition to restore the tenth-month salary, signed by twenty thousand citizens representing civic and labor organizations, parents' clubs, all members of the Commission Council, Mayor Robert S. Maestri, and most New Orleans members of the Senate and the House of Representatives.

One member of the board expressed puzzlement over this huge turnout since, he claimed, there was no controversy. Everyone on the board favored the tenth-month salary, he said, even an eleventh- and twelfth-month salary, but there just was not enough money. As usual, Reed would not accept the board's protestations at face value. She pointed out that the board had subtracted $750,000 from teachers' salaries at a time when it owed the banks $3 million. When the board had the opportunity to replace some of the salary funds after making $300,000 on the maturation of a ten-year bond, it decided instead to sell another issue of bonds requiring even more expenditures. Reed was tired "of hearing about a raise, raise, raise of teachers' salaries," she said. Teachers were not asking for a raise; they were asking for a restoration of salaries. Board member Isaac Heller responded to Reed by arguing that the board could get enough money to pay the teachers for ten months only if the Louisiana legislature gave more money to the board. Reed stood up again. "If the necessary funds are not available to pay teachers ten months' salary," she exclaimed, "close the schools now and you will see how quickly the funds will be provided."[82]

A few days later school board president Schaumburg announced that any surplus money allotted to the parish by the state Board of Education over and above the appropriations that had already been promised would be assigned to an extra month's salary for the teachers. T. H. Harris, state superintendent of education, had just announced increases in the state public school funds and had promised that teachers throughout the state would receive pay for a full ten months.[83]

The next week NOPSTA and the CTF held a mass meeting demanding restoration of the pay cut that had been in effect since 1932. Governor Leche attended the meeting at the Roosevelt Hotel and listened to Reed trace the history of teachers' pay cuts. She reminded the audience that, of the initial cut of

24 percent in 1932–33, only about 7 percent had been restored. Beginning teachers who made only $1,200 a year had been receiving a mere $720 a year. "Even on the ten month yearly plan we are still on the 1933 cut basis," she said, adding that New Orleans ranked the lowest in teachers' salaries of all cities of more than 300,000 population. "We would like to have this pay cut restored in full." [84] Leche told the crowd that he hoped Louisiana teachers would "eventually" be paid on a twelve-month basis. "I make no promises, however," he said. The teachers presented the governor with a petition containing seventeen hundred names, demanding restoration of teachers' salaries. [85]

The CTF and NOPSTA continued to fight with the board for full restoration of salaries. The two organizations formed a joint salary committee to study the problem and coordinate the battle. At the August board meeting, Myrtle Rey announced that she wanted to file a formal complaint about the board's refusal to meet with the salary committee. John F. Bowen of the Central Trades and Labor Council, speaking on behalf of his AFL fellow-workers, reminded the board that the federal Wagner Wage-Hour Act provided for talks between workers and their employers, and he recommended that the board grant the teachers' request for a conference. Once again, Reed's temper flared when faced with the board's intransigence. After receiving a negative response from Isaac Heller to her question about whether the board had a salary schedule ready, she asked to know what the board did have. The pleasure of the teachers' company, Heller replied. Reed, angry and frustrated, demanded to know why there was so much secrecy about the salary schedule. She received no response. [86] As usual, the board refused to share any of the decision-making process with its employees. Salary restoration and a single-salary schedule seemed as elusive as ever. Teachers still wondered whether the single-salary schedule endorsed by the board in 1934 was "ever going to change from a principle to a practice," questioning whether "by adopting the single-salary in principle only does not the Board get all its advantages and do not the teachers get all the disadvantages?" [87]

In August 1937 the Orleans Parish School Board finally announced salary increases and a nondiscriminatory, single-salary schedule based exclusively on experience and qualifications. The schedule remained free of gender bias and removed differences in salaries between high school and elementary school teachers. In 1938, as part of state Superintendent Harris's program of consolidating the power of the state over parish school boards, the state Board of Education ordered all parishes in Louisiana to adopt a similar single-salary schedule. The resolution specifically prohibited discrimination between men and women teachers.[88] Salary inequities, however, still remained between black and white teachers, with black men and women receiving significantly less pay than their white counterparts. While white teachers won significant pay increases as part of the new salary schedule, achieving 80 percent of the goal for salaries proposed in 1934, black teachers received no pay raise.[89]

By the summer of 1940 the Orleans Parish School Board's financial condition had deteriorated, and it announced a possible 12.5 percent cut in salaries for the upcoming school year. In early August Reed and a delegation of teachers met with Governor Sam Jones and the state superintendent of education to discuss the problem. As Reed later reported, state officials employed "some of the most remarkable arithmetic in the world" to explain why they could not help the teachers. Because of the uncertainty teachers faced year after year over how much they would actually be paid, Reed declared, the teaching profession in New Orleans could "attract only ragtags and bobtails." She urged congressional candidates to incorporate federal aid for schools in their platforms.[90] School board member Isaac Heller advised the teachers "to whip up public sentiment" in favor of more money for the schools.

Several teachers were angered by Heller's suggestion. "The teachers don't know which way to turn," Grace McGeehan replied. "We appeal to the board and they say they are only a disbursing body, then we go to the governor and the state superintendent and they refer us back to New Orleans on the principle of home rule. So we approach the mayor and he says the matter, being a parish affair, is beyond his jurisdiction." McGeehan noted that teachers' salaries might not be the board's main concern, "but it's a drastic thing for us. We're always being cut or threatened with a cut. You advise us to stir up sentiment to get our just dues, but I say that it is the duty of the board to bring the situation before the people." Myrtle (Rey) Gamus agreed with her colleague, describing the present situation as "the old-fashioned runaround," as the school board knew that this situation was developing, but it did nothing about it. "The teachers want their money," she said, and they "should not be placed in the position of begging for it."[91]

At the end of August a citizens committee, composed of Reed, former Young Men's Business Club president Louis G. Riecke, Attorney General Eugene Stanley, and Martha G. Robinson of the Woman's Citizens' Union, a nonpartisan women's political organization, discovered that the city and the state owed money to the school board, partly because of illegal tax deductions made in 1935 and 1936. The state attorney general agreed that the city had been illegally deducting costs of collection from school taxes, thus depriving the school board of a total of about $120,000. This amount combined with other underpayments totaled about $500,000 that the city and state combined owed the board.[92]

When Isaac Heller remarked that the board ought to "kiss and make up" with the city and the state and relinquish its financial claims against them, Sarah Reed replied that the teachers did not "want to become the victim of a $500,000 kiss. We don't mind the School Board's kissing anybody, but we don't want to be the victims by the pay cut route. We're very much afraid that while they're osculating, we'll be in a bad way because we can't pay our rent, or meet our doctors' bills, or buy our groceries." The debts were legal, Reed argued, and the school board had a duty to the schools to recover them. "Sitting back in swivel chairs and urging people to 'kiss and make up' isn't doing that duty." [93] Martha Robinson concurred. "Funds legally belonging to the schools should be collected regardless of the time involved in the necessary litigation," she said. "Failure to fulfill the public trust, such as the administration of school taxes, is not excused by a 'gentleman's agreement' which makes a mockery of law observance." [94]

In September 1940 Reed and a delegation of teachers from New Orleans went to Baton Rouge to discuss the financial situation with the Board of Liquidation, a state agency with authorization over New Orleans's bonded debt. The agency agreed to cover the deficit owed the school board. Sarah Reed's skill as a lobbyist for the teachers helps to explain the stipulation by the Board of Liquidation that teachers' salaries could not be cut. Governor Sam Jones also sided with the teachers. After evaluating the school board's budget and finding a $74,000 "cushion" fund for "contingencies and emergencies," the governor requested that the board use part of this fund for teachers' salaries in hope of averting the threatened 12.5 percent pay cut. The school board finally agreed to dedicate $24,000 to salaries. That, plus the $94,522 received from the Board of Liquidation, was enough to maintain salaries without a reduction.[95]

The delegation headed back to New Orleans, happy over its successful negotiations. At a mass meeting of teachers at the Monteleone Hotel, the delegates recounted the day's events to the teachers, praised the citizen's group for its help, and planned a banquet to celebrate their first paychecks in September.[96] On the eve of the meeting at which the school board was slated to approve an amended budget that would keep teachers' salaries at their current levels, Sarah Reed and CTF president Irene Kupiec were deluged with flowers and thank-you notes from New Orleans teachers. The summer-long fight mounted by the teachers' union had reached a successful conclusion. At its

meeting the next day, the school board voted against the pay slash and maintained salaries at 1939 levels.[97] A few days later, the teachers sponsored a formal "victory dinner" at the Jung Hotel, attended by more than six hundred
people. For her part in the salary campaign, Reed received a standing ovation
that lasted several minutes.[98]

Even members of the Schoolmasters Club, generally hostile to Reed, were
grateful to her for helping to protect their salaries, as indicated by the letter
they sent to the CTF making special mention of Reed's achievements.[99]
Although much of Reed's work as a lobbyist for the teachers took place behind
the scenes without any fanfare or publicity, teachers were well aware of her efforts. At the end of the 1940–41 academic year, teachers took advantage of
a CTF program at the Jung Hotel in New Orleans, originally scheduled as a
discussion of school finances, to pay special tribute to Reed and her work in
preventing the pay cut. Reed received a series of spontaneous ovations from
teachers and testimonials by the state attorney general, school officials, and
concerned citizens.

Attorney General Stanley told the gathering that Reed "did more, and better
lobbying, than all the high-priced corporation agents at the legislature, and
it was due to Mrs. Reed that you finally achieved the things that have come
to pass. She worked not for herself, but for you." A. P. Harvey, formerly of
the Central Trades and Labor Council and now state labor commissioner, observed, "There are people who talk about conserving everything from fish to
trees but when you talk about fair and decent pay for human beings, such
as underpaid teachers, 'problems' develop." According to Harvey, teachers
might have been experiencing pay cuts even as he spoke "had it not been for
Mrs. Reed and her work on [your] behalf."[100]

The campaign had not been an easy one, as the teachers heard from Louis
Riecke of the Young Men's Business Club, who had worked with Reed in the
salary campaign. "There were no cuts, in the end, but a lot of abuses, I can tell
you." Although he was unable to attend the dinner, Representative Hale Boggs
wrote Reed a congratulatory note, commenting that the testimonial was
"fitting recognition for the many years of service which you have given to the
cause of the public schools. I wish I could have been with the group."[101] The
evening ended "with Mrs. Reed moist-eyed, but declining to speak."[102]

It was a rare sight to see Sarah Reed speechless, and the moment didn't last
long. "Rest is rust," Reed often said, maintaining a schedule that kept her constantly occupied. "When I go to bed I find myself galloping, galloping," she
once wrote her niece. "Some new problem seems to develop overnight . . . but
whatever it is, not a minute is to be wasted."[103] She and the union had experi-

enced some remarkable victories since the CTF's inception: teacher tenure, the restoration of salary cuts, a single-salary schedule. But glaring injustices remained. Issues of social and economic justice absorbed Reed's attention throughout the 1930s and 1940s, as teachers continued to look to her for help in their battles with the school board.

5 Women's Issues

In keeping with her long-standing concern for the rights of women, Sarah Reed took on two issues in the mid-1930s that directly affected her female colleagues: the prohibition against married women teachers in the public schools and the salary inequity faced by the mostly female graduates of normal schools who did not hold B.A. degrees. The latter issue struck Reed as a matter of economic justice. While she supported higher education for all teachers—her three advanced degrees meant she had no personal stake in the battle herself—she was moved by the plight of women who had successfully taught in the public schools for many years but were, she thought, unduly penalized in the new 1937 salary schedule for not holding a college degree. Reed was seldom able to resist a plea for help from her colleagues, and this issue proved no exception.

The issue of married women banned from teaching was one dear to Reed's heart. She had herself been fired from her teaching position when her marriage became public knowledge—even though that had happened only after the death of her husband. Now Reed saw an opportunity to correct this injustice for all women teachers. One of the results of the new tenure law was to throw into doubt the validity of the school board's long-standing prohibition against the employment of married women. Section 172 of the Rules and Regulations of the Orleans Parish School Board read: "The marriage of a female teacher ipso facto vacates her position and is considered equivalent to a resignation."[1]

Bars against the employment of married women were common in public school systems, as well as in businesses, throughout the country. From the nineteenth century onward, many organizations discovered that prohibitions against the employment of married women could be economically profitable, as well as psychologically reassuring to those who feared that women's paid employment might undermine traditional gender roles.[2] Policies that banished women from the workplace after marriage enjoyed broad public support. As historian Claudia Goldin observed, "There was a reason to fit anyone's prejudice, ranging from the moralistic—that married women with children should stay at home and take care of them—to the Victorian—that pregnant women would be objectionable in the classroom—to the economic—that married women were less efficient than single women and became entrenched."[3] To some extent, these attitudes hurt middle-class women more than they did others, since exclusionary rules abounded in occupations that required advanced education and training. The prohibition against working wives intended to keep intact the patriarchal status quo by forcing middle-class women to stay at home with their families.[4]

Prohibitions against hiring married women proliferated in the 1930s as male heads of households grew desperate for work. In 1932 the federal government issued its first marriage bar when section 213 of the National Economy Act prohibited the employment of persons whose spouses were also on the U.S. payroll. Although the law as passed did not specify that women should be fired instead of men, the intent was clear and, in fact, the bill had read "married women" rather than "persons" before a House committee altered it. As it was, wives generally resigned anyway because they earned less than their husbands. Between 1932 and 1937, sixteen hundred female government employees lost their jobs because of section 213. Although the act was repealed in 1937, the head of the Women's Division of the Democratic National Committee, Molly Dewson, referred to "that dumb clause" as the "one black mark" against Roosevelt in regard to women's issues.[5]

The federal example prompted many state governments to take similar action. By 1940 nine states had curtailed the employment of married women in state governments and twenty-six had introduced legislation to ban married women from state employment so that their jobs would be open for single women and men. In some cases, governors simply issued executive orders to curtail the employment of married women. As federal and state governments legitimized a practice that had previously been in place in many school districts and businesses, new prohibitions against married women's employment began to appear in manufacturing occupations that had not previously practiced such discrimination. Even department stores began refusing to hire wives.

The Depression, then, saw a strengthening and expansion of proscriptions that served to keep married women at home, where many people felt they belonged anyway.[6] As one civic organization put it, married women ought to return to domestic life because "they are holding jobs that rightfully belong to the God-intended providers of the household."[7]

A New Orleans woman agreed that something needed to be done about married women holding jobs. In a letter to the editor of the *New Orleans Times-Picayune,* she blamed employed married women for her single children's inability to find jobs. "It used to be when a girl married, that meant an opening for someone, but not now. They hold their positions so they can dress up, but the men do not have that finer feeling for married women when they are out working and keeping a nice, respectable girl out of a place."[8]

Marriage bars were opposed by the Women's Bureau, the Women's Trade Union League, the League of Woman Voters, the National Woman's Party, and the Business and Professional Women's Clubs, which maintained that a wife's income was often crucial to the well-being of her family and that women had every right to be employed. It seemed, however, that nearly everyone else—including many single women—agreed that hiring married women during the Depression was wrong. A 1936 Gallup poll found that 82 percent of all Americans felt that married women whose husbands had jobs should not be employed. George Gallup concluded that he had "discovered an issue on which voters are about as solidly united as on any subject imaginable—including sin and hay fever."[9]

Long-standing pressures to exclude married women from schoolteaching reached new levels of intensity during the Depression. A 1928 survey by the National Education Association showed that 61 percent of all school systems banned the hiring of married women and 52 percent routinely fired women who married during the school year. The 1930s saw an increase in both practices. An NEA survey in 1930–31 found that 76 percent of 291 cities surveyed would not hire married women, and 63 percent fired women who married while under contract.[10] By the beginning of World War II, the portion of school districts that would not hire a married women had increased to 87 percent, and 70 percent of all school systems would automatically fire a woman who married while under contract.[11] In San Francisco, a married woman was told to get a divorce if she wanted a teaching job.[12]

Even some universities asked married women to resign during the Depression.[13] A 1938 study found that only among nurses and female college professors and presidents was there a smaller proportion of married women than could be found in the ranks of public school teachers, only 18 percent of whom were married. The proportion of married women engaged in all occupations was found to be 29 percent. "Evidently women teachers often are forced to sacrifice their profession on the marriage altar," the study's author concluded.[14]

In light of the strong national prejudice against the employment of married women during the Depression, it is little short of amazing that the marriage bar in the New Orleans public school system came down as early as 1936. In large part, this gain for the economic rights of women was testament to the persistence, influence, and legal perspicacity of Sarah Reed. Although the legality of excluding married women from the teaching corps in New Orleans had been debated as early as 1921, it was not until Reed forced the issue in 1936 that the board rescinded its restrictions.

Surprisingly, the first woman elected to the Orleans Parish School Board, herself a married woman, opposed dropping the marriage bar when that course of action was first suggested in 1921. When another board member had voiced doubts about the legality of prohibiting the employment of married women and had moved that the board drop its matrimonial bar, Fannie Baumgartner said that she could not support the motion. While she approved of hiring married women as substitute teachers (which was also prohibited at the time), she could condone employment of married women teachers only "under certain conditions that would have to be stipulated." As there was no second to the motion, the matter was dropped.[15] When a married teacher demanded a teaching job the next fall, a board member again moved that the board grant her request. School board president Daniel Murphy denied the motion.[16] The issue surfaced again in 1929, when a teacher who had secretly married in May demanded that the school board allow her the paycheck it had withheld for June. A city attorney reported to the board that because of its rule denying employment to married women, the teacher had no right to be paid for any time after her marriage, even though she continued to teach until the end of the school term.[17]

Some confusion ensued later that year when the state Department of Education issued a circular to all parish superintendents and school boards concerning a ruling made by the state's assistant attorney general: that the power to prohibit married women from teaching rested only with the state Board of Education and not with parish boards. Therefore, the assistant attorney general concluded, any rule restricting the employment of married women made by local parish school boards was illegal. Further, even if local boards did have the authority to deny employment to women because of their marital status, "the School Board would still be without authority to dismiss a teacher who holds a contract with the board, at any time during the session, for the mere reason that she had married after entering into the contract, unless it was stipulated in the contract that she should remain single during the term of her employment." The attorney general referred to Act 100 of 1922, which stipulated that a teacher could be discharged only for reasons of "incompetency, inefficiency or unworthiness," and that any teacher charged with any of these offenses had to be "given a full opportunity to be heard." [18]

The secretary of the school board immediately wrote the state superintendent of education asking for clarification of the circular. The Orleans Parish School Board, he said, had always had the impression that it was free to make its own rules.[19] The superintendent agreed and told the New Orleans school board that the attorney general's opinion did not apply to Orleans Parish.[20]

Some Orleans Parish school teachers, including Sarah Reed and members of NOPSTA, were unhappy with the superintendent's ruling. In November 1932 *Quartee* noted that there was "muttering" over the school board's "arbitrary ruling" regarding marriage and that many felt that their legal rights were being violated. In an article titled "Are Married Women Better Teachers?" the writer cited a case brought by a New York woman who married after she obtained her high school teaching license and was subsequently denied a teaching position on that account. Lucy Dietrich appealed to the New York state education commissioner, who in 1919 ruled in her favor and declared the marriage bar null and void. "What New Orleans needs is a test case like that of Mrs. Dietrich," *Quartee* suggested. "Someone of heroic mold and a well-off husband should make the demonstration. Let her fail to resign, attempt to continue, and fight her dismissal—with the Association behind her. Obviously, it should be a woman who has no intention of going on as a teacher, who does not need the extra income. Otherwise the results might be tragic." [21]

The *Quartee* article provoked both negative and positive responses from its readers. One man wrote the editor refuting the contention that married women ought to be allowed into the profession. Women, he said, ought to realize that marriage was their true career. "When a married woman devotes most of her energy to an occupation other than that of wife and mother, she is forgetting her true purpose; she is violating her biological importance and society as a whole suffers," he argued. A woman cannot make a successful marriage, "the safeguard of society," if she devotes herself to teaching. Women teachers who remained single, sacrificing "lovingly and unselfishly," deserved to be looked upon as the "real mothers of the race," he contended.[22] Not all women thought that such accolades were sufficient reward for the discrimination they faced. One woman protested that denying business and professional women the right to marry and continue their work was "an intolerable social injustice — putting it mildly. The attitude issues from economic fallacy, prejudice and all-around primitive social thinking."[23]

In the summer of 1936, the year the new teacher tenure law was enacted, four women teachers in Orleans Parish married. Reed approached Gladys Castel de Ben, Yvonne Crespo LaPrime, Nellie Pearce Cupit, and Martha Wegert Comeaux and asked if they would all reapply for teaching jobs in the fall in order to test the school board's marriage bar. LaPrime later told a reporter, "I was never one to carry banners or fight for things, but this seemed the only thing to do. Maybe I was just naive. I know that someone would have challenged this ruling sometime, but without Mrs. Reed, I'm not sure I would have had the courage. She did all the talking. . . . She told us when to write the letters, to whom, and what to say." Reed asked the four teachers to return to their former schools on the first day of class in the fall and to sign and date the teachers' book so they would not lose their tenure. "Then we went home," LaPrime said, "because there was no place for us."[24]

In their complaint against the school board, the fact that none of the four women had agreed to dismissal by voluntarily resigning and that each had reported for work on the first day of the fall session counted heavily in their favor. LaPrime and her colleagues asked that they "be retained as teachers on the ground that the vacating of our office as teacher never took effect and could not take effect until the beginning of the next school term."[25]

Reed, using her knowledge of the law, explained to LaPrime that New Orleans schoolteachers were first given tenure under section 66 of Act 100 of 1922, where the reasons for dismissal were spelled out. Marriage was not one of them, she noted. According to the courts, school boards could not add other reasons for dismissal. Even when the tenure laws stated that teachers may be fired "for any other good and sufficient reason," school boards could not say that marriage is sufficient cause "since any such action would be contrary to sound public policy," Reed said.

When the state legislature passed the budget law in 1934, giving the state control over school boards, it stated that boards could make their own rules as long as they were consistent with the law. The Orleans Parish School Board had not reenacted its marriage bar; consequently, no rule regarding marriage had been in effect during the time of the budget law, "and even if such a law had been readopted during that time (and it was not) it would not have been effective since it would not have been in accord with sound public policy which endorses marriage. Such a rule would have been inconsistent with law. To adopt the marriage law in any form now after the budget law has been repealed would be contrary to law and prohibited as 'ex post facto.'" The board's marriage law, "inoperative always in my opinion," Reed concluded, was now "doubly dead." [26]

LaPrime's attorney, Edward Rightor, echoed Reed. "I cannot see where getting married is immoral, a willful neglect of duty or evidence of incompetency," he said, delineating the only requirements for dismissal listed in the tenure law. Furthermore, he added, "a lady teacher who is removed because she has assumed the state of double blessedness would be correct in charging that the School Board acted beyond its powers." [27] As for the school board's reaction, LaPrime described the school officials as "disgruntled" because their work at the beginning of a new term was being disturbed by "these women interrupting them, wanting to hold on to their jobs and upsetting the apple cart. They kept telling us that there was no way we were going to be reinstated." [28]

In October 1936, after Reed and the four women took their case to the attorney general's office, the state's second assistant attorney general sent a ruling to the school board stating that any woman who married before Act 164 of 1934 and left her position voluntarily would thereby lose her tenure rights. However, he continued, in the case of women who married after the enactment of Act 164 of 1934, particularly as late as the summer of 1936, who did not resign, and "who have filed written protests and tendered themselves for service at the beginning of the school term in September, 1936, we are of the opinion that if they had acquired the status of a regular and permanent teacher, that the mere fact that they had married would not deprive them of their status." [29]

The teachers and Reed received the good news unofficially from the governor before the school board members learned of the ruling. As LaPrime remembered, "We were finally asked to meet with A. J. ('Gus') Tete, assistant superintendent. He told us firmly that we were to stop writing letters, that he did not wish to continue seeing us and that reinstatement was out of the question. Then one of us—I can't even recall which one—piped up, 'But the governor said ...' Mr. Tete froze and quickly phoned Nicholas Bauer, superintendent of schools. Soon after, no later than a month, I'm sure, we were reinstated." [30] The board tried to withhold salary payments for September and October, the period before reinstatement, but the women insisted on payment because without it their tenure could be questioned. They finally received their checks in March. [31]

The state supreme court upheld as law the attorney general's opinion after Annabelle Robertson Miester, another Orleans Parish teacher who had married in the summer of 1936, filed suit against the Orleans Parish School Board in December of 1936 to win back her teaching job. The court ruled in her favor, agreeing that "the ruling of the Orleans Parish School Board in not permitting her to retain her teaching position is contrary to the provisions of Act 164 of 1934 and Act 79 of 1936 and that your relator is entitled to retain her position as a regular and permanent teacher of the Orleans Parish School Board."[32] Miester, like the others, had never resigned, and the school board restored her to her former position.[33]

NOPSTA welcomed Miester back to the teaching corps in a happy editorial in *NOPSTA News*, congratulating her on her victory. Miester's success, the association observed, gave all female teachers "an added sense of security." NOPSTA acknowledged that the task of bringing suit was "a trying ordeal" but hoped that Miester's "accomplishment will help us all to have the courage of our convictions."[34]

Not all women agreed that married teachers should be allowed to retain their jobs. Normal school students and recent graduates saw their chances for gainful employment dwindle in light of the ruling in favor of married teachers. Fifty-three members of the class of 1936 of the Margaret C. Hanson Normal School in New Orleans signed a letter written by their class president to the school board. How, she asked, would they ever find a job if women continued to keep their positions after marriage? "Are not appointments few and difficult enough, without being fettered with yet another shackle? Incompetency! Neglect! Immorality!" she exclaimed. "How few teachers have been forced to resign because of one of these features! . . . Certainly no teacher, intelligent as she is supposed to be, would give up her position and wed a man who is incapable of supporting her and who could not continue to give her as much as, or more than, she now has."[35]

The normal school students had reason to worry. As of January 1, 1940, Orleans Parish School Board records showed that 85 percent of teachers who married kept their jobs. In the academic year 1936–37, the period of the new tenure law and the married woman ruling, there was a rash of marriages— 122 in the parish. Eighty-six women married during the next year, and another eighty-six in 1938–39. By 1940, out of 1,722 women teachers, 263 were married.[36] The board declined to appeal either the attorney general's ruling on LaPrime, de Ben, Cupit and Comeaux or the court's decision in the Miester suit.

Although the board could not from then on dismiss women under contract who married, it still refused to hire women who were already married. In 1942 the board agreed to allow married women to serve as substitute teachers as a result of a wartime scarcity of substitutes.[37] The continuing teacher shortage elicited a plea for hiring married women teachers from the New Orleans Council of Parent-Teacher Associations in 1946. The board decided, however, to retain its policy of not employing married women as permanent teachers. The PTA persisted in pushing for this change, but the school board steadfastly adhered to its policy, citing a tendency for a woman with young children to neglect classroom responsibilities while worrying about her own children. If her husband or children were ill, the board told the PTA, the woman had to stay home and take care of them, making it necessary to hire a substitute. Moreover, awarding teaching jobs to married women would leave no openings for young people completing their training. The board stated that its policy was to hire younger teachers, and married applicants were usually older than women just graduating from college.[38] In fact, the board had a written policy of not hiring women over the age of forty, as well as the one refusing employment to married women.[39]

The PTA asked the school board to reconsider its policy, questioning its reasoning in not hiring married women in order to keep the average age of the teaching corps down. "You don't have to hire everyone who applies," its secretary observed. The PTA believed that the board should concern itself with choosing the best possible applicants rather than trying to spread jobs around.[40] The Classroom Teachers' Federation joined the PTA in its campaign for hiring married women, as did the National Council of Jewish Women. The board remained unmoved by these requests and kept its rule until 1950, well past the time when most other school districts had dropped the prohibition.[41] In most cities, both types of marriage bars had ended by the conclusion of World War II. Only 18 percent of public schools in the United States still excluded married women by 1951.[42]

In addition to married teachers, another group of women looked to Sarah Reed for help—nondegreed teachers, most of whom held certificates from two-year normal schools that entitled them to teach in the primary grades. As usual, Reed put her lobbying and organizing skills to work in uniting teachers at odds with each other. As with issues dividing male from female and union from nonunion teachers, the differences between degreed and nondegreed teachers were exacerbated by board actions that seemed calculated to prevent teachers from establishing a united front. The board seemed as determined as ever to maintain its authority. The issue of how much teachers without degrees should be paid, a minor issue in reality, became a symbolic one involving the perception of power and the maintenance of the status quo.

Until 1932 the school board paid teachers with college degrees $150 a year more than teachers who did not have degrees. During the Depression years 1932–37, the differential decreased, with degreed teachers receiving only $75 a year more. When, in September 1937, the school board finally announced that it had adopted a single-salary schedule, based on training and experience, that wiped out differentials between male and female teachers as well as between elementary and high school teachers, it increased the salary gap between degreed and nondegreed teachers to $550 in favor of degree holders. According to Reed, "The non-degree teachers felt that this was an unjustifiable, unscientific, and intolerable difference."[43] A large group of teachers from NOPSTA and the CTF joined Reed at her regular appearance at the school board meeting in September 1937, and they presented a petition calling for increases in salaries for members of the teaching corps who did not hold college degrees but were graduates of normal schools. The nondegreed, the teachers charged, "were not given a living wage." As usual, Reed had a specific suggestion to remedy the situation. If necessary, she said, the money expended for supplies and coal could be reduced to supply the funds needed to raise the wages of the nondegreed teachers.[44]

At its regular November meeting, the Teachers' Federation approved recommendations of its salary committee, including a revision of the board's salary schedule. The union schedule called for a minimum salary of $1,200 and a maximum salary of $2,600 a year. An increment of $150 would be added to the basic salary for the B.A. degree and an equal amount added for the M.A. degree. The CTF schedule included automatic annual increases of $140. The school board's budget provided for a minimum salary of $980 without a degree and $1,000 with a degree for beginning teachers, a salary difference of only $20. At the maximum level, however, the differential increased significantly: nondegreed teachers would receive only $1,650 compared with $2,200 for degreed teachers, or a difference of $550.[45]

The Teachers' Federation did not oppose financial rewards for degrees. When the board had temporarily suspended its usual increment of $150 per degree, the Teachers' Federation had been among the most vocal groups arguing for its restoration.[46] The federation agreed with the board's efforts to promote advanced education for its teachers by offering additional money for each degree earned, Myrtle Rey explained, but she complained that the nondegreed received such little compensation that they would have a difficult time at retirement, given the minuscule pensions they would receive. In any case, she pointed out, under a new ruling by the state Department of Education, a teacher without a degree could not be hired in the public schools after 1940, thus eliminating the nondegreed problem in the future.[47]

On December 10 the Teachers' Federation presented the school board its proposed salary schedule, under which nondegreed teachers would receive $150 less than teachers with B.A. degrees. A representative of the Central Trades and Labor Council endorsed the federation's salary schedule, as did the chairman of the local American Association of University Professors. Myrtle Rey concluded the federation's presentation by acknowledging that not all teachers in the system agreed with the CTF petition and salary schedule. Some degreed teachers feared that the board would have to cut their salaries in order to give the nondegreed more money, she said, and they did not want to risk their own livelihoods. Isaac Heller told the teachers that the board could not act on the petition at present. While he recognized the right of groups and individuals to make speeches before the board, he went on to say, "regardless of the eloquence of the speakers," the board could not allocate funds it did not have. According to Reed, however, there was a margin of safety of $336,000 in the present budget, more than enough to eradicate the gross disparities.[48]

In opposition to the CTF's petition, a faculty member from Warren Easton High School submitted a letter signed by teachers with college degrees expressing their approval of the board's salary schedule. In the opinion of this group, the board ought to retain the high differential in order to provide incentives for advanced study and to promote "the progressive improvement of the educational system." The Schoolmasters Club agreed, arguing that "every possible incentive should be given the non-degree teacher to induce him or her to further study." The male teachers, most of whom already held degrees, were quick to praise the "Board's interest in raising the educational standards for the teaching corps of New Orleans."[49]

Other high school teachers also supported the high differential, arguing that in order to earn a degree teachers often had to sacrifice earnings they could have made by teaching summer school, as well as sacrificing afternoons, nights, weekends, and summers for six to eight years to take classes and study. "Progressive, ambitious teachers" had a "formidable financial investment" in their educations that deserved some financial return, an association of high school teachers told the board. Moreover, the teachers maintained, "excellence in teaching is likely to be associated with the higher levels of professional preparation." If it decreased the differential between degreed and nondegreed teachers, the board would do "irreparable wrong" to the system it was committed to improve, the association argued. "It would stifle ambition and progressiveness and foster professional disinterestedness [sic].[50]

The Teachers' Federation worried about the division in the teaching ranks caused by the discrepancies in the new salary schedule. Teachers had not forgotten the conflicts resulting from the fight over equal wages for women. As CTF executive secretary Manfred Willmer told Alonzo Grace, who was heading up a study of the city's educational system in 1938, "The discrimination against women in salary schedules was the cause of a long and somewhat bitter fight between various factions of teachers in our city and some of the sores have yet to heal, although we have had for some time a state law prohibiting salary discrimination against women teachers." Before the new salary schedule was introduced, it had seemed to the Teachers' Federation that all salary discrimination might finally end "and the teaching corps would be solidly united by the disappearance of all cliques and groups within teacher ranks," Willmer wrote.[51]

The federation had hoped that eliminating salary differentials would result in "more harmony, more unity of purpose" among New Orleans teachers, according to an article in the CTF *Yearbook*. "The unfair discrimination against the non-degree teacher shattered the unity that might otherwise have materialized." When the nondegreed found that their salaries were $550 less than the degreed teachers', they "felt an injury had been done."[52] In fact, the salary inequity had caused severe problems within the teaching corps. As Myrtle Rey told Governor Leche, "It has created a schism within the ranks of teachers; enmity and distrust between degree and non-degree teachers. Faculty relationships have become strained, lifelong friendships have cooled."[53]

Despite the board's apparent lack of interest in their pleas on behalf of the nondegreed, NOPSTA and the CTF continued to appear at board meetings to present petitions and to inquire as to the status of their request.[54] The teachers grew increasingly frustrated with the board's refusal to take action on the matter. At one point, Myrtle Rey told the board that one thing she had learned as a teacher was that it was often necessary "to repeat and repeat," so she was coming back before the board with the same request. According to the minutes of that meeting, "she thanked the Board for having adopted a single salary schedule, adding that the Federation had already thanked the Board about a million times for the schedule," but that the union still felt that the nondegreed should get more money. Reed backed up Rey, requesting to know how the board's budget was "working out." School board president Henry Schaumburg replied that, according to the accountant, "it was working out satisfactorily." In that case, Reed responded, "there would be available at the end of the year a reserve of $336,000 which the Board had not budgeted, and which could be used to make this increase for non-degree teachers retroactive." The board, no doubt feeling trapped by its own financial success and Reed's accounting acumen, replied that it "would have to wait until the end of the year to see."[55]

In fact, it took four more years for the issue to be resolved, years in which the board lost its collective temper over the teachers' repeated pleas and teachers vented their frustration over the endless "wait-and-see" attitude taken by the board. In October 1938 the board raised the salaries of superintendents, assistant superintendents, and supervisors, provoking Reed to remark that teachers had no objection to adequate salaries for others but that "when the Board does not make an adjustment for those on the lower salary brackets, the Board must not complain if the morale of the teaching corps is not high." This latest raise for administrators, she said, would only make things worse. Reed invited the board to "visit the classrooms of the teachers in the lowest brackets if they wanted to see overworked and unhappy teachers."[56]

Teachers were indeed unhappy. One disgruntled educator recalled the board's verbal tributes to teachers who had stayed at their posts during World War I and had kept working despite frequent pay decreases over the years. After vowing that "it would not forget the devoted service and sacrifices uncomplainingly borne," the teacher noted, the board had seemingly "forgotten one-half of this group whose service and devotion was applauded."[57]

Just as they had done in other cases when the school board refused to act in their best interests, teachers found that they had to go over the heads of school officials to accomplish their goal. As Reed pointed out, the school board's "denial of the Federation petition had become chronic, although the Board had the money to make the adjustment." The Teachers' Federation rallied considerable community support for its campaign. Many New Orleans citizens and organizations unsuccessfully requested the board to raise nondegreed salaries. After repeated failures on the home front, the federation once again traveled to Baton Rouge to fight for the rights of classroom teachers.[58]

The result, House Bill 498, requiring the board to raise salaries of teachers without degrees to a level of not less than $150 a year below the amount paid to teachers with bachelor's degrees, met with fierce opposition on the part of the school board. Although a proposal to adjust upward the salaries of a minority of the teaching corps does not, on its face, seem important enough to excite such intense opposition, when seen in the context of other threats to the board's autonomy, official efforts to defeat the bill become more understandable. Just a few months before the introduction of House Bill 498, an African American teacher in the New Orleans public school system had filed suit for equalization of pay. Although that suit offered the board a convenient excuse for delaying the nondegreed salary adjustment, it would mean much larger expenditures for the board if it succeeded. Even more significant, the board saw both the nondegreed bill and the African American suit as threats to its own decision-making powers.[59]

When Orleans Parish assistant superintendent Lionel J. Bourgeois appeared at the state capital to lobby against House Bill 498, he argued that it threatened the authority of local school officials by establishing a policy of state control over school budgets. And, he added, it would cost the taxpayers a lot of money, at least $240,000 more per year. Moreover, if passed, the bill would penalize teachers who had worked hard taking extension and summer school courses in order to earn degrees. All of the 659 nondegreed teachers in Orleans Parish could have earned a college degree, Bourgeois claimed. After all, 1,287 other teachers in the system had earned theirs. If it had to give raises to the nondegreed, the board would be forced to lower the salaries of degreed teachers. "The act, therefore, would result in a penalty to those teachers whose professional zeal impelled them to secure degrees and it would act as a reward to that small number of teachers who did nothing to advance their professional qualifications, at least by way of securing a college degree."[60]

In an all-out effort to defeat the bill, Bourgeois dragged out his most potent weapon—the race issue. As he told legislators, a "last minute analysis" of the bill showed that its passage would require the board to equalize the salaries of non-degree-holding white and black teachers in Orleans Parish. If the legislature fixed the salary of nondegreed teachers, all such teachers, regardless of race, would have to be paid on the same scale. If this act became law, the superintendent warned, the Louisiana legislature would be held responsible for this move toward racial equality.

The Teachers' Federation quickly disassociated itself from the racial issue. "The Negro question has no connection with this bill," the teachers advised in a flier issued to the public. "The big differential exists only in the salaries of white degree and non-degree teachers. The Orleans Board operates two salary schedules—one for white teachers and one for Negro teachers. This bill has no connection whatever with the Negro salary scale." If the supreme court decided to equalize Negro and white salaries, the CTF said, all teachers, not just the nondegreed, would be affected. "It is not fair to equalize the Negroes at the expense of the non-degree teachers," the CTF said, referring to the board's frequently reiterated excuse that if it had to increase the pay of black teachers, it could not afford also to raise the salaries of nondegreed teachers.[61]

Despite the objections of the school board and the superintendent, the bill to return to the $150 differential between degreed and nondegreed teachers passed the House on June 23, 1942, as a large delegation of New Orleans teachers looked on and applauded. Representative Alexander E. Rainold of New Orleans said that the bill would correct "a sad and serious injustice." The current $550 salary difference in Orleans Parish, he said, was the biggest in the state, perhaps in the whole United States. "It is hard to understand this big difference since those penalized teachers do the same work as the higher paid teachers. They have the same hours, duties, responsibilities, experience and success."[62]

Not everyone was as excited as the teachers over the bill's success. The *Times-Picayune* said that the bill amounted to "unwarranted and unwise" meddling by the legislature in the affairs of a local board. Even though the newspaper agreed that the school board was late in correcting the situation, "the tardiness of the Board is no excuse for legislative interference in the complicated matter of teacher ratings which, to be sound, must involve an assortment of qualification measurements." The New Orleans Association of Commerce and its educational committee unanimously voted to oppose the bill on the grounds that control of salaries ought to be left in the hands of the local school board, which would otherwise lose its ability to promote the further education of teachers. Furthermore, without new revenue of some kind, the bill would require salary reductions for degreed teachers.[63] The Bureau of Governmental Research, a reform organization of upper- and middle-class moderates, also called for salary decisions to be left in the hands of the parish school board. The law, the bureau claimed, "would deprive the School Board of its principal means of encouraging teachers already in the school system to improve themselves through taking additional teacher training work—either in summer schools or on periodic leaves of absence." Furthermore, the bureau warned, the unstable financial condition of the school board, possibly to be made worse by a court order requiring the board to equalize black and white teachers' salaries, might require lowering all teachers' pay. "This situation might well result in loss of better trained personnel to higher paid positions elsewhere," its educational committee chairman cautioned.[64]

Sarah Reed also lobbied the state legislature, where she countered every argument made by the school authorities and other opponents of the teachers' bill. "In answer to the charge that the state is attempting regulation of school systems, I would say that was done in the year 1922 by the very Act 100 which we are now trying to amend. Act 100 of 1922 was adopted for the purpose of uniformity which was then and is now recognized as necessary," Reed told legislators. "Similar legislation affecting sheriffs, police, and firemen are of a directory nature and the law books are full of it."

Reed reminded the lawmakers that Act 100 had established that those who earned teaching certificates would be allowed to teach and that such educators "had a right to believe they would not be discriminated against as they have been by the Orleans Parish School Board for the last five years. These teachers have lived in the hope that the Board really intended to correct this injustice." Instead, the board had continued to penalize the normal school graduates who held valid certificates from the state Board of Education. "These teachers," Reed argued, "have been the backbone of the system." The legislature had never intended, when it provided incentives for advanced degrees, "to sacrifice teachers who have given their very lifeblood to the school system."

"Think of it," Reed urged the legislators. "Two teachers are teaching side by side—they have the same work and both of them are holding life certificates—but their salaries are grossly unequal." It is an intolerable situation, she said, and one that existed only in Orleans Parish. "The Legislature, the parent body, should not allow this condition to continue. We would not have come to you had we not exhausted all the remedies available," Reed said. "We believe you will not allow injustice to be done in the name of local self government." [65]

The teachers' lobbying efforts in Baton Rouge won the bill for the nondegreed when it passed the Senate—in spite of the efforts of school authorities and others to defeat it—becoming Act 224 of 1942. Two months later, state Attorney General Eugene Stanley declared Act 224 unconstitutional because the law had amended a section of Act 100 that had already been repealed.[66] In the end, the differential never was significantly decreased.

The *Times-Picayune,* opposed to Act 224 to begin with, gloated that "the Legislature's method was as bad as its principle." The paper agreed that the board's reluctance to pay nondegreed teachers was probably not justified. "But that is a matter for the Board to correct." State legislators, the paper said, had been "much too susceptible to pleas of various groups for special favors," gained by persuading the state to "order around" local authorities and school boards. The federal government was also encroaching on local rights, the *Times-Picayune* warned, even to the point of controlling state elections, regardless of the unconstitutionality of such a move. "The poll tax bill is only one of several now being pushed in Congress by pressure groups to transfer state powers to the federal government." State governments were also acquiescing to "smaller pressure cliques" to control local affairs, the paper complained. "Occasionally the usurpers are thwarted by their own bungling, as in this school board case, but such instances are mere sidelights on the main show in which the big governments go right on consuming the small governments." [67]

The dispute over the nondegreed teachers exemplified both the school board's attitude toward its educators and Sarah Reed's philosophy regarding teacher unity, the importance of economic independence, and the primacy of economic justice. The board felt safer when its teachers were fighting among themselves. As New Orleans teachers were receiving among the lowest salaries of urban teachers in the United States, the board had good reason to fear the demands that a united teaching staff might make and the power it might muster to achieve them. The school board wanted to preserve its power over hiring, firing, and establishing salary scales for both white and black teachers. The teachers' habit of going directly to the state legislature to have their demands met threatened and angered the board, which still resented the limitations on its powers imposed by Huey Long and state Superintendent of Education T. H. Harris, who had worked to centralize control of education in the state government, taking away much of the power of local parish school boards.[68] Ever since Huey Long crushed the Regular Democrats of New Orleans, broke their control of state politics, and consolidated power in the state capital, his little "District of Columbia," as Long called it, New Orleans officials had resented the dictates of the state legislature and laws regulating what New Orleans administrators could and could not do.[69]

The tendency of the legislature to side with the teachers threatened local officials who, with the memory of Long still fresh, felt their grip on authority slipping away again under Franklin Roosevelt. The New Deal government and the changes it inspired were upsetting the local social and economic status quo. Moreover, the federal government threatened to interfere with the South's racial arrangements. The school board was no doubt familiar with federal court rulings in favor of African Americans in several salary equalization cases across the country, and now it was faced with the same kind of suit. The school board felt its power challenged on all fronts.

Time and time again, Reed and her colleagues had to appeal to higher authorities because of local opposition to change and reform. With great consistency, the board proved unsympathetic to the needs of its teachers, who were forced to go to the state legislature, where they found sponsors for their bills and lobbied for their passage. With the weight of a large teachers' voting bloc and the support of organized labor behind them, teachers met with more success on the state level than they did locally, where the Old Regular machine successfully controlled school board elections.

As legislative chairman of the CTF, Reed's work in the state legislature proved essential to the teachers' efforts. Her union's affiliation with the AFL contributed to the success of her lobbying efforts. After the organization of the CIO in 1935, the more conservative AFL began to seem like a reasonable alternative to Louisiana legislators who, while violently opposed to the CIO, did not want to be labeled antilabor by their working-class constituents. As an AFL affiliate, the AFT undoubtedly benefited from reaction against the CIO.[70]

Reed was also instrumental in maintaining a measure of teacher unity in the face of the school board's calculated efforts to foster division. In part, her actions reflected a labor movement perspective, with an emphasis on the tactical importance of bargaining from a position of rank-and-file solidarity. Strength through unity was one of Reed's abiding beliefs. But her devotion to the teachers' cause also sprang from bonds of loyalty and friendship, as well as broader humanistic concerns. She could not stand idly by and watch while women she had worked with all her life were exploited. "Whatever is bad for one group of teachers is a threat to the well-being of all teachers," Reed wrote. "Today one group is penalized, tomorrow another group may be the victim. Divide and conquer is only possible if the teachers allow themselves to be divided and conquered. We belong together," she urged. "We will not long keep what freedom we have if we array ourselves in hostile camps. . . . Let us heal our differences while there is yet time. Tomorrow may be too late."[71]

6 Segregation and Subterfuge

The beginnings of the civil rights movement in the 1930s—what one historian has called "the first act of a two-act play"—transformed Sarah Reed's racial views and prompted her to join the emerging struggle for racial justice. National forces operating on the local level affected her both personally and politically. Prior to the 1930s, social reform in the South was limited for lack of outside support. With the emergence of a strong labor movement and a federal government concerned with social problems, southern liberals found the support they needed to push for social change. The Depression, the New Deal, and labor combined to shake Reed out of her inherited plantation culture prejudice and propelled her into liberal racial activism. Reed's conversion resembled the experience of Virginia Foster Durr, a leading civil rights activist. Like Reed, Durr came out of the Old South slave-owning tradition and did not question her racial views until she became a New Deal supporter. Before the 1930s, Durr admits, "I was a racist, plain and simple."[1]

The New Deal, the wellspring of Durr's mature political philosophy, also made a lifelong impact on Reed. In particular, the Roosevelt administration brought African American issues to national attention and raised the racial consciousness of many Americans, including Reed. For the first time since Reconstruction, the federal government included blacks in its professed goals and programs, albeit in a limited fashion. Both blacks and whites began to think that the New Deal represented an opportunity to fight racial discrimination.[2] Although their gains were small, blacks saw in the Roosevelt administration a chance for improvement, some recognition that the federal government was concerned with their lives. Their alliance with the federal government was one that would continue throughout the civil rights struggle.[3]

The burgeoning union movement, particularly the organizing efforts of the CIO, also fueled blacks' hopes and expectations. Committed to interracial labor unions, the CIO, which first entered Louisiana in 1936, actively recruited African Americans into its ranks and achieved considerable strength among dock workers, truck drivers, and maritime cooks and stewards in New Orleans.[4] The Communist Party also played a significant role in the labor struggles of the 1930s. Besides setting up many CIO locals, the party worked to organize sharecroppers in Louisiana's rural parishes. In 1936 the Communist-sponsored Sharecroppers' Union moved its headquarters to New Orleans and began organizing the Louisiana Farmers Union (LFU).[5]

The same year, Willie and Irene Scott, black tenants living on rented land at Sarah and Roberta's Weyanoke plantation, organized a local of the LFU. It took some courage to undertake this task in West Feliciana, a parish that one observer described as governed by "white supremacy, negro subservience, white economic dominance, and exclusion of negroes from certain civil rights." Aware of the intimidation and violence involved in maintaining this system, white union organizers were reluctant to enter the parish. The Scotts, however, established a local on their own initiative, and white organizers finally consented to assist their efforts. The Louisiana Farmers Union established four locals totaling about two hundred members in West Feliciana Parish. White landowners at first ignored the activity among their black tenants, assuming that the traditional white-black hierarchy would not be disturbed.

This assumption was shattered when it became known that a white organizer had spent several nights in the Scotts' cabin at Weyanoke. Such flagrant indifference to the social customs of the parish outraged whites who already disapproved of Sarah and Roberta's politics. Roberta, in fact, was as outspoken in the parish as Sarah was in New Orleans. Sarah, who disliked West Feliciana society, tended to leave local politics to Roberta, who was deeply involved in the civic affairs of the parish.[6]

Roberta's views frequently clashed with those of her more conservative neighbors. The Communist origins of the union confirmed many whites' suspicions that Roberta was indeed subversive. Both Sarah and Roberta were aware of the Scotts' organizing activities and supported them, telling their tenants only to "keep quiet" about what they were doing.[7]

Keeping quiet was a good idea, but it was difficult to keep a secret in a parish where whites were suspected of intercepting blacks' mail, including a letter to Willie and Irene Scott announcing the date of a union organizer's arrival at Weyanoke. On the indicated night, several white men broke into the Scotts' cabin and found Irene Scott alone. They beat her repeatedly, demanding to know where to find her husband and the organizer, who had unexpectedly arrived a day early and had already departed. One of the men, Irene Scott later stated in an affidavit, was Frank Percy, Sarah's former suitor. Scott identified all of the men as "well-to-do farmers and against the union." When the men went out to their car to get a rope, Irene Scott escaped, and she and her husband fled to New Orleans.[8]

The Louisiana League for the Preservation of Constitutional Rights investigated the affair. The group had begun in 1936 to investigate violence against the CIO in New Orleans. George A. Dreyfous, a prominent New Orleans attorney, and Mack Swearingen, a Tulane history professor, both founding members, traveled to West Feliciana Parish to talk to black and white residents. In addition, they interviewed several people in New Orleans connected to the incident, including the Scotts and Roberta Towles. "It is no accident that the first violence occurred on Miss Towles' plantation," investigators reported. "Her treason to the local mores is savagely resented, and at least two of the most prominent white men blamed her for the incident."[9]

The investigators concluded that matters in West Feliciana Parish pointed to "a gravely dangerous situation." The problem stemmed, they surmised, from the extreme poverty in the area and the "growing race or class consciousness among the negroes." The long-time white residents of the parish, reported the investigators, "arrive at conclusions principally through tradition, prejudice, and passion. Their thinking is confused, inconsistent and archaic." Although whites took little interest in the rest of the world, wrote Swearingen and Dreyfous, "they arrogate to themselves an assumption of aristocratic superiority over other people, which is at the same time ludicrous, pathetic, and above all dangerous. The negroes are progressing faster in social education than the whites. The whites nevertheless continue to regard the negroes as ignorant and docile children, dependent upon white paternalism."

Dreyfous and Swearingen recommended that their organization not attempt to prosecute the case in the courts. The attorney general, they said, would not accept any case concerning violence against blacks by whites, and a grand jury would not indict. "The situation really amounts to the exclusion of the negroes from court remedies and there is no way to correct this except in federal court, for which there is not sufficient evidence." The only realistic course of action, they concluded, would be for the league to "make a public statement, carefully worded in a restrained manner, in the rather feeble hope that public opinion will have some slight salutary effect in the Parish." The investigators urged caution and restraint in order to protect black union members who might be subjected to further violence.[10]

As founding members of the Louisiana League for the Preservation of Constitutional Rights and as indirect participants in the organizing attempt, both Sarah and Roberta were well aware of what had happened and why. The sisters were already sympathetic to the labor movement, and the violence visited upon black tenants at Weyanoke dramatically underscored the connection between unionism and civil rights. In the fall of 1937, after the Scott beating, Sarah and Roberta took their first steps in assisting black colleagues in the Orleans Parish school system. This is not to say that either sister went so far as to advocate integration publicly. The educational color line was a fact of life, and no one, Reed and Towles included, sought to overturn the formal structure of segregation in the 1930s. They did, however, begin working actively to promote interracial cooperation among teachers, thereby earning the animosity of many within the New Orleans educational establishment.

Issues of compensation provided the first opportunity for interracial action. When the press reported the new salary schedule of 1937, which included restoration of pay that had been cut earlier in the Depression, it stated that the schedule applied "only to white teachers." Veronica Hill, a prominent black teacher, who was out of town at the time of the announcement, read about the new schedule in a clipping her mother had sent. When she read the first part of the news, she recalled, "I was so happy. This was wonderful, I thought." Then she reached the "only to white teachers" line. "I couldn't get home fast enough," she said. "When I did get home all the complacency, all the quietness was over. The colored teachers were in a rage."[11]

Two weeks later, an interracial delegation of fourteen teachers, headed by Sarah Reed, Veronica Hill, and Myrtle Rey, arrived at the school administration building armed with a petition demanding raises, a new salary schedule, and a "fairer deal" for black teachers. The elevator operator told them he had been directed not to take anyone to the third floor, where a closed meeting of the Orleans Parish School Board was in progress. Not to be deterred from their mission, the women climbed the outside fire escape, found an open window on the fifth floor and entered the building, took the stairs to the third floor, and either slid the petition under the locked door, threw it through an open transom window, or handed it to the president of the board, who opened the door, depending on which version of the now-legendary story one believes.[12] The black teachers got their raises the next day.

For most African American teachers, these pay increases ranged from $17 to $41 per year, a tiny sum that seemed welcome only in comparison with the threatened reductions. Like the arrangement for white teachers, the black salary schedule provided that all instructors with equal education and experience receive the same pay, eliminating differentials between teachers in secondary and elementary schools. Like the schedule for white teachers, the black teachers' schedule raised differentials between degreed and nondegreed teachers. In the revised 1937–38 salary schedule, beginning African American teachers without degrees were raised from $803 to $820 a year. The previously adopted schedule would have reduced their salaries to $640 a year. The 1937 maximum salary for a nondegreed black teacher was $1,361 after eleven years, while a white teacher with the same credentials received $1,650.

African American teachers with bachelor's degrees earned a minimum salary of $909 in 1937–38, compared with a $1,000 minimum for whites. The maximum for blacks with B.A.s amounted to $1,440; for whites with college degrees the figure was $2,200. A black teacher with a master's degree could earn a maximum salary of $1,560; the maximum for a white teacher amounted to $2,320.[13] The large differences in salaries paid black and white teachers were not unique to New Orleans. Nationally, the average African American teacher made approximately 55 percent of a white teacher's salary.[14]

Shortly after the fire escape incident, Roberta, Sarah, and Myrtle Rey met with a group of African American teachers in Orleans Parish to discuss the possibility of black teachers joining the AFT. The African American teachers, who, recalled Veronica Hill, were still "all stirred up" about not receiving their raises at the same time white teachers received theirs, were receptive to the suggestion. It was the school board "blunder," limiting raises to whites only, that upset black teachers the most, Hill said. "So many people were afraid to protest, but this was the last straw. They began to understand there really was a need for organization."[15]

Black teachers had already organized the Louisiana Colored Teachers Association in 1901, as well as a New Orleans chapter of the LCTA, but they recognized the advantages of aligning with a national organization. Reed and Towles answered their questions about the union and urged them to organize their own AFT local. It would be an all-black union as the AFT's policy was to conform to local practices in matters involving race. If a community's schools were segregated, so, too, were the local unions, and there was no talk of modifying this custom.[16]

In speaking to her black colleagues, Reed emphasized the importance of unionization for all teachers. Roberta gave a brief pitch for the AFT and outlined the process for joining the union, noting that local dues depended upon the decision of the members, that only seven people were needed to obtain a charter, and that ten dollars had to accompany their membership application to the national union. The African American teachers passed a resolution to join the AFT and collected $12.59 for the charter. Of that amount, $11 went to Roberta, who sent in the application, leaving $1.59 for the new organization's treasury.[17] Sarah and Roberta met two weeks later with what was by then the League of Classroom Teachers, American Federation of Teachers, Local 527, to discuss the possibility of sharing an executive secretary with Local 353 and to consider the need for salary increases for nondegreed teachers and for all black teachers. Reed pointed out that only 131 black teachers were receiving maximum salary, compared with 435 whites.[18] Edna M. Cordier was elected the first president of the League of Classroom Teachers, along with a board consisting of William Grant, Earl McWilliams, Peter Clard, Luvinia E. Strong, Hilda E. Turner, and George Carpenter.[19]

The league had great success in organizing, bringing more than 74 percent of the black teachers into the AFT in less than six months, a greater percentage of the teaching force than the white local ever succeeded in organizing. Union members tried to convince teachers that they would not lose their jobs if they joined the local. With the new tenure law in place, organizers could assure teachers that they had some protection. But even the tenure law did not completely reassure black teachers who worked for white school superintendents and an all white school board. "Whites expected, and usually received, abject deference from blacks," as historian Adam Fairclough has pointed out, "and teachers were no exception."[20]

Some black teachers, like some white ones, did not think professional people should have anything to do with unions. "They didn't think teachers ought to be associated with longshoremen. That sort of nonsense," Veronica Hill said. "We were called radicals, a group of malcontents." On the whole, however, black teachers recognized that they had little to lose and much to gain through association with a labor union; white teachers, more mired in the concept of professionalism, were harder to convince.[21]

In important respects, unionization meant more to blacks than it did to whites. Ever since the state constitution of 1898 disfranchised them, blacks in Louisiana were, as CTF executive secretary Manfred Willmer wrote the national office, "powerless politically." From a high of 130,344, the number of black voters in the state had fallen to 5,320 after disfranchisement; after the poll tax took effect, the number fell even further, to 1,342. By 1940 only 886 blacks were registered to vote in the entire state. Willmer warned his superiors in Chicago that it would be "almost impossible to get any public sentiment behind a program for the improvement of conditions in Negro schools." In such a bleak political environment, the labor movement—even one that adhered to the southern color line—provided one of the few allies blacks could find.[22]

The educational system in New Orleans contained vast inequities. Not only were black teachers paid less than their white counterparts who had the same education and experience, their working conditions were much worse. They had larger numbers of students, 50 percent more in some cases, and worked in dilapidated, unsafe buildings with inadequate supplies and textbooks. Black teachers held little hope for improvement, particularly after 1931, when the school board rejected money from the Julius Rosenwald Fund to help build a trade high school for black students. Even though there was then only one black high school in a city of 130,000 black residents and despite assurances that the school would hold classes to prepare students only for "negro trades," school officials refused the offer. One board member expressed the fear that building such a school would result in "all the negroes in the entire state coming to New Orleans."[23]

During the Depression both white and black schools were hard hit, but black schools faced the worst cuts. While black schoolchildren traditionally had received only a fraction of what was spent on white children in the public schools, during the 1930s that figure fell from 22 percent to 17 percent. At the same time, black teachers, who had received approximately 40 percent of the salaries paid to white teachers in 1930, were earning only about 32 percent of that amount by 1935.[24]

The dismal condition of black schools was well documented in a study of the New Orleans public school system directed from 1938 to 1940 by Alonzo G. Grace, Connecticut commissioner of education. The study resulted from a long campaign on the part of Reed, NOPSTA, the Teachers' Federation, the League of Classroom Teachers, the PTA's Emily Blanchard, Isaac Heller, and others to bring in an outside evaluator to analyze the city's public educational system. These people believed that the local school system was grossly underfunded and saddled with the costly burden of maintaining racially and sexually separate schools.

Reed issued the first call for such a study in a 1933 issue of *Quartee,* and in 1935 the New Orleans Council of Parents and Teachers passed a resolution asking for an "impartial study" of the New Orleans educational system. The PTA pointed out that according to the latest government statistics Louisiana ranked forty-fourth in the country in general education, forty-seventh in literacy, and forty-seventh in average attendance. The parents and teachers wanted an evaluation of the schools in New Orleans in order to make necessary improvements.[25] Manfred Willmer confided to an AFT official that the unions hoped that "this study will bring out the scandalous condition of negro schools and teachers."[26] Although resistant to such an endeavor, the school board finally agreed to cooperate.[27]

Grace found many problems in New Orleans schools, including the system's provision for only eleven years of education when nearly every other American city offered twelve. In addition, a smaller percentage of New Orleans children were enrolled in high school than in any comparable southern city.[28] He discovered the most glaring deficiencies in the system, however, in the black schools. Responding to a questionnaire sent to teachers as a part of the Grace study, Reed pointed out that blacks in New Orleans needed "better schools, better equipment, better paid teachers." She paraphrased Booker T. Washington, stating, "The only way to hold a man in the gutter is to stay there yourself," and commented, "Our white people must understand what that means." The study's conclusions closely paralleled Reed's observations, revealing "a wide gulf in educational opportunity dating far back into the history of the state and region."[29] Schools for African American children were inadequate in number and quality. Classes were overcrowded, building facilities substandard, and schools suffered from insufficient staff and a shortage of qualified teachers. Unfortunately, little was ever done to implement the recommendations of the study, and the public school system for both whites and blacks remained, for the most part, in the gutter Reed warned against.[30]

In their efforts to help organize African American teachers and to improve black education, Reed and Towles, like other activist liberals during the New Deal, worked to assist blacks without explicitly challenging segregation. But even these limited reform measures were scorned by most southern whites. Reed's participation in the Southern Conference for Human Welfare (SCHW), a group that inspired a great deal of hostility among southern traditionalists, placed Reed even further outside mainstream southern thought.

Organized in 1938, the SCHW was a reform group composed mainly of CIO unionists and southern liberals. The organization grew out of a response to the National Emergency Council's "Report on the Economic Conditions of the South," a document penned primarily by southerners who wanted to see the region's economy improved and made more equitable.[31] Linking racial discrimination to poverty, southern liberals believed that racism prevented their region from developing its true economic potential. The SCHW aimed to reform the South, both socially and economically.[32]

More than twelve hundred "lonely southern liberals," in Gunnar Myrdal's words, "experienced a foretaste of the freedom and power which large-scale political organization and action give" at the inaugural meeting of the SCHW, held in Birmingham in November 1938.[33] Under the chairmanship of University of North Carolina president Frank Porter Graham, the meeting featured talks by Eleanor Roosevelt, Supreme Court Justice Hugo Black, and U.S. Senators John Bankhead and Claude Pepper. Both black and white delegates attended the conference, including Herman C. Nixon, Clark Foreman, James A. Dombrowski, Virginia Durr, and Sarah Reed, representing the New Orleans Classroom Teachers' Federation. Reed persuaded the Orleans Parish School Board, a group not particularly supportive of the aims of the SCHW, to pay for her trip and to give her time off from teaching school.[34]

The delegates presented Justice Black with a statesmanship medal, honoring him as "the Southerner who has done most to promote human welfare."[35] Voter registration, antilynching laws, and federal aid to education ranked high among the reforms sought by the SCHW.[36] The conference also passed resolutions condemning the U.S. House Un-American Activities Committee and calling for the abolition of poll taxes and for full citizenship for all Americans regardless of race.[37]

CIO organizer Lucy Randolph Mason articulated an enthusiasm many conference participants must have shared: "For years I have known that the South cannot be saved by its middle class liberals alone," she wrote, "that they must make common cause with labor, the dispossessed on the land and the Negro." Finally, she exclaimed, southerners were attending a conference dedicated to human welfare that brought all of these groups together. "Some liberals may find it too shocking to have the other three groups so articulate about their needs," Mason concluded. "But this is the basis of progress in democracy, economic justice and social values in the South."[38]

The SCHW's liberal stands on racial issues alienated many southerners, including Birmingham police commissioner Eugene ("Bull") Connor, who informed conference delegates that by holding an integrated meeting they were violating Birmingham's segregation ordinance. The delegates agreed to conform to the law in this case and separated the races on either side of the auditorium, but they voted never to hold another segregated meeting. Although the gesture posed no direct challenge to Jim Crow laws, it was a significant move for southern liberals who usually avoided confronting the segregation issue. It also damned the group forever in the eyes of more conservative white southerners, already in revolt against New Deal initiatives, who disparaged SCHW members as "racial equality reformers."[39]

The New Deal orientation of the SCHW angered many southerners who were becoming increasingly disenchanted with Roosevelt after his attempt to "pack" the Supreme Court and his efforts to defeat his foes in the congressional elections of 1938. Southern critics of the New Deal were particularly concerned that the customary "patterns of dependency" in the South were endangered by minimum wage legislation, antipoverty programs, labor organizing, and "the expression of political awareness and interest among traditionally disfranchised groups."[40]

In general, southern conservatives resented the attention that liberals were paying to their region and worried that the social, political, and economic status quo would be disrupted. They were angry over Roosevelt's pronouncement that the South was the "nation's number one economic problem," fully understanding the implication that only liberal laws and legislators could improve their region.[41]

At the same time that southern liberals were beginning to grapple with the region's racial mores, blacks were mobilizing the forces that would eventually bring dramatic transformations to southern society.[42] Their first target was education, an area in which discrimination was clear-cut and pervasive. A national movement to improve classroom conditions for black children and to equalize salaries between African American and white teachers had been underway for some years by the time the League of Classroom Teachers organized in New Orleans. In 1934 the Garland Fund had donated ten thousand dollars to the National Association for the Advancement of Colored People, "to be used exclusively for a campaign of legal action and public education against unequal apportionment of public funds for education and discrimination in public education."

Little was accomplished on these fronts until 1938, when Melvin Alston, a black schoolteacher in Norfolk, Virginia, filed suit against the local board of education for practicing salary discrimination against African Americans. After lower courts rejected his suit, the U.S. Circuit Court decided in his favor in 1940, agreeing that a separate salary schedule for black teachers who had equal qualifications and responsibilities was in violation of the Fourteenth Amendment's due process and equal protection clauses. The court called salary differentials "as clear a discrimination on the ground of color as could well be imagined," and it mandated equalization of salaries. The U.S. Supreme Court refused to review the decision in the Alston suit, thus establishing a legal precedent in favor of equal salaries.[43]

The driving force behind the salary equalization suits was Thurgood Marshall of the National Association for the Advancement of Colored People. Although Marshall and the NAACP planned an eventual attack on school segregation, in the short run they tackled salary discrimination as a means of furthering racial equality. It was a slow—but significant—process. The NAACP lawyers took on state after state; by 1941 African American teachers had secured salary equalization in eight southern states.[44]

In New Orleans, the League of Classroom Teachers, taking advantage of the momentum created by the founding of the union and their success in securing salary increases, petitioned the Orleans Parish School Board for equal salaries in 1938. The teachers pointed out the many disparities that existed between the white and black educational systems in New Orleans: the board spent $62.52 for every white pupil, compared with $30.84 for each black child; the average white teachers, with a pupil load of thirty-five, received $47.77 per pupil in annual salary, while the average black teacher, with a pupil load of fifty-five, received only $21.78 per pupil per year.[45] A 1935–36 NAACP survey showed that Louisiana as a whole paid white teachers an average of $931 a year compared with the $403 average for black teachers.[46]

As it was obvious that the board had no intention of responding to their petition, black teachers arranged a meeting with Thurgood Marshall to discuss plans for a lawsuit. The group decided that Marshall and a local black lawyer, Alexander P. Tureaud, would handle the case as soon as they found a suitable plaintiff—not an easy task. Teachers were afraid of losing their jobs if they challenged the powerful school board. They knew that their counterparts in other southern states had been fired after presenting similar suits for salary equalization. Finally, in 1941, an untenured teacher at the Ricard School in New Orleans, Joseph P. McKelpin, agreed to help the committee, and in May Tureaud went before the Orleans Parish School Board with McKelpin's petition for equalization of black and white salaries.[47] Tureaud told the board that its separate salary schedules were discriminatory and unconstitutional in that they were based solely on race and color. The petition called for "a salary schedule free of all racial discrimination or differential." The board put the matter aside, telling Tureaud that the petition would be considered at some later date.[48] At its next regular meeting, the board refused the petition.[49]

In June 1941 Attorney General Eugene Stanley had met with a large group of teachers, state legislators, and businesspeople in New Orleans to discuss the federal court decision requiring equal pay for black teachers. "The Civil War is over," the attorney general said, "and we have no intention of starting it again." However, he clearly was not in accord with the decision and openly suggested that the school board might be able to circumvent the courts. "I want to call your attention to the way Southern states handled the question of equal accommodations for Negroes in street cars," Stanley said. "We provided accommodations for Negroes in the same street cars, and we still kept the so-called Jim Crow laws. We may be able to settle this question in somewhat the same way; I am sure that we can manage it in a way that will mean that the tax-payers' pocket will not suffer." Stanley later said that there was talk of reclassifying teachers in some way. Board member George Treadwell told the gathering that the 1940 Alston decision presented a "problem."[50]

The day after the board rejected McKelpin's petition, black leaders turned, as they had previously done in several other states, to the federal courts for redress. On June 14, 1941, Tureaud filed McKelpin's complaint with the U.S. District Court. The attorney argued that his client and "all other Negro teachers and principals in Orleans Parish are being denied the equal protection of the laws in that solely by reason of their color and race they are being denied compensation from public funds for their services as teachers equal to the compensation provided from public funds for and being paid to white teachers with equal qualifications and experience for equivalent services." The complaint called for the court to disallow the school board's practice of establishing teacher salaries according to race.[51]

The suit worried the local white press as much as it did Louisiana officials. The *Times-Picayune* editorialized about the possible effects of the McKelpin case, suggesting wholly negative results for white teachers. The paper pointed out that either large amounts of new revenue would be necessary to pay black teachers the same amount as whites or "perhaps the qualifications of the main body of teachers would have to be reduced." According to the newspaper, school authorities doubted whether they could raise the additional money, "especially for a purpose which they do not believe would be a blessing in every respect to the educational system." The editor raised the specter of outside agitators wreaking havoc with the local status quo, thus indirectly referring to Thurgood Marshall and the NAACP's role in the McKelpin case. "The issue seems to have been transplanted to Louisiana from other areas where Negro organizations have invoked the Fourteenth Amendment in the pay equality drive," the paper said. "It derives its importance from the fact that in recent cases the federal courts have seen much more than appears to the eye in the amendment's requirement that a state must afford all citizens the 'equal protection of the law.'"[52]

In September 1942 Judge Wayne Borah of the U.S. District Court ruled in *McKelpin v. OPSB* that the Orleans Parish School Board's customary practice of paying blacks smaller salaries, even when they had equal qualifications and experience, was "unlawful, unconstitutional, and . . . in violation of the equal protection clause of the Fourteenth Amendment of the Constitution of the United States and of Section 41 and 43 of Title 8 of the United States code." The school board was "permanently enjoined and restrained from discriminating in the payment of salaries against the plaintiff and any other Negro teachers and/or principals in the public school system of New Orleans, and in favor of any white teachers or principals in the public school system of New Orleans, on account of race or color." Judge Borah encouraged both Tureaud and the school board to recommend means whereby salary equalization could be accomplished.[53]

The school board wanted to extend the equalization process over a period of five years. Some teachers, both black and white, also wanted some sort of gradual process implemented. White teachers were concerned that their own salaries might be reduced in order to increase black salaries, particularly if equalization had to be achieved immediately. Nondegreed teachers of both races were also worried that their incomes might be reduced to offset raises that would go to degree-holding black teachers.[54]

Sarah Reed called A. P. Tureaud to discuss these concerns with him. As Tureaud related the conversation to Thurgood Marshall, Reed was afraid that white teachers would not cooperate with their black colleagues if they felt their own livelihoods were at risk. Reed reminded Tureaud of the bitterness between degreed and nondegreed teachers over the pay differential bill and urged him to consider "any reasonable proposition" the school board might offer to achieve equalization.[55] Reed, herself a longtime supporter of salary equalization for all teachers, was obviously having a difficult time in securing the support of her own union on this issue.

Marshall opposed the board's five-year plan. In fact, he told Tureaud, it "stinks."[56] He advised Tureaud to wait for a better offer. "Please bear in mind that we are in no hurry. They are in the hurry," Marshall wrote. "The time element is running against them, and not against us, and all we have to do is to sit calmly by. It is just like a checker game, and it is now their move; and I don't see why we should make a move and leave ourselves open."[57]

In the end, the court accepted a compromise worked out between the school board and the African American teachers that allowed the board two years, until September 1943, to put the new salary schedule fully into effect. Until that time, beginning with the academic year 1942, all African American teachers' and principals' salaries would be "increased by amounts equal to one-half the difference between the present salaries of said Negro teachers and principals and white teachers and principals of similar qualifications and experience."[58]

The joy that Tureaud and the black teachers felt over the decision in their favor was diminished considerably when McKelpin was fired soon after the announcement of his victory. It was obvious that white school authorities were not going to surrender gracefully. Some white teachers were also alarmed by the ruling. The all-white Louisiana Teachers' Association complained that "under the stress of war time conditions" the ruling had created educational problems of "extreme gravity." In an attempt to consolidate opposition to equalization, the LTA hinted that white teachers' salaries might be lowered to give blacks more money and argued that all of the available resources of the organization should be used either to oppose lawsuits brought by blacks or to find "remedial measures that will minimize the evil effects resulting from decisions unfavorable to white teachers."[59]

The NAACP responded to the LTA by publicizing the fact that no white teacher's salary had ever been reduced to equalize blacks' salaries. "In all of the cases in which Negroes, through the orderly processes of a democratic government, have obtained equalization of their salaries, not a single white teacher has received one cent cut in pay," the civil rights organization pointed out. The NAACP asked the governor to use his influence with the state Department of Education to ensure that no system would be devised to thwart the court ruling; the NAACP also informed the governor of the LTA's intention to evade the demands for equal pay.[60]

The LTA went ahead with its strategy to scuttle the court's requirement to equalize the salaries of black teachers with those of whites, finally settling on a "merit-responsibility" system, similar to one used in Florida for the same purpose. The Florida system had withstood charges of discrimination and unfair administration when Hilda Turner, an African American teacher in Hillsborough County, Florida, brought suit against the local school board. Turner lost when the federal court upheld the "merit-responsibility" system. Louisiana decided to adopt the same system, adding "merit and responsibility" to experience and education as the primary components in determining salary levels. Parish superintendents would be responsible for rating teachers, and any teacher who did not agree with the rating could appeal to the parish school board, whose ruling would be final.

The plan immediately drew objections from New Orleans teachers' associations whose joint tenure fund committee, on which Sarah Reed served, went to Baton Rouge to protest the proposal at a meeting of the state Board of Education. The committee's resolution contended that the plan was "based on such intangible qualities as ability and personality which would make teachers a political football and is a direct attack on the tenure system, which is the teacher's protection." One teacher suggested that the new system would allow principals to fire teachers whenever they wanted, and Reed argued that the plan would "put the teachers back into medieval history."[61]

Many white teachers realized that "merit-responsibility" could be used against them as easily as against black teachers. Neither outcome was desirable as far as the more liberal elements of the teaching community were concerned, but the race issue was seldom mentioned by whites. They observed the long-established custom of keeping race out of public debate, even when it was a crucial component. As a colleague in the CTF wrote Sarah Reed on another education issue, "For public discussion the race problem is out. The meat of this question must be white if we're to get anywhere at this time."[62]

In the meantime, Reed worked behind the scenes on the racial aspect of the merit-responsibility bill, asking Tureaud and the NAACP to help document that abolishing the regular salary schedule for one based on merit and responsibility resulted in salary discrimination against African American teachers. "We all know that that is the purpose for the change," the NAACP assistant special counsel wrote Tureaud, "but I know of nothing I can send Mrs. Reed which would establish as a fact this purpose and show how the new set-up is used to the prejudice of Negro teachers."[63]

The New Orleans white press came out against merit-responsibility without referring to the race issue that had prompted it. The *Item* alleged not to know "what this scheme is or what the occasion for it is, if any," but opposed it anyway, on the grounds that "nothing that undermines the teacher's protections against political favoritism or selfish personality should be tolerated." The paper also predicted that the policy would not stand up under court scrutiny if it were adopted.[64] The *Times-Picayune* reminded its readers that political considerations controlled school boards throughout the state, determining who became superintendent and who was hired to teach. Even without repealing the tenure law, adopting the merit-responsibility proposal "would arm politics-minded school authorities with a bludgeon as effective in most cases as the power of arbitrary discharge." Administrators would be able to use the nebulous qualifications of merit and responsibility "to cut the pay of teachers slated for punishment so drastically as to force them out of service." Tenure, as a practical protection, would be destroyed.[65]

Historically, teachers had objected to merit-based pay plans wherever they had been suggested. Chicago teachers protested such a plan in 1903 when they were trying to establish regular salary scales. The real purpose of the proposal, they felt, was to ensure that a recent salary increase that had not yet been completely funded would not materialize. In Atlanta, teachers experienced a similar situation in 1916 when, after one year under a merit plan, the total payroll was reduced by fifteen thousand dollars. Teachers realized that the intention of the plan all along had been to reduce costs and to punish certain teachers. The merit plan adopted in New Orleans in 1914 had been used to justify higher salaries for men and led to protests by women teachers and disunity in the teaching force. Later protests over merit plans usually were fought in defense of single-salary schedules. As a historian of the merit system concludes, teachers fought the "merit pay principle as a throwback to the earlier system of teachers being rewarded on the basis of the local board's undocumented opinion of their worth."[66]

At a state Board of Education meeting held to discuss the proposed system of rating Louisiana teachers, Reed, as the joint tenure committee's representative, reported that teachers were satisfied with the current process of using education and years of experience as the basis for determining salary levels. She reminded the board that a merit system had been tried in the past in New Orleans but had been abolished because of its unfairness. "It would be terrible to put us back in the boot-licking business. You know there are many teachers who became rather proficient as bootlickers. But I don't believe in solving one problem by creating another. This is a vicious proposal," she charged. "It amounts to taking away our present tenure law by subterfuge. You know now that teacher promotions are given in dark and devious methods but the situation will be much worse when we have to depend on the opinion of others as to our individual merit."

Myrtle Rey Gamus objected that the new plan would give the parish school superintendent "the power of a political god." When the state superintendent read the portion of the proposal stating that each teacher's merit rating would be determined by the parish superintendent, "loud laughter on the part of most of the teachers present caused him to pause until order was restored." Laughter also greeted the section that guaranteed the teacher's right to appeal his or her rating to the parish school board, which would make the final determination. The president of the LTA, E. R. Hester, told the board that he was acting as the spokesman for the teachers, the majority of whom had approved of the merit-responsibility plan. Most of the teachers at the meeting, however, denied the validity of his statement.[67]

Despite the opposition, the Louisiana State Board of Education approved the adoption of the merit-responsibility system, leaving the final decision up to local parish school boards. The state board might have been influenced, in part, by the assurances of the LTA president, who told one superintendent that the merit-responsibility resolution was never meant to be immediately implemented in all parishes. Instead, Hester recommended that parishes prepare a merit-responsibility plan but use it only if faced with a salary equalization suit. Realizing that some white teachers feared that the resolution might undermine tenure protections, Hester explained that there was a kind of "gentleman's agreement" not to adopt the plan unless it would serve white teachers' best interests. White teachers had "to trust each other," Hester said, and stand together against this newest form of 'carpet bagger' invasion." Consequently, he had requested superintendents and school board members all over the state not to implement the act unless it became necessary. He did not want teachers to feel "that their LTA leadership has betrayed them." If there was ever any doubt about the real motivation for the merit-responsibility resolution, Hester put it to rest with his openly discriminatory rationale.[68]

The school board must also have been impressed by state officials' estimate that it would cost Louisiana approximately $3 million a year to raise African American salaries. Only one board member, Tulane president Rufus Carrollton Harris, voted against the plan. Governor Sam Jones condoned the board's action. In fact, according to one observer at the meeting, Jones acknowledged that the equalization of blacks' salaries was the real reason for the passage of the resolution.[69] After the board's vote, some observers at the meeting cried out, "Is this your baby, Governor?"

When Reed called upon the governor to address the crowd, Jones complied, saying that the state was ashamed, both because of the low salaries it was currently paying all teachers and because of the low income of the state's population in general. Ignoring the real intent of the vote, and trying to put a progressive face on a deeply reactionary move, Jones told the teachers, "I would be unhappy if as a result of this resolution a single individual would be discriminated against, but I would be equally distressed if it does not eventually result in bettering the condition of the colored teachers. We must live together, side by side, and work out our problems together." Denying that the plan would increase the politicization of the schools by giving extraordinary power to the parish superintendents, Jones said he trusted that superintendents would not hold a "blackjack" over the heads of teachers, as many of them feared.

Reed was not impressed. "What am I to tell my children in the classroom to whom I am teaching the principles of Americanism?" Reed asked the governor. "Is this a voluntary sidestepping of the Constitution? . . . This merit—or demerit—system will open the schools to every known form of oppression,"

Reed charged. "Many more teachers would have come to the meeting," she continued. "You wouldn't have been able to hold it in this room but so many teachers told me they couldn't come here because they would be marked people if the resolution passed. If the teachers are going to teach the children democracy, they themselves should be able to live and enjoy democracy. . . . The teachers who didn't come up here today were smart. We know we are marked people for opposing this." [70]

The *New Orleans Item* agreed with Reed and Rufus Harris that the plan would put the teachers back into "the political serfdom from which the Tenure Act has lifted them. That is not Americanism," the *Item* editor maintained. In fact, he continued, "the State Board of Education did a radically wrong thing which can't fail to be mischievous and is wellnigh sure to bring back the evils of political and personal malpractice which the protesting teachers anticipate." *Merit* and *responsibility* were such indefinite terms, the editor notes, that they would "mean only what principals, superintendents, or school boards say they mean in each teacher's case." The teachers were worried that such a rating system would subject them to "every whim, caprice, selfish personal interest or political purpose of those above them. We can't see that they are anything but right." [71]

Teachers from the Orleans Parish Tenure Committee, which consisted of members of the Orleans unit of the LTA, NOPSTA, and the CTF, sent out fliers and organized meetings to protest the merit-responsibility plan. The committee argued that the teachers already worked under a merit system, the teacher tenure law. The new plan was nothing more than a "vicious attack" on tenure and (coming as close as they would to the race issue) "a subterfuge to dodge fairly and squarely the economic problem of equalizing the salaries of all teachers of equal qualifications and experience," stated one such flier written by the joint tenure committee after a mass meeting of teachers. The committee placed the onus of responsibility for the plan on the LTA, which it claimed had misrepresented the general attitude of the classroom teachers. The New Orleans League of Women Voters supported the dissenting teachers by sending letters to state Board of Education members, noting that the LWV was "fully aware of the race issue involved" and calling the proposed solution an "evasion," one that "holds trouble for the future." [72]

State school officials tried to gain the support of New Orleans teachers by admitting, as the state superintendent of education did at a meeting of the tenure committee, that the state board had adopted the resolution simply to avoid lowering whites' salaries so as to raise those of blacks. Reed persisted in her opposition, telling Superintendent John E. Coxe that "this plan cannot work. We are trying our best to get our schools out of politics and in one movement they are put right back in. We are going to continue to fight and will not stop until the resolution is repealed in its entirety." [73]

In the end, Orleans Parish never implemented the merit-responsibility resolution, although it was adopted in some other parishes. The Orleans Parish School Board, already obligated to equalize pay because of the *McKelpin* decision, was aware that evasion of the law would probably fail in the courts, and in September 1943 black teachers in New Orleans received paychecks equal to those of their white peers. [74] Reed was pleased. It had been a difficult fight. As she told her niece, "Our teacher association Don Quixotes have their hands full at present, not shooting windmills but windbags—members of the state school board—and windbags are harder to hit effectively." The proposal, she wrote, would have been used both to evade equal pay for blacks and to get rid of "troublesome" teachers. No doubt Reed realized that she might well have been among the first to go. [75]

Sarah's father, Daniel Turnbull Towles. Courtesy Special Collections, Earl K. Long Library, University of New Orleans.

Sarah's mother, Sarah Ker Towles. Courtesy Special Collections, Earl K. Long Library, University of New Orleans.

Weyanoke plantation, West Feliciana Parish, Louisiana. Courtesy Special Collections, Earl K. Long Library, University of New Orleans.

Sarah Butler Towles, c. 1906.
Courtesy Special Collections,
Earl K. Long Library, University
of New Orleans.

Elkanah (Eck) Reed. Courtesy Special
Collections, Earl K. Long Library,
University of New Orleans.

Newcomb College Class of 1904. *Back row, far right:* Sarah Butler Towles. Courtesy Special Collections, Earl K. Long Library, University of New Orleans.

Right to left: Frank Percy, Edward M. Percy, G. Carter Percy, Katherine M. Towles, Sarah Butler Towles, William T. LaSassier (1906). Courtesy Special Collections, Earl K. Long Library, University of New Orleans.

Sarah Reed surrounded by students and friend Theresa Elam after her victory in the 1948 "un-Americanism" case. Courtesy of the *New Orleans Times-Picayune.*

Sarah Reed at the Louisiana legislature, ca. 1961. Courtesy of the *New Orleans Times-Picayune.*

Sarah Towles Reed at the Louisiana legislature, 1972. Photo by John Messina.

7 Challenging Authority

In the 1930s a conservative backlash against the labor movement, radical political activity, and New Deal legislation gave rise to an anti-Communist movement that foreshadowed the McCarthyism of the 1950s. Red-baiters of the 1930s paid particular attention to the schools and initiated a loyalty oath movement that specifically targeted teachers. Not surprisingly, they found in anti-Communism a convenient weapon with which to fight a variety of liberal initiatives, including teacher unionism. As prominent liberals and unionists struggling to advance the cause of New Orleans teachers and public education, both Reed and her sister Roberta repeatedly clashed with the Crescent City's conservative community and its powerful economic interests. Civil rights for labor and labor leaders in particular were endangered, Tulane history professor H. C. Nixon warned in 1937, and all liberals were likely to be red-baited. "In fact," he wrote in *NOPSTA News*, "a liberal today in the South might be defined as a person who has been called a Communist and isn't."[1]

Teachers have often been included in the ranks of suspect groups, particularly during times of "superpatriotic sensitivity."[2] During World War I, New York City school authorities fired several teachers suspected of antiwar activity, some because of their socialist affiliations. School boards frequently dismissed teachers on charges of "conduct unbecoming a teacher," a phrase that usually amounted to a veiled charge of disloyalty. After the war, authorities continued to scrutinize teachers for signs of disloyalty.[3] The commissioner of education in the Harding administration promised to eliminate "Communism, Bolshevism and Socialism" from American schools, and several college professors and public school teachers lost their jobs as a result of subsequent purges. Although the teaching profession was scarcely a hotbed of radicalism, just enough Communists and socialists found their way into American classrooms to lend a kernel of plausibility to right-wing charges. Antiwar socialists had, in fact, founded the AFT to protect themselves from political attacks. The union lost members during the Red Scare, as most teachers refused to align themselves with the organization because its radical and liberal leanings made it a target for red-baiters. Approximately five thousand teachers had quit the AFT by 1923.[4]

New York institutionalized the search for subversive elements in the schools in 1919, when the state legislature charged the Lusk commission with investigating Communism in the schools. Many New York legislators were convinced that an investigation might be necessary after the New York Board of Education required teachers to sign a loyalty oath as a condition of employment in 1917 and hundreds of teachers refused. The Board of Education investigated thirty of the dissenters, all members of the AFT, and fired three teachers who admitted to being pacifists. One of these teachers accused the board of singling him out because of his union membership. An investigation of the AFT resulted, with New York City's Local 5 receiving the brunt of the attention. The dismissal of the teachers was upheld and the loyalty oath remained until 1923, when Governor Al Smith repealed it.[5] Even after the Red Scare faded, teachers remained the subjects of investigation by patriotic organizations. Union leaders and teachers who showed evidence of radical or even liberal political beliefs were carefully watched and sometimes harassed. Opposition to loyalty oaths, association with radicals, even unconventional behavior could jeopardize a teacher's job.[6]

The movement to require loyalty oaths for teachers subsided during the late 1920s, but resurfaced in 1931 following Communist demonstrations in Cleveland, Chicago, New York, and Washington, D.C., and riots in New York City touched off by a Communist rally in Union Square. The Daughters of the American Revolution led the new agitation for these laws, announcing, "The departure from American ideals under the guise of liberalism, internationalism, advanced thought, and radical theories, has progressed sufficiently to arouse the concern of those who believe that nationalism is synonymous with loyalty to country, and that in the adherence of youth to this ideal lies the future of America." Six states passed loyalty oath bills in the first year of the DAR campaign.[7]

Communist activity also prompted the creation of the Fish committee of the U.S. House of Representatives, a forerunner of the House Committee on Un-American Activities, charged with investigating Communistic tendencies among suspect groups of Americans. Republican Representative Hamilton Fish told the House that Communism within the United States threatened internal security. Before the end of 1931, Fish called Communist Party leader William Z. Foster to testify before his committee.[8] Seven years later, Congressman Martin Dies of Texas, chairman of the Special Committee on Un-American Activities, breathed new life into Congressional anti-Communism. Within days of its founding, the committee reported that it had found Communists in 640 organizations, 483 newspapers, and 280 labor unions.[9] The Dies committee specifically targeted the AFT after the AFL announced in 1939 that it might break its ties with the teachers' union if the AFT continued to allow Communist teachers in its ranks. Dies also warned the American public that the federal government contained "hundreds of left-wingers and radicals who do not believe in our system of private enterprise." Among the most dangerous "purveyors of class hatred," Dies argued, were Frances Perkins, Harold Ickes, and several other prominent officials in the Roosevelt administration.[10]

The hatred that many conservatives felt toward the New Deal often found its expression in aspersions against liberal Democrats' loyalty to their country. Members of the business community who detested the New Deal used anti-Communism as a way of discrediting both organized labor and progressive legislation. The U.S. Chamber of Commerce and the National Association of Manufacturers funded major campaigns to malign the Wagner Labor Relations Act and to promote right-to-work laws, smearing opponents as Communist-inspired.[11] The Veterans of Foreign Wars and the American Legion were also highly influential in setting public opinion against organized labor and linking it with Communism.

Because of its ties to organized labor, the AFT was the American Legion's primary target in the educational community. A legion pamphlet, "The ABC's of the Fifth Column," claimed that 80 percent of AFT members were Communists and that the rest were Communist sympathizers. A legion commander reported that the AFT had not displayed an American flag at its 1936 convention, concluding from this omission that Communists controlled the union.[12] William Randolph Hearst joined the legion's campaign against progressive teachers and unions when his newspaper chain carried a series of articles by legion commander Joseph V. McCabe in 1935, which suggested that teachers quit meddling in social and economic issues and leave the business of running the economy to businessmen.[13]

By 1936 twenty-one states and the District of Columbia required teachers to take loyalty oaths as a condition of employment.[14] Some Americans wanted Congress to pass a federal resolution asking all states to require such oaths.[15] Congress did pass a bill in 1935 that required teachers in the District of Columbia to sign an oath that they were not teaching Communist doctrines. The law was repealed in 1937, but not before teachers understood how easily their First Amendment rights might be diminished.[16] Despite their objections to being singled out as potentially subversive, teachers and college professors remained the main focus of the loyalty oath movement. Some states prohibited Communists from teaching in the public schools; others banned teachers' membership in supposedly subversive organizations. Georgia and Texas legislators required teachers to swear that they would not teach anything concerning government, economics, or social relations that contradicted Americanism.[17] Most states were more likely to make teachers promise simply to uphold the Constitution of the United States.[18] Teachers' groups and others, including the American Civil Liberties Union (ACLU), protested the oaths, and Republican presidential candidate Alf Landon objected that such laws made teaching a "suspect profession."[19]

An economic motive was also at play in the loyalty oath movement. Patriotic societies, among the most militant in their demands for Communist-free schools, were dedicated to preserving veterans' programs. With calls for tax reductions during the Depression often directed against veterans' payments, patriotic organizations such as the American Legion tried to turn the public's attention to possible cuts in education instead. Loyalty oaths discredited teachers, while at the same time bolstered public esteem for patriotic groups. The American Legion, with its massive treasury and 1 million members, including 16 U.S. senators and 130 members of the House, was among the most vocal of those calling for loyalty legislation.[20] The legion had other allies as well, one of the largest being the American Coalition of Patriotic Societies. The coalition, composed of eighty-five groups, included the Betsy Ross Corps, the Anglo-Saxon Federation, the Immigration Restriction Association of Chicago, and the Junior American Vigilante Intelligence Federation.

In New Orleans, Communist activity in the 1934 municipal elections proved to some citizens the need for loyalty legislation. Communists put forward a list of demands including unemployment relief, the right of workers to organize, equal pay for black teachers, and equal treatment of blacks. In a campaign flier, Communists announced that the conditions for the working class were worsening daily in New Orleans. Workers faced hunger and even starvation, they said, but when they tried to improve their situation by organizing, they were "met by the forces of 'law and order.' . . . Militant strikers fighting for better living conditions are arrested and jailed. . . . The right of free speech has been denied, and workers' meetings broken up by the police." [21]

In addition to attacks from Communists for discriminating against black teachers, the Orleans Parish School Board came under fire from anti-Communists for allowing a party member to lecture at a public high school. Parents of Eleanor McMain High School students and some members of the board were particularly upset that approximately two hundred blacks had attended the talk sponsored by the New Orleans Public Forum, an organization founded in 1934 by business and professional men to discuss economic issues. The board unhesitatingly prohibited the organization from conducting any more talks in a public school building. [22]

The interracial nature of the forum, which seated blacks and whites in the same room, troubled many people. Clearly the talk had been inspired by Communist proponents of integration. The speaker had not intended to "enlighten" his audience, claimed board member Theo Hotard. He had instead "calculated to sow the seed of discontent within the bosoms of those half-starved, half-clad members of humanity, those people who have suffered most from this depression, those people whom the Communists figured would grasp at a straw in hope of alleviating their distress." [23] Hotard claimed that handbills advertising the lecture had been distributed to workers of both races. The speaker, Hotard said, had told the audience that Communists "were planning a revolution among workers because the capitalists won't give up their power" and that the Communists "favored complete equality of the races." School board president Schaumberg suggested that to avoid any problem in the future, lectures for blacks would have to be held in black schools. [24]

Not all members of the school board agreed with the board's ruling against the New Orleans Public Forum. Isaac Heller, an ACLU attorney and son of the South's most prominent rabbi, Max Heller, wrote an article in response to the decision for *Quartee*, "The Right to Free Speech." He urged teachers to practice intellectual freedom as well as to preach it. Dismissing the likelihood of official reprisals, he reminded teachers, "Our system can never progress without intelligent cooperation, which means, at times, harsh and open criticism." [25] Heller also informed the New Orleans press that he supported the right of anyone to speak before school groups or in school buildings. His was a minority position on the board, he said, but he felt it was important to express his opinion "in view of the activities of certain groups in this city which would permit the exercise of this constitutional right only to those whose views exactly coincide with what they themselves happen to believe at the moment."[26] Heller chided his political opponents on the board, noting that "if the lectures on Socialists and Communists were disagreeable to us, then we should likewise object when the forum presented a lecture on the New Deal. Is the forum to be limited to those theories with which the majority of the school board is in accord?"[27]

Emily Blanchard of the New Orleans Council of Parents and Teachers agreed with her fellow New Deal supporter that the Public Forum talks should not have been banned from the public schools. "Stifling this liberal education movement," she said, tends to justify "the nation's opinion of the backward South." Moreover, she continued, "Our school board seems bent on demonstrating a political theory not remotely concerned with democracy. One suspects that the board has gone Fascist." Blanchard assured the readers of her open letter that she was not a Communist, "nor even a parlor Socialist." She was, rather, "such a thoroughgoing Democrat that a display of fascism on the part of public officials alarms her. She would remind these ardent officials that the New Deal includes a square deal."[28]

Other New Orleanians applauded the board's actions. The Louisiana Coalition of Patriotic Societies (LCPS), founded in 1936, considered the schools a prime target for subversive activities and sought to monitor the activities of teachers. The coalition promoted teacher loyalty oaths, alleging that in recent years there had been "a vigorous campaign conducted to inculcate Communistic doctrines in our schools, colleges and churches." According to the patriotic organization, "Speakers, disguised as educators, writers and sociologists" had spoken before various groups "advocating doctrines known to be inspired by the Soviet and other vicious movements in America." Specifically, the coalition pointed out, Communists had persuaded school administrators to keep the Reserve Officers Training Corps (ROTC) out of high schools. "Their work in New Orleans is only part of a national program to weaken our military and naval forces so as to make this country defenseless in case of a national emergency."[29]

In 1936 the patriotic society supported an ultimately unsuccessful proposal to attach a loyalty oath proviso to the teacher tenure bill. Even conservative teachers' groups protested the idea. The editor of the *Faculty*, the Schoolmasters publication, could not see any point in the oath, since the "conditions which prompted authorities in certain sections of the country to insist upon all teachers taking an oath do not exist here."[30] School board member George Treadwell, responding to the editor in the next issue of the *Faculty*, disagreed. He could not understand "why any loyal American citizen should have any objection to taking an oath of allegiance to his government." In fact,

Treadwell speculated, perhaps the very existence of the opposition to such an oath indicated its advisability.[31]

The CTF and NOPSTA opposed the oath, arguing that "a law that forces obedience through fear is as harmful to teaching progress as inertia or ignorance."[32] NOPSTA feared that attacks on teachers would only spread and that the oath was just one symptom of a larger movement against academic freedom.[33] While NOPSTA, the CTF, and others worried about attacks on civil liberties and applauded the defeat of the bill, other New Orleanians warned against "masquerading Bolsheviks and Communists prating about universal brotherhood of man," in the words of an attorney who spoke at Flag Day ceremonies at City Park in 1936. He cautioned his audience to be "ever alert and vigilant."[34]

Some citizens heeded his advice. The Young Men's Business Club passed a resolution recommending the investigation of Communism in the public schools. In a reversal of its earlier uneasiness about loyalty oaths, the Schoolmasters' Club jumped on the patriotic bandwagon and joined the Louisiana Coalition of Patriotic Societies in endorsing the oaths.[35] The suspicion that radical philosophies were beginning to corrupt the city's youth led some groups to do more than rely on pledges to preserve democracy. The Kiwanis Club sponsored a series of lectures for high school students on the advantages of American institutions. The *Item* praised the idea and expressed the belief that if students understood the government, they would be less susceptible to propaganda expounded by Communists and Fascists.[36]

When yet another bill came before the state legislature in 1938 that would require a loyalty oath of all public employees, the Teachers' Federation objected to teachers' new classification as a "suspect group," and called the oath bill a "threat to academic freedom and to the civil liberties of teachers and other public employees."[37] A representative of the Louisiana League for the Preservation of Constitutional Rights wrote Representative Frank J. Stich, a sponsor of the bill, that he did not understand a provision that would require public employees to defend the Constitution of the United States and that of Louisiana against all foreign and domestic enemies. "Inasmuch as we are not now at war, I am not aware of the fact that we have any enemies and in any event I do not know what a domestic enemy is." Furthermore, the idea of employees owing "faith and allegiance" to the Constitution struck him as undemocratic. "I was under the impression that citizens of the United States were free people and did not owe faith and allegiance," he continued, "these words being customarily used in connection with subjects of an autocratic government."[38]

The CTF mounted a strong opposition to the bill and organized a group of teachers and other citizens to go to Baton Rouge to protest it. At a legislative committee hearing, the Louisiana League for the Preservation of Constitutional Rights argued that the bill was a threat to freedom of speech and academic freedom and that it would promote "undemocratic suspicion and espionage." The bill was finally withdrawn. As Harold Lee of the LLPCR wrote the American Civil Liberties Union, "This was a more complete defeat than if it had been voted on and defeated." [39]

In 1938 school board member Isaac Heller came once again to the defense of free speech after parents complained that Communist literature was being sold outside a local high school while lectures sponsored by the League for Industrial Democracy (LID) were held in the school's auditorium. Heller challenged the parents' assumption that the speakers were Communists. As a member of the LID, Heller assured the board that league members were not Communist Party members.[40] Instead, LID was unofficially affiliated with the Socialist Party. Founded in 1905 by Upton Sinclair as an educational organization called the Intercollegiate Socialist Society, its name was changed to the League for Industrial Democracy in 1921. It was led throughout the 1920s by socialists, including Norman Thomas, whom the league and its student section supported for the presidency in 1932.[41]

Sarah Reed was also a member of the League for Industrial Democracy. In 1935 a Tulane student wrote her asking for help for a "handful of radicals now on the campus" who wanted to strengthen the Student League for Industrial Democracy (SLID) at Tulane. As a member of the league and a teacher, Reed might be able to identify radical students that SLID could recruit before they "go over to some fascist, quasi-fascist, or liberal movement," the student said. The job might be more difficult now, he warned, because both students and faculty were beginning to voice their opposition.[42]

Reaction to radicalism of any kind was indeed hardening by the late 1930s. The presence of Communists in New Orleans added a new dimension to the growing undercurrent of labor unrest that would culminate with the 1937 organizing campaigns of the newly formed Congress of Industrial Organizations. The CIO, which relied on trained Communist organizers for its early recruitment drives, sought to build a labor movement that was openly interracial. The group began a massive organizing drive in the South in 1937, the same year that Communists held their first All-Southern Communist Party Conference in Chattanooga. While the entire Communist population of the South amounted to scarcely three thousand members, such open activity alarmed many Southerners.[43] The militant sit-down strikes of 1937 also lent credence to the idea that labor was becoming too radical, too demanding.[44]

In New Orleans, the campaign to organize both black and white dockworkers into the CIO's West Coast–based International Longshoremen's and Warehousemen's Union in 1937 sparked police raids on CIO headquarters, arrests of union leaders, and destruction of membership cards. A CIO-organized strike by truck drivers in 1938 culminated in violence, massive arrests of picketers, and more police raids on CIO headquarters. New Orleans police arrested more than seventy-five CIO truck drivers in "preventative arrests." The acting police superintendent reassured citizens that "all agitators" sent from San Francisco "to agitate among the Negroes and get them to join the CIO" would be banished from the city. There was "no room in New Orleans for the CIO, Communists and reds," he said, "and if I can run them out of New Orleans, I'm going to do it." [45] In fact, New Orleans showed itself to be particularly intolerant of labor activity, as its police force continued to raid CIO meetings and looked the other way while armed men beat their prisoners. [46]

The Louisiana League for the Preservation of Constitutional Rights reported that the police openly admitted to civil-rights violations against the CIO, including raids and seizures without warrants, arrests without booking prisoners, refusing prisoners the right to engage an attorney, secret arrests, holding prisoners so that no one could find out where they were, and forcibly ejecting suspects from the city. [47] Such activities earned New Orleans a place on the American Civil Liberties Union's list of eleven major "centers of repression," where the most incidents of antilabor violence took place in 1937. [48] By 1939 the city had climbed to the top of the list of civil-liberties violators, competing only with Tampa and Little Rock for this distinction. [49]

A resolution introduced by Representative Frank Stich of New Orleans and adopted by the Louisiana legislature in 1938 denounced labor militancy as "Communistic" and referred to the union leaders as "imported and alien radicals" whose "insidious propaganda . . . has been directed to the organization of Negroes in this state." The "seeds of Communism" had "unfortunately taken root and unless drastic steps are taken at once it will spread to the rural parts of the state and white supremacy will be endangered," the resolution warned. [50] Louisiana lawmakers denounced the "alien emissaries" who had been disseminating subversive propaganda and advised agencies of the state and local governments to "take all steps necessary to suppress, stamp out and eradicate Communism and its attendant evils." [51]

Communism, the CIO, and racial equality became the watchwords of a powerful conservative counterattack against the economic and cultural challenge of labor's left wing. [52] According to the *St. Louis Post-Dispatch,* in a long 1936 article entitled "Red-Baiting in a Big Way in New Orleans," the forces of anti-Communism and antilabor had relatively little to worry about since they were stronger than labor or radicalism of any kind in New Orleans.

Nonetheless, the paper continued, business and professional men were not taking any chances and had joined together to fight Communists, although the paper estimated that there were fewer than a hundred of them in the city. Socialists, labor organizations, public speakers, and liberal college professors—"anyone who it is feared might promote the organization of labor in a city where unions are so weak that girls work in factories for as little as 7 and 8 cents an hour"—also came under attack.[53]

The Louisiana Coalition of Patriotic Societies, the *Post-Dispatch* reported, was the main force behind the crusade against subversion. Emmett L. Irwin, president of the coalition, told the newspaper that the organization's membership numbered between six and seven thousand and included leading New Orleans citizens. The coalition had close affiliations with many other organizations in the city, including the Daughters of the American Revolution, the American Legion, the Veterans of Foreign Wars, the Army and Navy Club, and the Daughters of 1812. The LCPS also had ties to the New Orleans Association of Commerce and several other civic associations.[54] The primary goal of the organization was to "promote patriotism." In the thinking of the coalition, this meant "undivided allegiance to the United States" and resistance to "efforts of unassimilated or hyphenated groups to use the Government of the United States for the furtherance of the politics of foreign governments, states, peoples, and organizations." The coalition pledged to "expose and combat the political and economic fallacies of socialism, communism and fascism" and to preserve the Constitution. It also advocated immigration restriction in order "to keep America American."[55]

Its president described the activities of the Louisiana Coalition to the *Post-Dispatch:* "We keep tabs on people," he said, "note down everything anyone suspected of subversive activities does, watch him and then the minute he steps out of line, we get him." Objects of this kind of surveillance, Irwin said, were people in such subversive groups as the American Civil Liberties Union, the League for Industrial Democracy, and the League Against War and Fascism. If a teacher said anything the group felt was suspect, Irwin said, the coalition went to the parish school board. The Louisiana Coalition criticized Tulane professors who advocated the expansion of the federal government's role in such areas as banking, transportation, and communications, and it condemned Orleans Parish School Board member Isaac Heller for voting against organizing a high school unit of the Junior Reserve Officers Training Corps.[56]

The Association of Commerce's National Defense Committee also supported the formation of a high school ROTC unit.[57] The issue of whether the military ought to be represented in public high schools sparked a great deal of controversy in the mid-1930s. When the issue first arose in New Orleans in 1936, in the form of a request by the National Defense Committee to establish a ROTC unit at a public high school, forces both pro and con appeared before the school board. Lining up against the proposal were the PTA, NOPSTA, the Central Trades and Labor Council, several women's organizations, labor representatives, and members of the New Orleans Youth Council, and Sarah Reed, representing the CTF.[58]

Opponents of ROTC won, at least temporarily, when the school board declined to start a unit in the New Orleans public schools.[59] Four years later, however, Fortier High School principal John Conniff, former assistant superintendent of public schools in Orleans Parish, created an unofficial military unit at his school.[60] Although the undertaking was not a regular ROTC unit, it was organized along similar lines. Sarah Reed's public opposition to her principal's pet project did not go unnoticed by Conniff, who used this issue against her in their subsequent dealings.

Conniff did not like Roberta Towles any better than he liked her sister. As membership chairman of the Teachers' Federation, Towles, described as "energetic, adroit and unconquerable," was heavily involved in union activities.[61] She and Sarah worked together on many projects, including the organization of the African American teachers' union. Throughout their long careers, Towles and Reed frequently teamed up, and their activities on behalf of the union often irritated school authorities. The two sisters, a board member once said, "constantly oppose everything the School Board tries to do."[62] Sarah and Roberta's close connection left both of them vulnerable to sanctions from school administrators, who used procedural and pedagogical issues to mount what was essentially an ideological attack upon the women.

The first episode in what would be a prolonged campaign to weaken the influence of the sisters began on February 9, 1938, when Superintendent Bauer informed Roberta by letter that he was transferring her from Fortier High to the Charles J. Colton High School in two days. Colton was a downtown school, several miles from Roberta's Uptown residence near Fortier. In her new position, Roberta would have three new subjects to teach to more than two hundred students. Naturally, Roberta considered this transfer a demotion and, coming as it did in the middle of the academic year, an abrupt, unexpected, and inconvenient one at that.

Roberta requested a public hearing before the school board. It turned out to be a perfunctory meeting as the board did not really investigate the matter and would not permit questioning of Principal Conniff or Superintendent

Bauer, although both were present. The Classroom Teachers' Federation believed that school officials were singling out Towles because of her position on the union's executive board. The school board evaded the issue by stating simply that transferring teachers was the prerogative of the superintendent, whose decision was not open to debate. In a memorandum sent to its members, the Teachers' Federation charged that the board had ignored its own rule, namely, "No principal shall show partiality in favor of, or prejudice against, any teacher." Clearly, the federation argued, Conniff had shown prejudice against Towles, and it urged union members and all those who believed in "fair play" to protest vigorously the board's cover-up of the violation.[63]

One federation member described Towles as being "confronted by the vicious circle of autocratic hierarchies." The school board would do nothing, thus following the direction of the superintendent, who would do nothing because he had agreed to follow the recommendation of his principal, who said that he could do nothing because the board and the superintendent had already made the decision. "This is the well-known Army game of 'passing the buck,'" the writer concluded, noting that "the abuse of power at Fortier has had a disastrous effect upon the entire teaching corps in that it has destroyed morale and has created a widespread feeling of inferiority."[64]

At the public hearing before the school board, Reed charged that Conniff had asked for Roberta's transfer because he disapproved of her teaching methods.[65] At a meeting between the Teachers' Federation and Conniff, the principal had criticized Towles for allowing her students too much freedom in the classroom. Experimental teaching methods were not allowed at Fortier, Conniff said. He also accused Towles of spending too much class time discussing current problems. ATF executive secretary Manfred Willmer pointed out that Conniff was contradicting the current program of the Louisiana Department of Education, which directed teachers to experiment with new teaching techniques and programs allowing greater classroom freedom and encouraging pupil participation. "If one teacher can be penalized for using progressive teaching methods," Willmer said, "the many progressive teachers throughout the state may also suffer penalties."[66]

Reed told the *Times-Picayune* that Conniff had said that her sister's "teaching was out of keeping with the teaching pattern used at Fortier and that it made the pupils dissatisfied in other classrooms at the school."[67] Willmer also took his argument to the newspapers, pointing out that Towles was a pioneer in progressive education. In her history class, Willmer said, she tried to relate current events to historical ones, and she encouraged students to actively participate in the workings of the classroom by planning class activities and by discussing their studies as a group. Willmer pointed out that while some teachers in New Orleans had been praised for implementing this type of pedagogy, Towles had been "punished by summary transfer from one end of the city to the other, which is not only a personal inconvenience, but which also served to interrupt and destroy the work she has already done." [68]

Part of the explanation for Towles's transfer stemmed from the conservatism of her principal. Traditional educators such as John Conniff considered progressive teaching methods subversive. Conniff revealed his traditional orientation in a letter to the Orleans Parish superintendent, in which he described the Teachers College of Columbia University as "one of the most weakening and damaging influences in American education." He blamed Teachers College graduates for "the prevailing revolt against authority and work in the performance of daily duty in the school, in the home, and in the community." Teachers College was widely known for its emphasis on progressive education. Largely inspired by the writings of John Dewey, these progressive educators at Columbia in the 1930s, including George Counts, William H. Kilpatrick, and Harold Rugg, were dedicated to the idea of the school as an agent of social change, a frightening concept to someone who was satisfied with the way things were. [69]

Conniff criticized textbook companies for listening to "these so-called experts" and producing books full of "new-fangled ideas." [70] Although Conniff did not specify just which textbooks upset him the most, he was, no doubt, familiar with the furor produced by the textbooks written by Harold Rugg. Rugg's obvious contempt for capitalism and its social injustices infuriated conservative educators. One right-wing critic accused the progressive educator's texts of "promoting unrest, of fomenting class struggle, of proposing unworkable government planning, and of retailing inaccurate views of the Constitution." [71]

John Conniff and like-minded administrators and citizens worried about trends they saw emerging in the 1930s. Radical philosophies seemed to be gaining currency in many areas, including education. Teachers College was at the height of its influence, and John Dewey was espousing his own brand of socialism in books and national magazines. [72] Departures from normal classroom routine endorsed by progressive educators—field trips, active student participation in class, and group projects—were criticized for their "communistic" implications. The New Orleans Schoolmasters Club charged that the progressive educational philosophy of fitting the school to the child lacked "discipline" and "masculinity." [73] Some opponents of the New Deal focused their disapproval on progressive education, which had gained many followers during the 1930s, and they attempted "to save the schools from subversion" by eliminating progressive teachers.[74] Like other critics of progressive education, Conniff feared the political and social consequences of educational reform. He wanted the schools to retain their customary role as conservators of the status quo, and he was prepared to make sure that his school, at least, stayed on the traditional track.[75]

To accomplish his goal, Manfred Willmer believed, Conniff intended "to preserve autocratic classrooms at his school." The principal was equally determined, according to Willmer, to weaken the influence of the Teachers' Federation by indirectly informing other teachers that they, too, could be punished for union activities. As Willmer wrote AFL president William Green, "This transfer, coming as it did in the middle of a semester, has caused a great deal of hardship and inconvenience, and appears to be a punitive measure taken against Miss Towles because of her activity in this organization." School authorities had encouraged the formation of a "company union," the executive secretary told Green, and were trying to persuade teachers to switch over to the officially sanctioned organization. "Our current campaign therefore is one of crucial importance for the teachers' union in this region," Willmer said. He asked the AFL leader to write the Orleans Parish School Board and the superintendent in support of the CTF's efforts on behalf of Towles. Local authorities were susceptible to outside influence, Willmer concluded, and the CTF was confident that publicity generated by Green's letter would help its cause.[76]

In March of 1938, the president of the "company union" described by Willmer went before the board to announce the formation of the Orleans Public School Teachers' Association. Joseph Schwartz informed the board that teachers had organized the association to promote "a spirit of friendliness and cooperation between the administration and the teaching corps." Despite Schwartz's claim that most New Orleans teachers were "anxious to cooperate with the Board in a truly professional manner," the effort to form a new union quickly collapsed.[77]

The Teachers' Federation continued to fight the Towles transfer, but the board refused to reverse its decision despite protests from a wide range of organizations and individuals, including a vigorous letter of protest from AFL president Green. When a union member requested permission to read the AFL president's letter to the school board, president Henry Schaumburg ruled that the board would not hear anything else related to the Towles case. A member of the Central Trades and Labor Council questioned this decision, prompting board member Theo Hotard to remark that he could see no reason for "this constant agitation," especially coming as it did primarily from the Teachers'

Federation, a labor organization. After all, he pointed out, the downtown students Towles would now teach were children of the working class, whereas her Uptown students were more likely to be from the "silk stocking" class.

The attempt to quiet the union by implying that it did not care about the needs of working-class children angered Reed, who stood up and pointed out that there was a more relevant issue involved—the arbitrary nature of the transfer. President Schaumburg ruled Reed out of order. She continued speaking anyway. It was not the inconvenience of the location that was most upsetting to her sister, Reed said. Roberta had accepted teaching assignments farther from home than this one, even across the Mississippi River. What Miss Towles objected to, Reed explained, was that Principal Conniff had never had a conference with her about her teaching, he had never visited any of her classes, and she had received no explanation for this sudden move. Teachers understood that the board had the right to transfer them, Reed continued, "but when a teacher has served a Board faithfully for nearly 30 years, some reasonable explanation should be given for the transfer." Reed suggested that the board initiate an appeal process for transfers and warned that "such cases as the transfer of Miss Towles simply drove the teachers to the legislature in Baton Rouge to obtain relief." Teachers, she pointed out, continually had to seek bills in their behalf and they were "tired of having to appeal to the Legislature to pass such laws."

The distinction between Reed's activities and those of her sister became blurred for a moment when Hotard asked Reed whether she had visited him at home and referred to Conniff "in uncomplimentary terms." No, Reed said, she had not discussed Conniff in such a way; she had simply mentioned that he was "ill." At this point, all order broke down at the meeting, and Myrtle Rey began reading aloud from a magazine article by the president of the University of Chicago about democracy in the schools. Hotard declared her out of order and adjourned the meeting.[78]

The action taken against Roberta was, in some measure, directed also against Sarah. Roberta probably seemed a more vulnerable target than her outspoken and politically influential sister. Transferring Roberta may well have been a warning to both sisters as well as to other Teachers' Federation members that they should take care in challenging the authority of school administrators. Both sisters were also considered political radicals by some members of the New Orleans community, and action taken against either of them would have sent a clear ideological message to teachers in general.

The broader implications of the episode were made explicit later in the summer of 1938 in two radio broadcasts devoted to the Towles case. In the first address, Willmer articulated the American Federation of Teachers philosophy of education. Schools should be "fortresses of democracy where the children of the nation might learn to know and to practice democratic techniques of self-government," he said. The New Orleans public schools failed to live up to this ideal. "They have not been able to educate for democracy," he claimed, "because the democratic process is unknown in the schools." He attacked the decision to transfer Towles, noting that although the tenure law protected a teacher from arbitrary dismissal, "through the power of arbitrary transfer of teachers from one school to the other, a principal may completely destroy the happiness, security and professional well-being of any teacher."[79]

In his rebuttal, Lawrence Stone of the American Legion branded the Classroom Teachers' Federation executive secretary, "somewhat fancifully" as Willmer later described it, as a "left-wing Socialist," and then attacked Towles and Reed because they, together with several "Socialists and Communists," had blocked the introduction of ROTC at Fortier. "From that point," Willmer wrote, "he went on to a denunciation of Communism, mentioning the transfer case incidentally in order to make his inference more apparent."[80]

In the midst of this controversy, Conniff made a strong anti-Communism speech at Fortier, dragging out, as Willmer put it, "the familiar, shopworn red herring."[81] Conniff warned his faculty and students that he considered advocating "Communistic tendencies in any manner, shape or form whatsoever, in this school or out of this school . . . the highest type of disloyalty, a disloyalty that is traitorous and treacherous to the principles and practices of all loyal and patriotic citizens of our city, of our State and of our country." Conniff warned that no Communistic "tendency by hint, suggestion, innuendo or otherwise will be countenanced, or tolerated for a moment in this school." On the grounds that "loyalty is the most valuable quality any human being can possess," Conniff urged his faculty to be "ever ready to flay alive the venomous Hydra-headed monster, Communism, wherever and whenever it lifts its hideous head to the light of day."[82]

Willmer found the speech at Fortier noteworthy for several reasons. "It occurs to me," Willmer wrote, "that a man who thinks 'loyalty is the most valuable quality any human being can possess' is hopelessly out of place in the schools of democratic America." Willmer also thought that "such loose talk about [a] 'venomous Hydra-headed monster' borders dangerously on the pathological." Willmer worried that an obsession with "loyalty" had infected the whole New Orleans school system.[83]

Although loyalty was never articulated as a reason for Roberta Towles's transfer, her case represented the first episode in what was destined to be a protracted campaign of right-wing intimidation of local teachers. In the Towles affair loyalty meant allegiance to an authoritarian administrator and his personal concept of patriotism. One thing it apparently did not mean, as far as Conniff was concerned, was allegiance to a labor union that opposed military training for high school boys and consistently challenged the authority of men in power.

The Teachers' Federation adhered to the ATF motto, "Education for Democracy, Democracy in Education." Federation leaders believed in a democratic school system, one in which teachers joined with administrators in decision making. The "loyalty fetish" as Willmer put it, clearly worked against this kind of participatory organization. "With this conception of loyalty so rampant," Willmer said, "our gestures in the direction of teacher participation have been largely farcical, and teachers have participated only to endorse what has already been decided."[84] The Teachers' Federation saw the attack on Towles as symptomatic of the attitude of school authorities toward teachers. In a letter to school board president Henry Schaumburg, the CTF complained that Conniff and the board "consider those who have taken up this matter for Miss Towles, and Miss Towles herself, as nothing more than bondsmen who must say no more than 'Yes Sir' or 'No Sir' to any instructions given by those in authority or lose their jobs. . . . You have considered only her obedience to authority."[85]

The Central Trades and Labor Council campaigned on Roberta's behalf, passing resolutions and sending out petitions to make the school board "realize the injustice which has been done to Miss Towles." The Labor Council observed that because Towles was one of the most active members of the teachers' union, "members of organized labor are now under the impression that she has been discriminated against because of her activity in that organization." The council urged the school board to grant a hearing on the subject to help dispel the fear that the board was using transfers to punish teachers.[86]

At the annual national convention of the AFT in 1938, delegates passed a resolution that linked Towles's transfer with her successful work in building the membership of the CTF. In a tenure system, it pointed out, transfer was the only means whereby a principal or a board could discipline its teachers, and because Towles's work with the union was so well known, it was "evident that the transfer method of intimidation is to be used to discourage activity in the labor movement and the further organization of teachers as trade unionists." Arbitrary transfer would weaken teacher tenure and teacher security, the AFT warned, as well as undermine academic freedom. The union officially protested and condemned "the arbitrary and punitive transfer of

Miss Roberta Towles as unscientific, undemocratic, and un-American."[87] After the convention, the chairman of the AFT sent superintendent Nicholas Bauer a letter informing him of the resolution that had been unanimously passed by representatives of more than thirty thousand AFT members.[88]

Since the state attorney general had already ruled that the school board did have the authority to transfer teachers, even during the school term, the AFT's protests went unheeded, and Roberta was not transferred back to Fortier.[89] The defeat in the state legislature of a Teachers' Federation bill that would have required written notice of causes for transfer, a reasonable time frame for the transfer to take place, and a right of appeal further strengthened the superintendent's and school board's positions and precluded the possibility of a reversal of their decision.[90]

The outcome of the Towles case gave hostile school board members a green light to tackle Reed at the first available opportunity. Reed and the Teachers' Federation were obvious targets for those who wanted the schools to remain free from controversy and all taint of radicalism. The union was always controversial, and as one observer noted, "to many people Reed *was* the union."[91]

In 1938 the Schoolmasters Club, which opposed Reed and the Teachers' Federation on most issues and which was by then a charter member of the Louisiana Coalition of Patriotic Societies, began meeting with others in the coalition to discuss the activities of people and organizations the two groups believed were exhibiting "un-American" inclinations.[92] The Teachers' Federation was one of the groups the Schoolmasters found objectionable, but they were not yet prepared to accuse the union of un-American activities.

The Schoolmasters agreed with the American Association of University Professors' opposition to labor affiliation, citing in its journal the AAUP's fear that such affiliation might curtail academic freedom.[93] The unionization of teachers was highly controversial in Louisiana, as elsewhere. The Louisiana Teachers' Association fought labor affiliation at every opportunity. When teachers in Caddo Parish considered joining the AFL, LTA president E. R. Hester described the union movement as part of a national effort to undermine the authority of state teachers' organizations. "Organization of the teachers into labor unions is very dangerous to our educational system," he said. "Sabotage of the teachers' associations might be followed by sabotage of our textbooks and the filling of them with labor propaganda for inculcating it in the youths of the land."[94]

The CTF tried to assure Hester that it had no interest in interfering with his organization. Unlike the LTA, the New Orleans Classroom Teachers' Federation believed that labor allies could only help in the uphill struggle that teachers faced in securing fair wages and decent working conditions. The CTF was just as concerned as the LTA about the status of teachers as a professional group, it wrote Hester; it simply differed on the best way to accomplish their common goal of professional recognition. "If the entire teaching corps of New Orleans were federated," the CTF suggested, "there would be more solicitude for the professional status of the teacher, a smaller differential between the $10,000 salary of the superintendent and the $2500 maximum of the classroom teacher . . . and more real concern in the results achieved in more uplift and in the future of the pupils."[95]

Hostility toward labor unions remained linked to a suspicion that Communists were using unions to subvert American society through indoctrination of schoolchildren. In 1938 the Coalition of Patriotic Societies sent state Superintendent of Education T. H. Harris a letter warning that "a few unpatriotic teachers" in the public school system were "taking advantage of their positions . . . to expound in insidious ways their unhealthful and vicious views on government." Harris responded by warning parish school officials against the "teaching of communism" in Louisiana public schools. Communists, Harris agreed, were particularly inclined to use this tactic to corrupt American society. "It is my judgment," he continued, "that a teacher who not only embraces that system of government but attempts to indoctrinate his pupils with it has no place in our system of schools and should be eliminated from it."[96]

Although the *Times-Picayune* acknowledged that many people "would guard just as zealously the freedom of thought as others would prevent the infiltration of foreign doctrines," the New Orleans daily saw some merit in Harris's warning. The Coalition of Patriotic Societies "would hardly act on mere supposition," the paper stated. Harris had said that the coalition contained "many of our best and most thoughtful people," and the paper agreed; it cautioned against the possible hazards of teaching "isms" to youngsters, especially when "informed adults" had trouble understanding them.[97]

After the Soviet-Nazi nonaggression pact in 1939 and the end of the Popular Front era, the political climate became less and less tolerant of radical or unconventional ideas, and teachers were subjected to closer scrutiny than ever before. The idea of a Communist conspiracy at work in the United States spread rapidly in the early 1940s, convincing some liberals that red-baiters had been right all along. Even the ACLU endorsed an anti-Communist statement and ousted radical Elizabeth Gurley Flynn from its board. A new Red Scare erupted in many areas of the society, including but not limited to academia. Unions, the CIO among them, denounced Communism and ejected Communist leaders. Congress passed the Smith Act in 1940, making it illegal to advocate the overthrow of the government. The Justice Department and the Naturalization Service began to question Communist Party members. On college campuses, radical groups that had flourished in the 1930s folded in the 1940s. Some universities barred Communists from teaching.[98]

Investigations and other policies aimed at rooting out Communists from the educational world gained momentum. The New York state legislature's Rapp-Coudert committee began its investigation of Communism in the New York schools in 1940. In the same year, president A. G. Ruthven of the University of Michigan declared that freedom of expression and assembly did not give students and faculty the right to work against the American form of government. Teachers should recognize that they were obligated to the state to teach their students respect for the government, and they needed to "rid themselves of the notion that romanticism, sentimentalism, and indiscriminate tolerance are essential components of democracy," he told the National Association of State Universities at its annual convention. Such ideas were "only evidence of indecision and fuzzy-mindedness."[99]

The National Education Association, the largest teachers' organization in the nation, succumbed to anti-Communist paranoia when it recommended in 1941 a purging of teachers whose conduct was deemed "inimical to the best interests of our country." At its annual convention, the NEA organized a commission to investigate allegations of subversive teaching and adopted a resolution that opposed the employment of any teacher who advocated, or who was a member of a group that advocated, changing the government of the country by other than constitutional means.[100]

Even the AFT felt compelled to take action against its Communist members, expelling the Communist-dominated Local 5, the Teachers Union of the City of New York in 1941, along with two other locals, the New York College Teachers' Local 537 and Local 192 in Philadelphia. The executive committee of the AFT claimed that such action was necessary because Local 5 was "not in harmony with the principles of the American Federation of Teachers and tended to bring the AFT into disrepute and because its existence is detrimental to the development of democracy in education."[101]

Reed was among those who protested the expulsion of Local 5. The national Committee to Save the AFT asked Reed to join forces with other union members who felt it was a mistake to expel radical locals. Reed agreed and the executive board of Local 353 wrote the AFT executive council in Chicago requesting it to call off its investigations into locals and the revocation of charters. "We are in the midst of a great battle for the schools," sympathetic members of the CTF said. "We plead with you not to play into the hands of the enemies of the schools by promoting and continuing internal dissension." Reed telegraphed Local 5 in New York City, expressing her concern and offering her help. Vice president Dale Zysman wrote her back, thanking her for her interest. "We have been attacked by reactionaries of every stripe and color—both inside and outside the AFT," he wrote. "The charges against us are all patently false and represent nothing but a jumble of untruths." [102]

The fear that Communism would make the most headway via the school system manifested itself most strongly in Louisiana in a 1940 bill proposed by the Louisiana Coalition of Patriotic Societies. The bill would have prohibited teachers from joining Nazi, Fascist, or Communist groups and would have made it a misdemeanor for a teacher to advise a student against joining the military. [103] The bill was defeated, with some critics charging that it would permit a "witch hunt against teachers." [104]

The New Orleans States supported the bill and warned its readers that schools in some larger cities had been charged with going "pink." While the paper did not think that would happen in New Orleans, it advised its readers to guard against the possibility, "particularly during the trying times just ahead when the impact of world disorder may place the educational system in danger of an infiltration of foreign isms." All isms were equally bad, in the opinion of the paper, which noted that "reds, pinks, socialists, Nazis, Fascists and similar groups" had had some success in infiltrating the schools and filling the textbooks with their dangerous philosophies. Even respected educators had been accused of propagandizing for one or another of the isms. "It is not always easy to detect the subtle indoctrination of un-American doctrine," the paper cautioned. "We hope that the New Orleans school system is thoroughly free of this taint, as we believe it is. The important thing is to keep it that way." [105]

The Young Men's Business Club (YMBC) in New Orleans wrote its own Americanism proviso, resolving that "anyone connected with the State and/or Orleans Parish Public School system who teaches or preaches un-American ideologies and/or belittles our American form of government, upon being found guilty of these practices by duly constituted authorities, shall be discharged for disloyalty to our free American institutions and form of government." The resolution further stated that "Americanism should be taught in the schools with the purpose in view of developing in the school children a strong spirit of patriotism and deeper appreciation and understanding of blessings and advantages of the American democratic mode of life." [106]

Although the YMBC resolution did not go any further than the club's membership and although the state law was defeated, the sentiment inherent in both expressed itself in other ways. As the new school term got underway in the fall of 1940, Orleans Parish school superintendent Nicholas Bauer ordered all the public schools in the city to devote a minimum of ten minutes a day to an "Americanism program." Bauer specified that all schools would be required to use as their slogan: "Americanism—the Blessings and Responsibilities of a Democracy." Every principal and every teacher in the system, Bauer said, would be expected to use this slogan; no exceptions would be made. "We are not afraid to touch on isms," Bauer told the New Orleans Principals' Association, "but we want you to come back always to the thought that the American way of life is the grand way of life." [107]

Americanism was in part a patriotic response to the world conflict the United States was about to enter. Many Americans were genuinely afraid of ideologies they thought would undermine American strength and morale during this frightening time. Americanism could also be a weapon used to attack groups that held liberal or radical political beliefs and who threatened the established order. Sometimes such threats to the status quo involved criticism of political corruption. Such was the case in New Orleans when supporters of educational reform pinpointed unrealistically low property tax assessments as one of the reasons for the poor economic condition of the city's public schools. Assessors commonly pegged property far below market value in order to gain support for the political machine. Schools, largely dependent on property taxes, suffered as a result.[108]

When the Classroom Teachers' Federation spearheaded the campaign to protect teachers' salaries from a proposed 12.5 percent pay cut in the summer of 1940, it pointed out that low tax assessments based on political favoritism significantly contributed to the economic problems of the public school system. The union, already suspect because of its left-liberal leanings, became an easy target for conservative businessmen who did not want to see their favored tax situation endangered. If teachers were held to special rules of good citizenship, the union could perhaps be silenced and its credibility undermined. Because of the election of reformer Sam H. Jones as governor in 1940, the beneficiaries of Long machine politics were already worried about their futures. The *Times-Picayune* sided with the reformers, pointing out that eliminating the unfair tax assessments "that attained scandalous proportions under the dictatorship" should end the cuts in teachers' salaries that were so common under the "Long-Leche-Maestri regime." [109]

The Americanism campaign picked up steam in September 1940 when the Coalition of Patriotic Societies of Louisiana again tried to make "un-American" activities illegal. The coalition suggested that the school board pass a rule to prohibit all teachers, employees, agents, and representatives of the Orleans Parish School Board from:

> 1. Holding membership in, or participating in, the activities of any group of organization, or joining with any individual, whose aim or purpose is the overthrow of the Government of the United States of America by force or violence; or the supplanting of it with any system of government now generally known as "totalitarian"— including the present systems of Russia, Germany and Italy (and Japan), or which is guided or controlled by or owes allegiance to any foreign government, party, political organization or individual; or which teaches or promotes class or religious hatred or strife; or which advocates the abolition of the right to private property; or which advocates refusal to defend the United States of America if it is invaded by arms; or which advocates refusal to serve in the armed forces of the United States, if and when called upon to do so by proper government authority.
>
> 2. Advising, urging, persuading or inducing any pupil in the Public Schools of New Orleans to join any group or organization, or any individual, that promises, fosters, upholds, believes in or attempts any of the activities mentioned in Paragraph No. 1 (above): or to adopt, pursue, effect or seek to accomplish any of the aims and purposes mentioned in paragraph No. 1 (above).[110]

During a meeting of the school board's Committee of the Whole to consider the LCPS resolution, Isaac Heller reminded his fellow board members that the U.S. Constitution granted rights that this resolution would deny. One of these rights was to advocate changes in the government. While the board could justifiably expel from the school system any teacher who promoted the violent overthrow of the government, Heller said, it could not fire a teacher for suggesting other changes in the form of government or society, such as elimination of private property. George Treadwell responded that it was fine for teachers to have their own views, but the board should not employ teachers who attempted to pass such opinions on to their students. The patriotic coalition's resolution would not prevent teachers from thinking whatever they wanted, Treadwell said, but it would stop them from sharing these thoughts with schoolchildren. Contradicting his own avowal that teachers should be free to think whatever they liked, Treadwell asserted that people who held views such as those prohibited in the coalition's resolution should not be employed as teachers since such beliefs would inevitably influence their teaching.[111]

The school board agreed to consider the coalition's resolution at an upcoming meeting. Opponents of the proposal immediately began protesting to the board. The Committee on Academic Freedom of the American Civil Liberties Union maintained that the resolution, however reasonable its objectives, would only encourage "witch-hunting." The mere existence of such a rule, the ACLU pointed out, would intimate that disloyal teachers actually existed in the New Orleans public schools. That suspicion would reflect badly on all school board employees "and, in a larger sense, upon the Board itself." As far as the ACLU could judge, such a resolution was uncalled for in New Orleans. It was, in fact, a "dangerous" gesture, particularly "in view of the source of this resolution." If enacted the rule would likely result in accusations against teachers who belonged to organizations that were not subversive but that might be unpopular. "The particular conception of patriotism which marks the Coalition of Patriotic Societies may be used as a yardstick to judge the patriotism of others," the ACLU warned. "Once such a process is started there is no end to it." [112]

New Orleans teachers were divided over the coalition's resolution. Many teachers resented the aspersions cast upon their loyalty by such rules. One classroom instructor pointed out that unlike most people, teachers started out the day with the pledge of allegiance and frequently volunteered for the Red Cross, the Community Chest, and the Draft Board. [113] Other teachers supported the coalition's resolution, including a group that wrote the school board to complain that "'academic freedom' is being used as a cover for 'academic license.'" [114]

The Louisiana League for the Preservation of Constitutional Rights warned that because the wording of the resolution was so vague, it could easily be used "as an instrument of persecution" to get rid of teachers for merely personal reasons. Additionally, the league noted, the rule could prevent discussion of such subjects as public ownership of utilities, including the Tennessee Valley Authority, and it would bar conscientious objectors from teaching. Furthermore, under the proposed rule, a pupil who had a grudge against a teacher could accuse that instructor of classroom indoctrination, thereby inhibiting discussion of any controversial subject. The league believed that during this time of world crisis it was necessary for all citizens to be loyal to their country, "but loyalty cannot be enforced with a whip." [115]

Herman L. Barnett, president of the Louisiana Coalition of Patriotic Societies, defended his organization's rule, arguing that it would act as "a deterrent" to prevent the kind of subversion the Rapp-Coudert committee was uncovering in New York. "It is fairly certain that our public school teachers are loyal Americans, but the adoption of this rule would have the effect of causing any teacher with any desire to inculcate any foreign 'isms' to pause and reflect before developing the symptoms which seem to have affected some teachers in other parts of the country," Barnett reasoned.[116]

The January school board meeting, at which the coalition's rule was to be discussed, was jammed with spectators eager to witness or participate in what Harnett Kane of the *New Orleans Item-Tribune* described as "a rampaging, roaring session on Americanism, fifth-columning and persecution of teachers."[117] Among those speaking in favor of the coalition's rule was Henry Warmoth Robinson, chairman of the legislative committee of the LCPS, who argued that the rule was a preventive measure consistent with the tenure law, since any suspect teacher would first be warned and given a chance to discontinue propagandizing before being dismissed. According to Robinson, the proposal would make the teacher watchful "so that she will not be an unconscious victim of her own perversion or her own intellect—to warn her that she shouldn't do these things."[118]

Others in favor of the rule included the Veterans of Foreign Wars and the National Defense Committee of the Association of Commerce, represented by Arthur DeLa Houssaye and James C. Poche, who regretted the necessity for such a rule but warned that "foreign propagandists" had already been working to influence teachers. Joseph Mendez of the Veterans of Foreign Wars commented that he had been "humiliated to learn that New Orleans is considered one of the hotbeds of communism. It is accepted generally that our schools have been invaded." Barnett reminded the audience of the "terrifying" disclosures about New York City teachers. One of the most prominent sponsors of the bill, T. Semmes Walmsley, former mayor of New Orleans, acted as a spokesman for the Coalition of Patriotic Societies. Such a rule was necessary to allow authorities to fire a teacher who was not patriotic, he asserted. The coalition did not mean to discredit the school system, believing that the teaching corps was "99% loyal to the United States"; nevertheless, the coalition felt that it was necessary "to purge from that group those persons who would teach the children who had been sent to them doctrines which their parents would not want them taught and which were un-American."[119]

Opponents of the resolution included Harold Lee, associate professor of philosophy at Newcomb College and president of the Louisiana League for the Preservation of Constitutional Rights, who argued that such a rule would actually "make education for democracy impossible." He pointed out that the rule would prohibit Quakers "such as William Penn or Herbert Hoover" from teaching in the schools and that, unlike the coalition's rule, United States law recognized conscientious objection to military service.[120] George Dreyfous, another founding member of the LLPCR, warned that the rule would, in effect, prevent the teacher from "teaching anything." The league did not believe that "graduates of the public schools will be prepared for participation in democratic government if they are taught only by teachers who must constantly fear that a realistic approach to the problems of government will endanger his livelihood."

In a formal statement, the LLPCR argued that "instead of being a patriotic suggestion," the proposed rule was "a highly unpatriotic one. Its adoption would sponsor a spirit of suspicion, fear and suppression in our schools that would disrupt united effort, and this spirit would quickly spread into the community at large." Furthermore, the league said, "According to this rule, any pupil who cherished spiteful feelings against any teacher could accuse that teacher of attempting to influence him. A teacher could not teach anything at all in controversial subjects such as the social sciences without laying himself open to this danger."[121]

A representative of the Central Trades and Labor Council objected to the wording of the rule, arguing that it would inhibit teachers from forming any groups or organizations. Sarah Reed agreed with her colleagues in both the labor council and the LLPCR that adoption of the rule would be "a step in the wrong direction." If the Coalition of Patriotic Societies was indeed worried about the schools, she wondered, where had it been last summer when teachers and other citizens concerned about the school system had been working to avoid a financial crisis?[122]

Isaac Heller, who had recently declined to run for reelection to the board, spoke at the meeting as a representative of the ACLU. He opposed the resolution, he said, because he did not think that patriotism could be legislated. Heller then offered an alternative rule that said simply that the board would "not permit the teaching of Communism, Nazism or Fascism and that it will not permit anyone who is a member of these groups to teach in the public schools." In proposing such a rule, Heller was, perhaps, only making the best of a bad situation. Aware that some kind of prohibition was inevitable, he may simply have been trying to get one passed that was not as objectionable as the one already before the board. In any case, the ACLU was not opposed to such rules, having written one of its own.

Finally, after two and one-half hours of argument, board member Theo Hotard presented the coalition's rule with several amendments; it was unanimously adopted. In its final form, the rule read:

All teachers, employees, agents and representatives of the Orleans Parish School Board, or in any manner connected with or employed in the public schools of the City of New Orleans, are prohibited from:

1. Holding membership in, or participating in, the activities of any group or organization and joining with any individual whose aim or purpose is the overthrow of the government of the United States of America by force or violence; or the supplanting of it with any system of government which is guided or controlled by or owes allegiance to any foreign government, party, political organization or individual; or which teaches or promotes class or religious hatred or strife; or which advocates the general abolition of the right to private property; or which conspires to defeat the purpose or intent of law governing conscription or national defense.

2. Advising, urging, persuading or inducing any pupil in the public schools in New Orleans to join any group or organization which promises, fosters, upholds or attempts to overthrow the government of the United States by force or violence.

It shall be the duty of the superintendent to call the guilty parties and first warn them of the violation of these rules, and if they persist in their violation of the rule they will be charged under the tenure law and given a trial before the Board with resources to court for final decision before dismissal.[123]

Most of those present at the meeting agreed that the new Americanism rule eliminated the worst "witch-hunt" sections of the original rule. Isaac Heller said that he had achieved most of what he had set out to do when he led the opposition to the coalition's rule.[124] Not everyone was as satisfied as Heller with the adopted rule. Harold Lee, of the Louisiana League for the Preservation of Constitutional Rights, said that although the amended rule eliminated provisions that would have barred Quakers from teaching in the public schools, it still "is subject to misuse and misrepresentation. . . . Elements who wish to persecute any particular teacher will find it much easier than before to fabricate charges against that teacher. Such elements must be guarded against and if they become active, must be opposed."[125]

8 The Teachers' Federation on Trial

Sarah Reed became the first target of the Americanism rule. Because she was a teacher, her political views were automatically held up to public scrutiny. As a labor leader and a liberal committed to equal rights for women and blacks, Reed's activities rendered her suspect to conservative New Orleanians, who made several attempts to discredit the veteran teacher over the course of the 1940s. They cited her outspoken views and liberal affiliations as evidence of "un-Americanism," the catchall category for virtually any doctrine or policy that threatened the status quo. She was, as she once said, a "marked" woman.

At a March 11, 1941, school board meeting, assistant superintendent Lionel J. Bourgeois informed members about charges made against Reed by some of her students at Fortier High School, where she taught civics. The charges resulted from an investigation by Fortier principal John Conniff, who had called students into his office and asked them if any of their teachers "were going against the democratic way of life." If so, the students were to make a statement to the chairman of the Association of Commerce's National Defense Committee, Arthur DeLa Houssaye.[1]

Coincidentally or not, seven of Reed's students were the only ones to make such statements, which questioned their teacher's patriotism and criticized her unorthodox teaching practices. DeLa Houssaye presented these affidavits to parish school superintendent Nicholas Bauer. The two men agreed that authorities should watch Reed carefully, and if she violated the newly adopted Americanism rule, the superintendent should call her into his office and warn her that he had noticed her activities. If she continued to violate the rule, the school board would be forced to take some kind of action against her. A few days later, DeLa Houssaye reported back to the superintendent that the Association of Commerce had not approved this arrangement; instead, it wanted Reed transferred immediately to teach a subject other than civics in another school.[2]

The superintendent took no action at first, as he had to make a trip out of town. When he returned, school board member George Treadwell brought the matter up with him and suggested that Bauer go ahead and transfer Reed since Conniff, her principal, had already made that request. When the board examined the affidavits in March, Treadwell explained that he was acting in a dual capacity since the affidavits had been presented to him both as a member of the National Defense Committee of the Association of Commerce and as a member of the school board. Treadwell said that he was not opposed to academic freedom, but that he thought the board had the right to monitor what was taught to children in the public schools. If a teacher gave the impression of disloyalty—either intentionally or accidentally—the board should transfer the teacher.[3] The school officials finally decided that the superintendent should show Reed the affidavits after deleting the names of the students and then question her about the validity of the statements. If she admitted their truthfulness, the superintendent would transfer her. If she denied the allegations, the superintendent would consult again with the board.[4]

Board member Louis Pilie objected to this plan. After all, he argued, Reed would not lose any pay if simply transferred to another school. Why, he asked, should the board shoulder the responsibility for letting her teach a subject such as civics, where she could do "a great deal of harm"? George Treadwell agreed. He did not want to bring actual charges against Reed, he said. He merely wanted her transferred to a subject that would not provoke controversy.[5]

Superintendent Bauer called Reed into his office and showed her the affidavits minus signatures, indirectly warning her that the board was keeping an eye on her classroom. Reed did not know how to respond. As she later wrote the superintendent, she had no idea what she was supposed to do about the statements. Reed objected that they were not signed, and she asked the superintendent if she was expected to answer charges from unnamed accusers, "or is it your thought that a teacher should be protected by her superior officers and made to answer only those charges which are made in the open, and with respect to which the signers are willing to appear?" Reed said that she was ready to answer for anything she said or did. "The point I raise at this time is whether or not it would be a wise precedent to subject a teacher to the insidious attack of individuals who, for reasons best known to themselves, will not disclose their identity."[6]

Reed maintained that the statements in the affidavits were "so obviously false and malicious that they do not merit consideration." She later reported to the board that when Superintendent Bauer first showed her the affidavits they were undated and unsigned. Five weeks later, he called her back to his office and gave her the names and dates. She still had no idea what she was expected to do about them, but she was becoming increasingly angry about the situation. "I believe that thirty years of devoted service to the schools of Orleans Parish is ample evidence of my patriotism and abiding faith in American principles and institutions, and entitles me to your confidence," she informed the board.[7] Although Reed had contacted an attorney, she did not, in the end, need his services. The board decided not to act on the allegations and, for the time being, put the matter aside. But as soon became evident, the campaign against Sarah Reed was only beginning.

After war broke out in December 1941, the school board began to consider lengthening the school day by one-half hour to accommodate mothers working in war industries and to allow time for a new "Victory Corps Curriculum" that required more science courses and more physical education. In March, Reed queried the school board concerning rumors about a longer school day beginning with the next term. The newly appointed superintendent, A. J. Tete, confirmed that the new high school curriculum would indeed require a longer day. Reed disagreed with the plan, arguing that schools should remain open for fewer hours to give teachers more time to help win the war by engaging in defense work.[8]

Reed continued to oppose the idea of a longer day. At a meeting in January 1942, she insisted that the schedule change would drive men from the teaching corps, since many of them left school at 3:30 to work in war industries. School board member Pilie questioned whether some male teachers were doing work after school that prevented them from doing their best work during school hours and whether "many of our teachers are asleep at their desks." Reed defended after-school work, arguing that the board could not expect teachers to overlook this opportunity to supplement their incomes, considering their inadequate salaries. Superintendent Tete promised to send a questionnaire to all teachers to identify those working in war industries.[9] Even before the questionnaire was mailed, however, the board resolved the issue of the lengthened school day by starting school half an hour earlier rather than ending later.[10]

The conflict over school hours and war work culminated in an incident that seemed innocuous at the time but that the school board and principal John Conniff seized upon as a pretext for removing Reed from the teaching force. In February 1943 the board suspended Reed for refusing to fill out Tete's form asking for information about teachers' after-school activities, both paid and voluntary. Reed had left the questionnaire blank except for her signature. When John Conniff saw Reed's empty form, he immediately wrote Superintendent Tete, complaining that Reed had refused to follow his instructions to complete the questionnaire. Reed had told Conniff that "it was none of the School Board's business and she didn't intend to furnish the information," the principal reported to the board. Reed also declined to put her refusal in writing despite his request that she do so.[11]

A few days later, Conniff sent for Reed and informed her that the school board and the superintendent had directed him to suspend her from her position. "In fifteen minutes, I had handed in my school records and was on my way to Canal Street a free woman; all of it quick and snappy just like that," Reed wrote her niece.[12] She went directly to the law offices of attorney Paul Habans. After hearing her explanation of the situation, Habans asked for time to research the relevant statutes. Not surprisingly, Reed was sure of her legal ground. "The law is on my side, Mr. Habans, but please check anyway," she said.[13]

Reed was right. The next day Habans said that she was entitled to seek a writ of mandamus compelling her reinstatement. Knowing that the court would ask her if she had exhausted all amicable means to get her job back before going to court, Reed asked her attorney to phone Superintendent Tete and tell him that she wished to be reinstated at once. When Habans called, he "found Mr. Tete very cocksure of himself and his treatment of me," Reed wrote. Tete told Habans that Reed could be reinstated if she just wrote "Nothing" on the questionnaire. "Tell Mr. Tete that's what I'm going to do. I'm going to write nothing on that questionnaire," she said. Habans told Tete that the board had removed Reed from her job without the benefit of proper procedure as outlined in the tenure law. "Why, we haven't removed Mrs. Reed," the superintendent replied. "This suspension would not go on indefinitely. In the course of time, we would call Mrs. Reed in, accuse her of something and give her a trial." Habans maintained that the board had violated the tenure law "the minute you took away her job and her salary."[14]

Reed immediately filed suit in civil district court for reinstatement and for a writ compelling the superintendent to show cause for suspension. Tete continued to argue that as soon as she answered the questionnaire he would reinstate her, and she repeatedly refused to complete it.[15] Reed regarded her suspension as a blatant attempt to circumvent the law and deprive her of the right to a hearing, where the board's true purpose and "inscrutable and unconscionable methods" would be exposed.[16]

Reed and Habans invoked the tenure law, Act 79 of 1936, which prohibited any teacher from being fined or suspended without written charges of immorality, neglect of duty, or incompetency as well as a hearing before the school board to determine guilt. Reed's petition alleged that the questionnaire and subsequent board actions "disregarded the established and constitutional rights of American citizens and the direct provisions of the state law concerning tenure. It also violates the entire spirit of the four freedoms."

Reed maintained that the questionnaire had no relation to her teaching duties or to any other school work "but, on the contrary, was an inquiry into the private occupations and personal pastime of teachers after school hours and not related to their professional occupation." She contended that teachers whose private lives and conduct "do not interfere with their teaching efficiency or violate public morals, cannot be made the pawn of school directors or the subject of their inquisition." The questionnaire, moreover, was "unrelated to School Board work." Reed demanded full salary restitution in addition to reinstatement.[17]

After Reed filed suit, the school board decided that a formal hearing was appropriate after all. Reed interpreted the change as evidence that the board recognized the weakness of its legal position and hoped to avoid further litigation. The board scheduled her hearing for March 17, 1943, and informed her that the inquiry could be either public or private.[18] A week before her hearing date, Reed requested an injunction forbidding the entire proceeding on the grounds that she could not get a fair hearing from a body that had already decided on her guilt. In her petition to the court, Reed alleged that because the "war work" questionnaire concerned activities unrelated to academic employment, she could not be charged with neglect of school duties for refusing to fill it out. Reed's lawyers claimed that a board trial was "calculated to annoy, to humiliate and discredit her in school circles and in the community, to lessen her efficiency" and that it constituted "a very definite attempt to break down her morale and self-reliance."[19] The judge, Frank J. Stich, a former state representative and sponsor of a 1938 anti-Communist bill in the legislature, "denied the injunction saying that the School Board was a high class group of men and would give me a fair trial," Reed wrote.[20] The judge postponed her court case pending the outcome of the board hearing.

Teachers and students strongly objected to Reed's suspension. One hundred eighteen Fortier students signed a petition to Superintendent Tete asking for her reinstatement.[21] The New Orleans branch of the Louisiana Teachers' Association published a resolution declaring that Reed's suspension violated her rights and "has brought humiliation upon the professional standing of all teachers."[22] NOPSTA published its own resolution, maintaining that Reed's dismissal had "created a feeling of unrest and insecurity among the whole teaching corps," a feeling, the association warned, that would "indirectly affect the children."[23] The High School Teachers' Association demanded that the board give Reed her job back without a hearing. NOPSTA informed board members that it would urge Reed to appeal to the courts for protection under the tenure law if the board did not reinstate her.[24] The League of Classroom Teachers voted to send a letter to Reed telling her it was "with her in her fight."[25]

In a letter to the Central Trades and Labor Council, the CTF informed its fellow-unionists, "One of the most active and charter members of the Teachers' Federation, Local 353, is under serious attack by the Orleans Parish School Board in what appears to be an effort to break the spirit of the Teachers' Federation and to lessen its influence in the educational world." The union warned the council that "the Teachers' Federation, Local 353 is now on trial in the case of Mrs. Sarah Towles Reed."[26]

At the March 17 meeting of the school board called to hear the charges against Reed, four teachers told the board that they, too, had failed to fill out their questionnaires. One teacher reported that only three of thirty-three teachers in her school said they had completed the forms, although all thirty-three forms had reached the superintendent's office with answers filled in. The teacher assumed that her principal had completed them. Superintendent Tete insisted that Reed was the only New Orleans teacher who did not answer the questionnaire. The *Item* reported that "at this statement a murmur went up from a number of teachers who were sitting at the meeting." If other teachers had also refused to complete the form, asked attorney Paul Habans, why, then, should "the finger of condemnation . . . be pointed at this teacher alone?" Reed had been, in his characterization, "a Joan of Arc among the teachers for many years. To be a leader means you must be shot at."[27] Louis H. Gosserand, assistant counsel for Reed, asked the superintendent why he did not call Reed into his office to discuss the situation with her before letting the school board suspend her. "I had hundreds of interviews with Mrs. Reed before, and I knew nothing would come of it," Tete replied.[28]

The hearing lasted all day. Reed later sent a copy of her favorite part of the proceedings to her niece. When her attorneys asked Tete at what time his supervision over teachers ended each day, the superintendent replied: "You must remember that I observe the orders of the Board. If the Board assigned me twenty-four hours a day to follow my teachers around, I would do it. I don't fix the time of my duties."

> Q: Do you feel the Board has the right to assign you to do that 24 hours a day?
> A: Right, or not right, if they assign it, I will do it.
> Q: Do you feel that you have the right to ask teachers to tell you what they're doing after 5:00?
> A: I don't conclude whether it is right or not. If the Board tells me to do it, I will do it.

"Isn't this truly a gem?" Reed wrote. "You can't possibly imagine what a kick everyone got out of this and the hearing," which she described as "a scream." Her break from teaching "was a perfect vacation," she said. Undoubtedly, the school board wished its vacation from Reed might have lasted longer. Reed tended to aggravate school authorities. In the middle of her legal dispute, she went before the board to protest another of their decisions, this one about the transfer of teachers, and she asked for a conference between the board and the teachers. President Theo Hotard said he would not agree to a conference with Reed because she objected to everything the board did and she "was constantly trying to upset the teaching corps and system." At a time when "the entire system was in an all-out effort for national defense," this kind of attitude was "next to sabotage and akin to treason," he said. Reed replied that she wished she had a stenographer present to record that comment. Hotard said that he would be pleased to say it again and slowly repeated his remarks.[29]

Reed was determined to win her case. She told reporters that if the board decided against her, she would appeal to the civil district court, the state supreme court, even the U.S. Supreme Court if necessary. "This is not a personal issue," she said. "I am here representing the teachers." [30] Reed did indeed have to appeal her case. Although the school board did not call her to testify at its hearing on her conduct, it found her guilty of willful neglect of duty. It then proceeded to reinstate her despite her refusal to complete the questionnaire. The board must have realized that it did not have a strong case against Reed and that, in light of all the support for her from teachers, students, and the public, permanently removing Reed from her position would not have been a popular decision. Although it lacked the nerve to fire her, the board asserted some measure of authority by withholding her pay from the date of her formal suspension, February 24, until the date of her formal reinstatement, March 18, the day that Reed went back to work at Fortier.[31] Reed even found some humor in the verdict, which apparently found her innocent of neglect of duty for part of the pay period and guilty during the remainder. "It's a brand-new verdict, part-time guilt. I have a new distinction," Reed said.[32]

Reed's supporters didn't find the verdict as humorous as did Reed herself. The "part-time guilt" and the fact that Reed seemed to have been singled out for punishment angered her supporters. In a letter to the editor of the *New Orleans States,* an anonymous writer asked, "How can she be guilty part of the time and not guilty the other part of the time? The school board trial brought out the fact that other teachers did not sign and fill out their copies of the paper in question. Why were they not treated as was Mrs. Reed? Is this a case of personal persecution as a result of all those unsuccessful interviews mentioned by Mr. Tete?"[33] Gladys Peck, a teacher, wrote Reed urging her, "Stick to your guns. . . . We need more leaders like you. The average teacher is afraid to raise her voice." The teacher may receive only crumbs, she wrote, "but she is afraid if she says anything she will not even have crumbs."[34]

The writer of another letter to the editor alleged that Reed's suspension had been based on a "trumped up issue, that the real one is this teacher's lack of docility to a set of officers so politically dominated and an educational system so creakingly ancient that the people of New Orleans in their own interest should have long since repudiated both!" As the writer pointed out, "If [the people of New Orleans] allow them to fire Mrs. Reed, do you think it likely that any New Orleans teacher will dare to protest anything they see fit to hand out?"[35]

Reed, for one, dared to continue her protest. She lost no time in filing a new suit to have the board's verdict set aside and to recoup the $200 subtracted from her salary for the "guilty month." On March 19 the school board sent Reed a check for $115.28 as salary for the period from February 10 through February 23.[36] In her appeal filed in civil district court, Reed asked the court to annul the board's judgment finding her guilty of willful neglect of duty. She also wanted the board to pay her the $200.52 withheld from February 24 to March 17. Reed's suit pointed out that several other teachers had also refused to complete the war work questionnaire and that yet others, also upset about the school board's effort to delve into their after-school activities, had simply filled in "none" on the form.[37]

Reed believed that her suspension constituted a test case under the teacher tenure law—the Teachers' Act, as it was called—and her fellow teachers agreed with her. In a joint resolution by NOPSTA, the CTF, and the New Orleans unit of the LTA, teachers maintained that the school board's decision meant that "the benefits of the tenure law have been dissipated and any teacher might be harassed and annoyed and even deprived of the right to practice her profession at the will of the Board."[38] The editor of the *New*

Orleans Item agreed with Reed and the other teachers. Since the Teachers' Act did not require teachers to report their after-school activities to anyone, the *Item* found it plain "as a pikestaff" that the board had "exceeded its authority." Although the money involved might be small and not worth a lawsuit, the paper said, "maintenance of the Teachers' Act in full integrity and force is very important indeed. At any rate, Mrs. Reed is still claiming her lost pay. Our guess . . . is that if she carries on she will win her suit."[39]

In its answer to Reed's suit, the school board alleged that Reed, "for many years past, has been disobedient, argumentative, obnoxious and contrary in the performance of her duties; that she has systematically and consistently sought to embarrass the members of respondent Board, the Superintendent of Orleans Parish Schools, and the principals of the schools at which she was teaching, by willfully refusing and neglecting to obey orders and instructions and by publicly and adversely criticizing actions of the Superintendent."

The board also maintained that its members were "business and professional men of high standing in this community." Nevertheless, Reed had "time after time, sought to override the wishes of the electorate of this community by annoying, humiliating and embarrassing the members of the respondent Board, the Superintendent . . . and her principals . . . in an attempt to impose her will, her thoughts, her ideals, her opinions, her doctrines and her methods of teaching upon this community." The board had refrained from bringing charges against Reed earlier, it claimed, "because of her long tenure of office, her age, and the hope that she would adjust herself to conditions prevailing in the Nation and cease her system of activities above delineated."[40]

During the district court trial Myrtle Rey Gamus, longtime teacher activist, testified that she, too, had refused to fill out the war work questionnaire but that another teacher had done it for her. "I did not think it was the business of the School Board what war work I did outside of school hours," Gamus testified.[41] Thirty-three Fortier teachers who had signed a petition asking that the board expunge its suspension order and pay Reed the salary it had withheld were summoned to the trial, and one of them was called to testify in support of Reed. In the petition the Fortier faculty members stated, "Aside from her contribution to education in New Orleans, her utter selflessness in her work and her interest in student and teacher problems should merit more than the passing appreciation given capable teachers, but rather the whole-hearted generosity comparable to hers. Nothing would be a finer gesture from the Orleans Parish School Board than a restoration of salary to Mrs. Reed and an expunging from the records of the whole incident which led to the present impasse."[42] Although politics seemingly had nothing to do with the charges brought against Reed, the political agenda behind the case was evidently clear to Reed's Fortier High School students who also filed supportive petitions with the school board. One petition described her as "a competent teacher [who] at no time has mentioned anything dealing with communism."[43] Another informed the board that "Mrs. Reed holds one of the most interesting classes in the Fortier High School."[44] Reed herself spent two days on the stand, consistently denying the charges of willful neglect.[45]

When Reed's lawyers introduced as evidence a report by a citizens' planning committee for public education, stating that Reed's civics classes scored higher in tests than students in other schools, the teachers attending the trial began applauding and cheering, halting the proceedings for a significant amount of time. Judge Stich scolded the teachers for their outburst and threatened them with contempt of court if they did it again. "I am surprised at you teachers," the judge said. "This is a courtroom, not a public hearing."[46]

The board offered, in its defense, letters from two of Reed's principals requesting her transfer from their schools. Conniff had asked the board to transfer Reed many times and had referred to her "unsatisfactory, disobedient and eccentric behavior" in his annual report. After Reed examined a letter from Conniff to Tete about her, offered as evidence, the board's attorney asked, "Did you refer to Mr. Conniff as a diabetic old crank?" "I did not even know he had diabetes," Reed answered.[47] Eleanor Riggs, her former principal at Wright High School, testified that she had asked for Reed's transfer because of the teacher's "antagonistic" attitude. To illustrate her point, Riggs told the court that on one occasion, after she had told Reed that she had to teach Latin, Reed began kicking books around her classroom in a fit of temper. "The peace of my school was threatened by Mrs. Reed's discontent," Riggs alleged.[48]

The board also offered as examples of Reed's uncooperative behavior excerpts from meetings at which Reed had criticized or questioned actions of the board, including her petitions on behalf of nondegreed teachers and her protests over arbitrary transfers of teachers. It also offered clippings from New Orleans newspapers to prove its charge that Reed had consistently sought to embarrass the board and the superintendent. In November 1934, for example, "Reed charged that teachers are being penalized so that the Board may be placed on a cash basis"; in 1936 she told the *Morning Tribune* that "she didn't need military training at her school as she went through a major engagement every day"; in 1937 Reed was quoted as saying that "the School Board has no right, as a public board, to hold an executive meeting and exclude the teachers, but this has never been put to a test." In her protest against her sister Roberta's transfer, Reed told the *Item* that Roberta "believes in teaching pupils rather than textbooks. It's just that we haven't converted the principals, in many cases, to going forward in instruction. So when a teacher goes ahead, she gets transferred, and the principal stays."

School board attorneys presented stories on the fire escape episode, in addition to other reports on Reed's many efforts to gain salary increases for teachers. They included as evidence a photograph of Reed and other teachers calling on the mayor about the proposed 12.5 percent salary cut, along with her comment that because of low salaries, the teaching profession in New Orleans "can attract only ragtails and bobtails."[49] In her defense, Reed pointed out that she had been the legislative chairman for teachers' organizations for many years and that her remarks before the school board and to the press had always been connected to issues relevant to teachers' interests.[50]

In addition to reviewing past episodes, the board introduced into the evidence the 1940–41 affidavits collected by the Association of Commerce. For the first time the student allegations against Reed were made public. The affidavits contained a wide assortment of charges against Reed, some of them humorous, some of them outrageous, many of them contradictory. The defense also entered into the records a memorandum from the superintendent regarding Reed's reaction to the affidavits. According to the memorandum, Reed had said that the statements could be divided into three groups: (1) those that she had definitely not made; (2) those that had been "twisted"; and (3) those that she had the right to make and which she acknowledged as having made.[51]

It seems clear that many of the statements were simply false, the result of either confusion on the part of the students or resentment against Reed for one reason or another. In any case, most of the statements would appear harmless unless interpreted as part of a larger, subversive agenda, a view taken by the Association of Commerce, before and after the statements were collected.

In the affidavit signed by Martin Kombar, a former Fortier student, Reed had purportedly referred to the U.S. Constitution as a "horse-and-buggy" document. She had belittled the Baptist church on St. Charles Avenue for spending $750 on a neon sign. She had advised a Catholic boy not to confess to a priest what he had done "as it is none of his business." According to Kombar, when Reed told the class about an upcoming visit from members of the school board, she said, "Boys, I want you to behave tomorrow. Some old men are coming to see the classes. It is a shame to make those old men walk up four flights of stairs."[52]

Another student swore that Reed was "opposed to our principles and Constitutional government, has no use for the capitalistic system, was discontented with conditions in the United States, and apparently sympathized wholeheartedly with the system then being conducted in Russia."[53] Another student said Mrs. Reed "would make a good communistic teacher." This opinion apparently did not deter him from reporting that on several occasions he had overheard Reed claim to be a fascist. In fact, the student said, Reed believed that fascism and communism amounted to the same thing: "that private ownership should be abolished; that there should be no class or racial distinction and that blacks and whites should mingle and be permitted to attend the same theatres, the same schools and meeting places."[54] Another student agreed that Reed often praised communism and spent a lot of time in and out of the classroom pointing out the good points of the communist system.[55]

Frank E. Lemothe Jr. told the Association of Commerce that Reed had criticized the school board for refusing to admit a student who would not salute the American flag, that she opposed military training "either in the schools or in the country," and that she opposed "the fortifying and preparing of this country for defense against aggression as it was useless inasmuch as we would fall apart from within." Two other students also mentioned Reed's opposition to military training at Fortier, her tendency to discuss communism, and her statement that "the South was not a fit place in which to live." She was also indifferent to religion, two students pointed out in identical affidavits."[56]

After hearing all the testimony, Judge Frank Stich ruled in favor of the school board. The *Item* had been wrong in its optimistic approval of Reed's chances of success. She did not receive her lost pay, and Judge Stich upheld the board in finding Reed guilty of willful neglect of duty. "The plaintiff not only failed, but she deliberately, willfully and militantly refused to fill in the questionnaire," Judge Stich said. "Her testimony in open court and her demeanor and action on the witness stand are conclusive of the fact that she did not ever intend to comply with the request of the School Board." Her attitude, said the judge, clearly indicated that she did not think the board had any right to inquire into her time after school. But the board did have that right, he ruled.[57]

The school board's case against Reed was based on Reed's attitude and demeanor as much as anything else. Just as her sister Roberta's transfer had been prompted by Roberta's refusal to conform to the opinions of her principal, the attempted dismissal of Reed grew out of a challenge to bureaucratic authority. Both style and substance were involved. Reed's social outlook was unpopular in itself, but her independent and combative public posture had rankled school officials for more than thirty years. It was time to put an end to it.

By striking at Reed, the board also hoped to undermine the influence of the Classroom Teachers' Federation, with which Reed was so closely associated.

Even before the trial began, the school board attorney made it clear that he was going to try to discredit the federation as well as Reed. He told the press that he would prove that Reed and the CTF had "for years made a persistent effort to bait the School Board and the Superintendent of Schools."[58] Reed continued to maintain that the questionnaire infringed upon the rights of teachers and denied the allegation that she had previously agreed to help the board find out how many teachers were engaged in war work. "I would cut my hand off before I would snoop on other teachers to find out whether they were asleep at their desks from exhaustion caused by their war work," she declared.[59]

Reed may have lost her legal case, but she did not lose her willingness to challenge authority or her dedication to progressive teaching techniques. Reed's classes continued to be as lively as they had been shown to be in the student affidavits introduced at the trial. The affidavits described students engaging in debates about a multitude of subjects and issues, many of them political and controversial.

They also indicated that some of her students were sometimes confused by what they were reading and hearing. One of the students who signed an affidavit complained that Reed seldom used a textbook in her classes but relied instead on magazines and newspapers, as if this fact in itself was damning.[60] To some people, it was. Textbooks were less likely to contain controversial topics and more likely to reflect a conservative outlook. Reed adhered to a progressive philosophy of teaching that often favored newspapers and magazines over texts. The shelves of her classroom were filled with magazines, including the *New Republic* and the *Nation,* some of her students reported, publications that would make her teaching methods suspect in many people's eyes. In a survey about schools and teaching methods, Reed once wrote, "Schools are too dull. . . . We busy [the student] in a textbook where he is kept from controversy. He is so chilled and so unreal when he emerges from the average school that he is a misfit for life." She had no intention of letting that happen to her own students.[61]

Reed also revamped the traditional authoritarian classroom, organizing her civics class as a kind of legislature, in which one boy held the position of chairman, calling the assembly to order and asking for reports from the class on world events, national and local politics, and other topics. Minutes of the class meetings kept by the day's secretary reveal that animated discussions were common and the topics of debate highly controversial for the time and place. On February 15, 1930, for example, Reed, as general chairman, asked the class to define loyalty. "Many definitions were given," the secretary reported. Two days later Reed asked for an explanation of democracy. "She also asked whether or not Negroes could vote." Later that week, the class discussed the "Negro question," the class secretary recorded, "and there were many opinions."

In one class Reed supplied some statistics and other facts about New Orleans and Louisiana, and a discussion ensued about why Louisiana ranked forty-seventh in literacy. In 1939 and 1940, Reed's classes discussed such subjects as the CIO, immigration laws, the fairness of the sales tax, economic conditions in the South, and the Spanish Civil War. One class considered "the individual." As the class secretary wrote, "This caused some argument on heredity, environment and associates. While talking about environment the discussion moved to the house and then to the housing problems of this city." One student's contribution to the news report concerned freedom of speech, which triggered a lengthy debate. In another class, "A big slum discussion immediately started but had to be put down to get on with the regular business."

Occasionally the discussions got out of hand, as on October 28, 1940, when "Mrs. Reed took over the class because of disturbances." The class spent the rest of the period listening to Reed lecture about constitutional amendments. Reed also gave tests. At the beginning of one class, the secretary wrote, "Mrs. Reed . . . suggested we have a test (wasn't given much support by class) but anyway the test went on." The first few minutes of many classes were spent reading magazines. Sometimes Reed led the discussions. Occasionally, Reed's own opinion about certain subjects appeared in the class minutes, as on February 28, 1939, when "Mrs. Reed criticized the outlawing of the sit-down strike by the U.S. Supreme Court." New Deal policies and Roosevelt's speeches were common topics in Reed's civics classes throughout the 1930s and early 1940s, and she sometimes editorialized about them. She did so on October 29, 1940, talking about a recent speech by the president, when she commented that "Mr. Roosevelt answered falsehood with facts."

Several of her classes analyzed the democratic and undemocratic features of New Orleans government. One student listed the undemocratic characteristics of the city's government in the 1930s: "Uncalled for arrests by police, police toleration of gambling resorts, refusal to let poll books be photographed, refusal to grant right of free assembly, and suppression of free speech."[62] Reed also directed her classes to make scrapbooks containing clippings from newspapers and magazines about the war in Europe or other world events. One student scrapbook made in 1936, titled "Current Events and USA Problems," contained articles on slum clearance, a food stamp plan for the needy, old age in America, and an article from the *New American* about the CIO's effort to organize the steel industry. The article concluded, "If the CIO can now get enough support to defeat the steel barons, a body blow will have been struck against the allied forces of greed and oppression in this country." Another scrapbook, titled "Concentration of Wealth," carried articles on United Fruit, DuPont, and the National Steel Corporation.[63]

Reed also required her students to write autobiographies. One student's contained a section that read: "Five democratic tendencies in me worth encouraging: (1) love of free speech; (2) love of free assemble [sic]; (3) my belief that there should be a fairer distribution of nation's wealth; (4) my liking for order, dislike of violence and turmoil; (5) my strong interest in local and national politics." It continued, "Five undemocratic tendencies in me worth watching: (1) dislike for Negro; (2) admiration for the smooth, efficient way in which dictatorial governments operate; (3) intolerance of other persons' viewpoint or opinions; (4) the tendency to be prejudiced against people because of their nationality; (5) belief that Negroes should not be educated."[64]

Obviously, Reed's high school students were not getting a traditional education in her classes. Reed unbolted the students' desks from the floor to encourage a more participatory, democratic classroom.[65] They took field trips to courtrooms, city hall, and the parish prison. At a meeting of the school board, one of Reed's civics classes presented two petitions, one calling for the building of an auditorium at Fortier, which the board agreed was a good idea, and another to lengthen the Christmas vacation, which the board turned down.[66] Reed's classes watched documentary films such as Pare Lorentz's *The River* and Ralph Steiner's *The City.* They collected food for the Alexander Milne Home School for Destitute Orphan Girls. Reed offered extra credit to students who helped convince people to attend important meetings, such as one held at the Roosevelt Hotel in 1940 for the purpose of informing the public about amendments to be voted on in an upcoming election.[67]

Time spent in Reed's classes left an indelible impression on many of her students, several of whom wrote her letters years after graduating to thank her. During World War II she received several letters from former pupils, one of whom wrote from a military camp at Wheeler, Georgia, to tell her that the discussions in her class "were my most enjoyable school days. Do you remember the arguments we had concerning William Green and John L. Lewis?"[68] Her former student Perry Willis, who was with the amphibious forces of the U.S. Pacific Fleet, wrote her from Okinawa: "Of all the professors and teachers I have ever come in contact with, you had the greatest effect on me. . . . Your impression stuck and left me with the memory of a very courageous, a very interesting, and a very free personality. You gave me a feeling of warmth toward others which I lacked, a feeling of respect for the rights of others, a feeling that all is possible through cooperation and friendliness and effort. Of course I've never lived up to the sparks you kindled but still they've remained there and that was something."[69]

Reed's pedagogy was a shining example of liberal-left educational progressivism at its best. Her teaching methods bore a strong resemblance to those advocated by John Dewey and used by Eleanor Roosevelt when she taught at the Todhunter School in New York.[70] According to her biographer, Blanche Wiesen Cook, Roosevelt believed that "education was the essential foundation upon which all democratic institutions rested" and she conducted her classrooms in a democratic manner, encouraging group discussions and using newspapers and magazines instead of textbooks. As Roosevelt said, it was the teacher's "function . . . to make history and literature and the seemingly barren study of the machinery of government somehow akin to the things the pupils are doing in their daily life."[71] Both Roosevelt and Reed saw a direct connection between political democracy in the larger world and democracy in the classroom, and they both sought to make the connection clear to their students. That was precisely what troubled Reed's conservative critics.

Despite the failure of her suit against the school board, Reed continued to seek justice from the legal system. As she had promised, she appealed the civil district court's decision and filed suit in the Orleans Parish Court of Appeals, maintaining that she had been made to suffer because of her work with the New Orleans Classroom Teachers' Federation. "Surely there is no duty imposed by law or in morals on any teacher to refrain from expressing her opinion, either as a citizen or as a representative of a group of teachers, on the acts and policies of a public body such as a school board," Reed's brief stated. It further alleged that many other teachers had likewise refused to complete the school board's questionnaire but had not been penalized for failure to do so.[72]

While the board claimed that it was soliciting the information in order to revamp school schedules to accommodate teachers' war work, the brief continued, in fact board member Pilie had stated the form's true purpose: to learn whether war workers were performing their teaching responsibilities properly. "The court has erred in assuming that to the School Board this questionnaire was a serious undertaking with a patriotic purpose for, as a matter of fact, no action resulted from the questionnaire (except the suspension of Mrs. Reed) insofar as the school schedule was concerned." The school board seemed unconcerned that many of the answers were obviously flippant: the word "Nothing" written across many forms in red crayon, in the same handwriting. The school board accepted all of them except Reed's. "The Court is in error in holding that appellant was not discriminated against by the Board. . . . Mrs. Reed alone was singled out for retribution and censure."

Moreover, the appeal read, the court was mistaken when it assumed that neither the superintendent nor the board were "guided by impure motives; unless we imply that they were guided by motives that were pure in spite and malignity." The introduction of affidavits by students "reflecting on her character as a teacher and a citizen," and private notes kept by the superintendent about his personal conversations with Reed over the years—"all of which were entirely unrelated to the instant case except perhaps to demonstrate not only an impure but a vicious attitude toward Mrs. Reed"—showed that the board had spitefully tried to malign the plaintiff.[73]

Reed lost again. On April 30, 1945, the Orleans Parish Court of Appeals affirmed Judge Stich's decision in dismissing Reed's suit against the school board.[74] The appellate court ruled that the war work questionnaire was indeed reasonable and in compliance with the recommendations of both the federal government and the State Board of Education to include more science courses and more physical education hours in high school curricula. The questionnaire, then, was not an invasion of privacy, as Reed had claimed.

The court did not accept the allegation that Reed had been singled out for persecution even though other teachers had also refused to fill out their forms. And, regardless of their refusal, their principals had filled out the forms for them, and the completed forms had been given to the superintendent. "In truth, plaintiff stands alone as the only teacher in the City of New Orleans who militantly refused to give the information requested," Judge E. Howard McCaleb Jr. said. It found "nothing in the conduct, either of the Board or its Superintendent, which would warrant a conclusion that their action was guided by impure motives." Even though Reed had "received leniency" from the school board in the form of reinstatement, she could not use that as an argument for receiving the rest of her salary.

"The record shows that plaintiff is a highly educated and intelligent lady and that she has, by her untiring efforts on behalf of the school teachers of the State during the last thirty years, attained prominence and respect in the community," Judge McCaleb continued. "But the attitude of defiance of authority displayed by her in the instant manner cannot be approved or condoned."[75]

After hearing the decision, the Teachers' Federation reminded its members that the real purpose of the questionnaire had been to find out "how many teachers engaged in war work were asleep at their desks." The union also pointed to the judge's words citing Reed's "untiring efforts in behalf of the school teachers of the State during the last thirty years." In the opinion of the federation, "Enough said!"[76] It was plain to them that the questionnaire had indeed been a ploy on the part of the board to ferret out teachers who may indeed have fallen asleep on the job trying to supplement their meager salaries through extra work in war industries.

In a memo to Superintendent Tete in October of 1943, several months after Reed's suspension, principal John Conniff complained to Tete that eight faculty members at Fortier, who were employed in night shifts at local plants, reported to school in the morning "in an unfit condition to offer efficient instruction to the students under their guidance. . . . Not only are they listless and tired, but they are frequently sleepy." Furthermore, they became "easily disgruntled," Conniff charged. This memo, which was not made public, shows that the teachers were probably correct about the real meaning of the questionnaire. They were just as accurate in their suspicion that the board used Reed's refusal to fill out the questionnaire as a convenient excuse finally to rid themselves of a troublesome teacher.[77]

9 Cold War Politics

The reemergence of the anti-Communist issue in an even more virulent form after World War II created philosophical and political problems for Reed and other liberals. The dissolution of the Soviet-American alliance gave conservative critics ammunition and forced liberals to rethink their Popular Front attitudes. As the Soviet Union moved into Eastern Europe and reports of Stalin's purges reached the West, Americans worried about the effects of Communist infiltration. In this Cold War atmosphere, liberals such as Reed became increasingly vulnerable to charges of subversion.

In 1948, in another attempt to rid themselves of Reed and discredit the Teachers' Federation, the Orleans Parish School Board resurrected charges of "un-Americanism" first leveled against Reed in 1941. Now that anti-Communism was a staple of American political thought, such accusations of disloyalty carried more weight. With Communism generally perceived as a genuine threat, the social ostracism and possible loss of employment that could result from the merest suspicion of subversion made standing up to such charges difficult.[1] As playwright Arthur Miller has pointed out, many liberals "were fearful, and with good reason, of being identified as covert Communists if they should protest too strongly."[2]

In August 1948, the same month that Whitaker Chambers went before the House Un-American Activities Committee and publicly accused Alger Hiss of engaging in espionage for the Soviet Union, Sarah Reed appeared before the Orleans Parish School Board for a hearing on charges of "not stressing the American way of life as superior in every respect to Communism or other 'isms.'" Although the board did not directly accuse Reed of advocating Communism, superintendent Lionel J. Bourgeois told her that "there is too much doubt as to whether or not you have done all that you should have done to proselytize for the democratic way." The board files contained evidence that justified this question, the superintendent said. Consequently, he had decided to transfer Reed from civics to another, less sensitive, subject. In her new position, she would be prohibited from mentioning Communism, socialism, "or any other foreign 'ism' in dealing with the children on school property and during school hours." Bourgeois further admonished Reed "that in any case where the American way of life is brought up in your class it will be your bounden duty to extol the merits of the American system."[3]

Bourgeois's accusation of "un-Americanism" was a serious one to make against a schoolteacher whose reputation would surely suffer from any kind of association with Communism. Any taint of a foreign ism would be enough to destroy a teacher's career. After nearly forty years in the New Orleans school system, Reed was nearing retirement in 1948. It is doubtful that she would have accepted a transfer in any case, particularly not at the age of sixty-six. There is good reason to conclude that the school board decided to take advantage of growing anti-Communist sentiment to rid itself of a longtime problem in the person of Sarah Reed. Bourgeois himself had experienced run-ins with Reed on a number of occasions. In 1945 he wrote Reed criticizing "the continuous faultfinding which characterizes your attitude to everything that is done at the Public School Administration." He would, he warned her, no longer "take time to argue with you regarding the merits or demerits of our efforts to improve public education in this city."[4]

The Cold War presented the board with a perfect excuse to undermine Reed's outspoken advocacy of teacher rights and academic freedom. Punishing such a well-known teacher also gave the board a chance to show the community that it was diligently guarding the schools against Communist influence. Someone as liberal as Reed, with her longstanding labor affiliation, close association with black teachers, and ties to the political left, presented an ideal target for anti-Communist crusaders. After years of fighting the school board and the local Democratic machine, Reed had alienated herself long ago from authorities committed to safeguarding the public schools from ideological contamination.

Although the specter of radicalism had concerned school authorities and others for many years, the possibility of political infiltration seemed all too real by 1948. In 1945 the Committee on Academic Freedom and Tenure of the American Association of University Professors (AAUP) warned of the likelihood of new attacks on academic freedom, particularly in the social sciences. The AAUP report came in the wake of the dismissal of president Homer P. Rainey of the University of Texas after he had accused the university regents of limiting academic freedom on campus. Because of "an impaired perspective" as a result of the war, the AAUP report stated, such attacks on university liberals were increasingly likely.[5]

Conservative forces determined to obliterate the heritage of the New Deal grew increasingly vocal following the war. Republicans took advantage of reaction against New Deal liberalism in the 1946 elections and made communism in government, the Roosevelt government in particular, a popular issue in the fall elections. House Minority Leader Joseph Martin told the public that the election of a Republican Congress would eliminate Communists and fellow travelers.[6] The election was, as one historian has characterized it, "a liberal disaster."[7] For the first time in sixteen years, Republicans gained control of the House and Senate, partly on the strength of their anti–New Deal and anti-Communist rhetoric. Only thirty-six of seventy-seven congressmen labeled as liberal by the *New Republic* were returned to their seats.[8] The election brought to Washington California's Richard M. Nixon, Indiana's William E. Jenner, and Wisconsin's Joseph R. McCarthy, who directed their early attacks against Democratic New Dealers before taking on Communists.

On the strength of their 1946 success, members of the Republican-controlled House Un-American Activities Committee, charged with investigating un-American propaganda and subversion, announced their intention to "expose and ferret out the Communists and Communist sympathizers in the federal government." President Truman responded to the success of red-baiting and gave it federal legitimacy in 1947 when, just nine days after announcing his intention to curtail the spread of Communism around the world, he issued Executive Order no. 9835 calling for a new loyalty-security program in the U.S. government, the first ever initiated in peacetime.

Truman's initiative, aimed specifically at Communists, provided a respectable rationale for local anti-Communist purges, and after 1947 the fight against internal Communism became a national crusade. With the enactment of the new federal program, anyone suspected of Communist ties could lose his job; in fact, "fellow travelers" also could be dismissed under this order, which prohibited federal employees from "sympathetic association" with Communist ideology.[9] Under Executive Order 9835 the Justice Department compiled a list of "totalitarian fascist, communist or subversive" organizations; membership in or association with any of these groups would serve as an indicator of one's loyalty and could also determine whether a suspect kept his or her job.[10]

Truman's executive order, geared more to defeat Republicans than to crush domestic Communists, touched off a spate of new loyalty oaths, security checks, and purges across the country. Disloyalty seemed more pervasive than ever as its meaning expanded to include donations to suspect groups and attendance at meetings of "radical" or even "liberal" organizations. The fear that "subversives might be lurking everywhere," as one historian has written, proliferated after the Truman order. In 1947 the ACLU reported an atmosphere "increasingly hostile to the liberties of organized labor, the political left and many minorities."[11]

The House Committee on Un-American Activities opened hearings in 1947 on alleged disloyalty in Hollywood. In the same year, a federal grand jury in New York subpoenaed dozens of past and present government employees accused of belonging to the Communist Party by two major informers—Elizabeth Bentley and Whitaker Chambers. These proceedings set the stage for the more famous HUAC hearings in 1948 featuring the Chambers-Hiss controversy.[12]

Although Truman denounced a HUAC hearing as a "red herring," he could not, as James MacGregor Burns put it, "bottle up the genie of suspicion he had helped release."[13] By 1948 both political parties were using red-baiting techniques to gain public support in an election year. The Republicans pushed for investigations of Communism in the federal government, while the Democratic administration buttressed its image as the watchdog of democracy by indicting twelve leaders of the American Communist Party in 1948 under the Smith Act, a 1940 statute that declared it illegal to "teach and advocate the overthrow and destruction of the government of the United States by force and violence." The prosecution of actual American Communists gave the administration the image it wanted and the public even more cause for alarm about domestic enemies.[14]

The backlash against liberalism that the United States experienced in the late 1940s and 1950s was exacerbated in the South by fear of the emerging civil rights movement. Change seemed to confront the South at every turn. Sharecropping was dying out. Blacks were moving into southern cities in ever increasing numbers, and they were being admitted to graduate schools and major league baseball teams. Truman's Committee on Civil Rights indicated some concern on the part of the federal government about society's treatment of African Americans, and in 1948 the president urged Congress to pass far-reaching civil rights legislation, including an antilynching act and laws abolishing the poll tax and segregation in interstate transportation. In the same year, Truman signed an executive order prohibiting segregation in the armed services and all other agencies of the federal government.[15]

Resistance to the growing civil rights movement mushroomed as the South made a final effort to arrest the momentum of change that undermined its customary racial arrangements. School authorities in New Orleans, as in the rest of the South, struggled to maintain the racial status quo. Responding to a request from Sarah Reed about the school board's policy on teaching race relations, Superintendent Bourgeois made it clear that the New Orleans Public Schools would tolerate no change as far as the "color line" was concerned. Teachers should concentrate on preaching "the gospel of opportunity within one's social group," he told Reed. "Under no circumstance should the teacher undertake to indoctrinate pupils with her own philosophy with regard to such concepts as miscegenation, fraternization upon the basis of social admixture of the races, segregation of the races wherever such has resulted from the polity of the state, and other kindred matters." Apparently fearing that she might indeed do all of the above, Bourgeois warned Reed, "Under no circumstances would the Orleans Parish School Board and I permit the classrooms to be used as fomenting grounds for radical gospels which can only end in social upheaval and sorrow."[16]

Given the strength and pervasiveness of such sentiments, it is hardly surprising that southern liberals simply did not have enough influence to prevent the Dixiecrats' 1948 fight for states' rights and segregation and their denunciations of unionism, Communism, socialism, and any other ism that did not accord with traditional southern values. Nor did liberals have the clout to deter "the rise of massive resistance" after *Brown v. Board of Education* in 1954.[17] In fact, liberal support had waned for some time in the South. Liberals reached the peak of their influence and prestige in the New Deal years when federal programs and policies had bolstered their self-confidence and power. With the federal government behind them, liberals were able to achieve a certain independence from state and local power. The New Deal "emboldened them, increased their influence and numbers, and broadened their vision of regional welfare into the economic and political realms."[18]

During the Truman years, however, federal support for liberal ideology began to erode. Attacked from the Republican right for being soft on Communism and sensing a loss of support from the left, Truman began to ally himself more with conservatives. In the 1948 campaign, he weakened the position of southern reformers by helping to identify former New Dealer and liberal champion Henry Wallace and his supporters with Communism, thus discrediting liberals of every persuasion. If they were indeed dependent upon the support of the federal government, Truman's choice in favor of conservatives was bound to have disastrous results for Southern liberals.[19]

In the South, conservatives targeted the Southern Conference for Human Welfare (SCHW) as one means of discrediting the New Deal and liberalism in general. The participation of Communists in the SCHW provided further ammunition for critics of the left-liberal organization who frequently linked civil rights activity with Communism. The SCHW was singled out early on for attack in New Orleans by Ivor Trapolin, chairman of the Young Men's Business Club's antisubversive committee and later the club's president. Trapolin kept a long list of suspected Communist sympathizers and made frequent reports to the media about his findings.[20] Trapolin's 1946 assault on the SCHW predated by a year a similar report issued by the House Un-American Activities Committee. In fact the Americanism Committee of the Young Men's Business Club and the HUAC staff cooperated in their investigative efforts. Like HUAC, Trapolin called the SCHW a Communist-front group, citing as evidence the conference's support for "the repeal of the poll tax, the passing of the FEPC bill, better living conditions for the working man, civil liberties, racial equality and more." The Americanism Committee concluded that the SCHW agenda aimed to provoke "mass dissension" in the South by "pitting class against class," with revolution as its ultimate goal.[21]

The transfer of the Southern Conference's headquarters to New Orleans in 1946 and its meeting there in November of that year undoubtedly precipitated Trapolin's report on the organization. The group drew considerable attention in New Orleans, partly because more than half its delegates were African Americans. At the New Orleans convention, the conference condemned racial discrimination in housing, education, employment, wages, transportation, and accommodations.[22] It also decided to fight segregation actively through its educational adjunct, the Southern Conference Educational Fund.[23] The YMBC reiterated its original accusation against the organization in June 1947, and Trapolin followed up with a radio show called "The Southern Conference—the Red Drive in New Orleans."[24]

In the same month Trapolin wrote Reed that the YMBC had noticed her name on the list of those attending a dinner sponsored by the Southern Conference. He asked her if she had given her permission to use her name on the program and whether she was, indeed, a member of the conference. He also advised her that the Young Men's Business Club of New Orleans was opposed to the SCHW because of its "definite Communistic tendencies." Because of its dangerous political leanings and because the House Committee on Un-American Activities had also concluded that the SCHW was a Communist-front organization, Trapolin reported that the YMBC's Civic Bureau planned to publicize the names of all New Orleans citizens who supported it.[25]

The kinds of accusations made by Trapolin against the SCHW were not uncommon in the post–World War II years. Senator Theodore Bilbo of Mississippi described the SCHW as an "un-American, negro social equality, communistic, mongrel outfit." [26] Efforts to discredit civil rights groups by accusing them of subversive intent were a standard segregationist ploy.[27] White supremacists used anti-Communism to advance their own cause, castigating any proposed societal change, including integration and unionization, as seditious and Communist-inspired. As one historian has observed, postwar Southern leaders tended to see integrationists and Communists "as two inseparable sides of a single coin." [28] During their "Operation Dixie" recruitment drive, CIO organizers were physically attacked throughout the South. One antiunion editor claimed that the CIO intended "to arouse class-hatred and race-hatred for the purpose of creating strikes, riots, bloodshed, anarchy and revolution." [29] In 1947 southerners took advantage of the new Taft-Hartley law, passed by a Republican Congress over Truman's veto the previous year, to ban the closed shop and limit unionization movements. In 1948 the segregationist Dixiecrat Party based its existence on the fight against the "interrelated evils of integration, unionism and 'communism.'" [30]

Attacks on liberals and radicals during the early Cold War had sexual components as well. Historian Sara Evans believes that postwar concerns about changes in women's societal roles and sexual mores reinforced geopolitical and cultural anxieties to create a nearly obsessive concern with Communists in the schools. Schoolteachers, who were overwhelmingly female, could be seen both as weak links in the chain of Americanism and as potential subverters of domesticity. The House Un-American Activities Committee gave credence to a Columbia University professor when he said, "The girls' schools and women's colleges contain some of the most loyal disciples of Russia. Teachers there are often frustrated females. They have gone through bitter struggles to attain their positions. A political dogma based on hatred expresses their personal attitudes." The committee concluded that "the Communists have always found the teaching group the easiest touch of all the professional classes." [31]

New Orleanians' concern about Communism, the *Item* explained on November 1, 1946, had prompted its series "Reds in New Orleans." One of the things Communists were doing in New Orleans, the newspaper reported, was working in the CIO, which had recently launched a new southern organizing drive. Communists in the CIO local of the International Longshoremen's and Warehousemen's Union were trying to influence the membership to employ "Soviet principles," the *Item* said.[32]

Reports of Communist activity in New Orleans alarmed many residents of the Crescent City. On the night of November 7, 1946, a group of men, accompanied by police officers and *Item* reporters, disrupted a Communist Party meeting. According to the secretary of the party's Civil Rights Defense Committee, the meeting had been publicly announced and police protection requested but not provided. Instead, police arrested everyone attending the meeting, and the court found them guilty of disturbing the peace. The men who had attacked the gathering were charged with inciting to riot, but their cases were dismissed because of lack of evidence.[33]

The *Item* reported that the fight broke out following a speech given by a "Negro Communist leader who credited Russian armies with winning the war and praised the Soviet Union as a 'better country than America.'" The police seemed to be waiting for some sort of signal to begin their attack on the meeting because, in an instant, "an expectant detail of police swarmed into the wild fracas and the meeting room . . . was cleared." Photographers were present to document the fight—a large picture appeared on the front page of the *Item* the next morning—and reporters noted every detail of the melee, including flying chairs, hurled tomatoes, eggs, and stink bombs.[34] Two days later, a lynch mob threatened the state chairman of the Communist Party, James E. Jackson. When he called the police, he was taken to jail and booked for disturbing the peace and criminal mischief.[35]

In January 1948 Henry Wallace, who had served as vice-president under Roosevelt and secretary of commerce under Truman, resigned as editor of the *New Republic* and announced himself as a candidate for the presidency. He promised that his first goal would be to eradicate racism, and he campaigned on a plank that included peace with the Soviet Union, support for labor, and civil rights for blacks.[36] His acceptance of Communists in his campaign organization outraged many Americans, including anti-Stalinist liberals. The "emerging political and intellectual consensus of 1948," as one historian has pointed out, doomed the Wallace campaign. This "increasingly illiberal era" viewed his candidacy as a threat to patriotism, Americanism, and conservatism.[37] The vast majority of American voters saw the Progressive Party as a dangerous departure from mainstream values. Wallace campaigners were physically attacked throughout the nation, particularly in the South, where the candidate's stand on desegregation and civil rights made him profoundly unpopular among whites.[38] The response to Wallace's campaign by the liberal establishment focused on his Communist supporters, while Dixiecrat presidential nominee Strom Thurmond reacted to Wallace by reaffirming the South's racial traditions, declaring that "there's not enough troops in the Army to break down segregation and admit the negro into our homes, our eating places, our swimming pools and our theatres." [39]

The *Times-Picayune*'s coverage of the Wallace campaign focused on Wallace's leftist sympathies as well as on his liberal racial stands. The headline for a story on the Progressive Party convention declared "Platform Points Up Reds' Rights," in case anyone missed the connection when reading about the Progressive Party's pledge to "fight for the constitutional rights of Communists and all other political groups to express their views as the first line of defense of the liberties of a democratic people." [40] The next day, the *Times-Picayune* ran a fierce editorial against Wallace, stating, "Here we have the closest approach yet recorded by any American party to the Communist 'ideal' of despotically centralized power administered by a ruling group of 'representatives of the people' to bestow blessings upon their wards." The paper compared the Progressive Party's platform to Hitler's Germany and Stalin's Russia.[41]

The 1948 election marked a turning point for the Democratic party in the South and for American politics in general. The South was already experiencing a conservative resurgence when the Dixiecrat revolt against the Democratic party broke up the South's New Deal coalition. The labor-left alliance that had given southern blacks their only real power base was obliterated, a development that would have disastrous consequences after 1954. At bottom, race lay at the foundation of southern dissatisfaction with both the Democratic Party and the Progressive Party. In the face of the civil rights movement and the economic and social changes brought on by the New Deal and World War II, the South became more dedicated than ever to states' rights and more determined to resist any disruptions of the "southern way of life." [42] And the inability of liberal organizations to provide any real alternatives in the South allowed conservatives to prevail in political and social policy making.[43]

Even after Wallace's loss to Truman, southern conservatives continued to view Progressive Party ideas with alarm, particularly when they involved issues of race. In New Orleans in February 1949, a group of sixty-four young people, many of them Tulane, Newcomb, and Dillard students, were taken into custody and fined for disturbing the peace after neighbors complained about noise coming from an "inter-racial party." Two young women, one of them Sarah Reed's niece Alice LeSassier, were identified as sponsors of the party and members of the Young Progressives, an organization of Wallace supporters. Alice's roommate, Arlene Stitch, told a reporter that the party had been held with the purpose of "extending the organization" in New Orleans. The newspaper, depicting Stitch as an outside agitator, noted that she had been in New Orleans for just three weeks. "I saw nothing wrong with having Negroes in my home, and I don't think we were disturbing the peace," she said. "The police came by four times before they began frisking my guests and taking them to jail. Every time they came things were quiet." Two Newcomb students reported that they had been surprised to find that the party was "mixed." They went on to say that the gathering was "definitely pink and bordering on the red side."[44]

In the spring of 1948 New Orleans attorney Cuthbert S. Baldwin told the Louisiana Bar Association that the courts needed to maintain a vigilant stand against Communism. He also called for the removal of Communists from all institutions of learning.[45] Schools and teachers inevitably felt the brunt of Cold War hostilities. By 1949 twenty-two states had established loyalty oaths for teachers, thirty-eight states had passed general antisedition laws, twenty-one had outlawed seditious teaching, and thirty-one prohibited teachers from belonging to seditious organizations. Twelve states permitted teachers to be fired for reasons of "disloyalty." An estimated six hundred teachers at all levels of education lost their jobs between 1947 and 1955.[46]

In 1948 the American Legion turned its attention once again to the classroom, pledging to help the teaching profession curtail the spread of Communism. At its 1948 national convention, the legion called for the "unimpaired" teaching of American history and civics in order to instill in students a "greater zeal for our form of government, its social and industrial systems."[47] The National Education Association advocated a similar goal during American Education Week in 1948. According to the NEA, it was "the responsibility of the schools to indoctrinate our youth in the American way of life so that they know it, believe in it, and live it continuously."[48]

The Orleans Parish School Board had made its stand in favor of patriotism when it adopted the Americanism rule in 1941, a move that was motivated in part by the war against Fascism. After World War II, however, an obsessive concern with Communism displaced all other ideological worries, and in 1948 the school board actively investigated complaints that public school teachers were imparting Communist doctrines to their students. On May 5, 1948, John

Kieffer, a Tulane political science professor, told the Young Men's Business Club that he had heard that some New Orleans students were following "the party line." That afternoon, Superintendent Bourgeois called a meeting of New Orleans public high school principals to investigate the charges. The principals supported Bourgeois's investigation but reported that the only suspects they had found up to that point had been two substitute teachers whom they had already barred from further work in their schools. Probably in reference to the 1940–41 affidavits against Reed, school board president Robert M. Haas disclosed that accusations about Communism being taught in the schools had surfaced several years ago, "but there was never anything concrete enough for us to work on."

The principals promised to check every student and every teacher in the public high schools for signs of possible Communist influence and to ask the students if they were receiving anti-American propaganda at school. "We should go as far as necessary," school board member R. Emmet Mahoney said, "and let the chips fall where they may." Another board member, William C. Fletcher, agreed, adding that "anyone who would distribute Communist propaganda in the high schools ought to be shipped the hell out of this country and back to Russia."[49]

The school board came under increasing pressure to weed out any possible Communist taint in the schools. In June the board of directors of the Association of Commerce, acting on a resolution written by its "national security council," recommended that all public school teachers be required to take a loyalty oath in the form of an affidavit denying any ties with the Communist Party. Inspired, no doubt, by the loyalty oaths required of all union leaders by the 1947 Taft-Hartley Act, the association believed that teachers should also swear that they did not "support any organization that believes in or teaches the overthrow of the United States government by force or by any illegal or unconstitutional methods." In the opinion of the Association of Commerce, the same association that had collected evidence against Reed eight years earlier, the oath was essential to the preservation of democracy. "Possibly the most fertile soil wherein the seeds of Communism might be sowed is in our institutions of learning where the children and youth of America are placed directly under the influence, guidance and control of its personnel," the association cautioned.[50]

Superintendent Bourgeois objected to the use of a loyalty oath although he affirmed the belief that "loyalty to American ideals had to be a primary consideration in employing and retaining public school teachers." The loyalty oath, he said, would only lead to resentment and subject teachers to possible humiliation. He said there was sufficient evidence that New Orleans school-teachers were loyal, and even teachers who might be Communists wouldn't hesitate taking an oath, regardless of their affiliations. "If all school administrators throughout the nation are vigilant," the superintendent said, "there is no serious threat of Communistic infiltration in the schools."[51]

The *New Orleans States* agreed with Bourgeois that a loyalty oath would be unwise. After some furor following Kieffer's accusation, the paper pointed out in June, subsequent investigations had found no evidence to support it. "As a matter of fact," the *States* editorialized, "if some of the teachers had been turned toward radical thinking in the past few years, they would have had plenty of provocation." Teachers had been badly overworked and pitifully underpaid. They were required to participate in collections, crusades, and civic drives on top of their regular duties. "We assigned to the teachers the most important work done by any public servant, and paid them the least; paid them less than the janitors of the schools and keepers of the grounds. The teachers waited patiently for justice and decent treatment. If any strayed from decency's path, we are not blameless."[52]

The editor of the *States* had not yet heard about the accusations against Sarah Reed. On May 10, just five days after Kieffer's talk, superintendent Bourgeois submitted to a closed meeting of the school board a summary of evidence regarding Reed's commitment to "Americanism." This material consisted of "unsolicited" statements from five of Reed's current students, plus material from her file, including the 1940–41 affidavits.

Superintendent Bourgeois outlined to the board his actions after Kieffer's comments appeared in the New Orleans newspapers, beginning with his meeting with high school principals in which they had discussed the veracity of such reports. The superintendent had subsequently dictated a questionnaire that he sent to every white high school student. The results, he said, indicated that there were no grounds for the Tulane professor's charges that New Orleans students had been infected by Communism, with the possible exception of a few Fortier students. Bourgeois had interviewed these students, who, he reported, had answered the questionnaire "in such a manner as to cast serious doubt about the teaching of Communism in the Fortier High School." According to the superintendent, the "students were admonished by me that they should be most careful and that they should make no statement based on hearsay; that the professional reputation of a teacher was her greatest asset and that while testimony to be given should be exact, moderation rather than zeal was what we desired." Bourgeois presented to the board on May 10 the following statements, excerpts of testimony given by the students and signed by them:

1. Mrs. Reed definitely pointed out certain phases of superiorities of Communism over the Democratic way; that when they [students] argued against Communism she would reply that they did not understand it. Signed: Guido J. Pizzeck

2. The Teacher [Mrs. Reed] definitely advocated Socialism in place of present system of Democracy. She prophesied that present system of government would eventually end in dictatorship and advocated equal distribution of nation's wealth. She advocated repeal of Taft-Hartley Act. She always brought out the bad points of our government. Signed: E. Bruce Edrington

3. [An affidavit identical to Bruce Edrington's.] Signed: Alan Adams.

4. In discussing the presidential situation the teacher [Mrs. Reed] advocated Henry Wallace. The student asked if she was aware that he was being supported by Communists, to which she replied that she was for Henry Wallace regardless. Signed: Glynn G. Fowler

5. Advocated the division of wealth in the country and advocated socialism. Signed: C. D. Hawkshead III

Bourgeois was concerned about these allegations, he said, although he did not think that by itself the testimony constituted sufficient grounds for bringing charges against Reed. However, he added, "I was quite disturbed about it, as it pointed to a situation which had been referred to me several times anonymously as warranting further study." After reviewing Reed's file, he had concluded that the evidence contained in it, coupled with the students' recent statements, presented sufficient cause to bring her case before the board in 1948.

Included in Reed's file were the seven student affidavits dating from 1940–41. In his May 10, 1948, presentation Bourgeois also included excerpts from the Orleans Parish School Board minutes for March 11, 1941, when the students' charges against Reed were first discussed. Bourgeois told the 1948 board, "Although there was a great deal of discussion by the Board on the above issues, no final disposition appears to have been made [in 1941], nor was any hearing had of Mrs. Reed before the Board. What is important now is that new complaints have been made of the same nature as those which involved Mrs. Reed several years ago." Bourgeois was reluctant to file charges "against a teacher who had labored so long in the public schools of this city," but, he claimed, the proposed transfer of teaching assignments would in fact protect Reed, as well as the students, from the "humiliation" of a trial.

He reminded the board of "the many difficulties it had encountered in its past official dealings with Mrs. Reed," recalling specifically "her refusal to obey a Board directive," her suspension, and her subsequent lawsuit against the board. He pointed out that she had lost the suit when the state supreme court sustained the action of the school board, holding "that the Board had dealt leniently with Mrs. Reed." He noted that two of Reed's principals had requested her transfer from their schools because of her "uncooperative" attitude. His memo also included John Conniff's letter of December 1940, in which the principal had complained that "Mrs. Reed is antagonistic to all recognized authority, exerts a damaging influence upon the patriotism of the student body and handicaps the school's Americanism programs, etc." In fact, Bourgeois declared, this statement was the determining factor in his decision to bring the matter to the board's attention.[53]

While there had been some discussion about transferring Reed to teach another subject in 1941, the board had taken no action. Now, however, Bourgeois had decided to recommend Reed's transfer to another area of teaching, one that she herself could choose, "with the injunction that in her new field she would abstain from discussing Communism and other isms and that she proselytize for the American system of Democracy." He recommended that the board give Reed an opportunity to appear before it; he would even "recommend forbearance should Mrs. Reed furnish proof of her intention that in the future she will so conduct her classes as to leave no doubts in the minds of the students as to what their loyalty should be to American ideals." The superintendent said he believed that he had been entirely fair to Reed in this matter, particularly in light of his efforts to avoid publicity about the proposed transfer.[54]

On May 24, Bourgeois wrote Reed informing her that he intended to transfer her from social studies to another, unspecified field because of complaints by students that she had not emphasized the superiority of the American way of life over Communism. He also informed Reed that the school board had been accumulating "a docket" on her for several years.[55] Failure to hear from Reed on this matter prompted another letter on July 23 from acting superintendent Edwin Eley, asking again to which field she preferred to be transferred.[56]

Finally, on July 30, Reed responded to both letters, explaining that legislative activities had prevented her from answering earlier. She asked the superintendents to take no action until she could discuss the matter with them more fully.[57] Bourgeois did not consider Reed's explanation adequate. "I am somewhat bewildered by the statement that you were unable to answer my letter of May 24 because of legislative activities. Apparently you have had the time to present your case to several individuals and agencies not connected with the School Board," he wrote. The superintendent explained that a committee of Tulane professors had requested a meeting with him concerning Reed's case and that other educators had inquired about the situation as well. He had also received a "threatening" letter from the acting secretary of the Central Trades and Labor Council.

"While I have no desire to air your case or to take any punitive measures against you," the superintendent wrote Reed, "I must remind you that as an employee of the School Board your first duty was to answer my communication of May 24, 1948." Bourgeois told Reed that he would give her five days to discuss the matter with him; after that time, he said, "I shall proceed to present my official recommendation to the Board as I believe it is my duty to do."[58]

Bourgeois resented Reed's efforts to make her case public; he must have assumed that she would not want the kind of publicity that would attend such charges and would accept a transfer rather than risk her reputation. It took courage to openly deny charges of disloyalty in 1948; a more cautious person would have acquiesced to the board's transfer in the hope that the matter would remain private. Reed, however, had never been cautious. "The matter of notoriety and publication of your case, due to your own activities, now makes it a practical impossibility to circumvent the many rumors that are being circulated," Bourgeois told Reed. She had the right to appeal her case to the school board, he said. "On the other hand, I firmly intend to review to the Board all of the evidence that has accumulated regarding the subject under controversy. Thereafter, the matter of publicity shall be beyond my control."[59] Reed answered this letter by setting up an appointment with the superintendent for herself and her attorney.

Reed had indeed spent much of her time since receiving Bourgeois's first letter in rallying her forces behind her. She and the Teachers' Federation organized a citizens' group, set up a committee of thirty teachers, and gathered supportive statements from parents and faculty members. The Central Trades and Labor Council agreed to pay all expenses necessary to fight the accusations against Reed.[60] The acting secretary of the labor council wrote a strongly worded letter to Bourgeois, informing him that "the officers and members of the Labor Movement in New Orleans will watch your every action and utterance, and if it becomes necessary we will advocate your transfer or removal, or there will be no cooperation from our group in connection with the Orleans Parish School Program." The union leader knew "of no case under the Nazis, or the Russians, whereby anything as drastic or as unfair has ever been attempted." If this "system" Bourgeois was introducing into the schools was "what my boy and other Americans have fought for," the labor secretary continued, "then God help us all."[61]

On August 3, C. C. Henson of the Louisiana Education Foundation and William Lester Kolb of Tulane University called at Bourgeois's office. As representatives of a committee of professors at Tulane and Loyola who had organized to support Reed, they discussed her case with the superintendent.[62] Bourgeois, displeased that Reed had decided to air publicly the charges against her, told the school board that he had considered the proposed transfer "privileged communication under the law" and that he had "rigidly abstained from publicizing her in the instant case." He also assured the board that he had "not the slightest personal animus" against her and was acting only to protect the students and Reed herself.[63]

On August 26, in a six-hour hearing concerning the charges brought against Reed, her students and colleagues overwhelmed the board with protestations of her commitment to democracy. Once again, Reed's allies and friends stood behind her, giving the board little choice but to exonerate her. Eight students spoke in their teacher's behalf; only three testified against her. At least forty other students and twenty teachers waited outside the hearing room, prepared to come to Reed's defense, and nearly two hundred students volunteered to do whatever they could to help her. The New Orleans Classroom Teachers' Federation surveyed 250 students, who all denied that Reed "had made statements which would reflect on democracy."[64] One seventeen-year-old boy wrote this statement for the defense: "I think anyone who is starting all this stupid stuff about Mrs. Reed is crazy, and furthermore, if you have never been taught by her in civics, how can you comment on her? And I say again she has a lot more sense than a lot of people I know."[65]

Some of the most interesting information to emerge from this hearing concerned the testimony of one of the students who had signed an affidavit against Reed in 1941. Edmund Brown revealed, for the first time, how he had come to make a statement in the first place. "Mr. Conniff called a few of us into his office," Brown recalled, and asked the students "if we felt that any of the teachers in the school were going against the Democratic way, and, if so, that we were to come down and see you [Arthur DeLa Houssaye, of the Association of Commerce, who was present at the August 26 hearing] and give you our opinion of the matter."[66] In view of this information, there seems little doubt that Reed had been targeted from the first by her principal and/or the Association of Commerce. In fact, Reed's case presents a nearly textbook example of how the 1940s Red Scare was used against liberal and controversial teachers for reasons that were entirely unrelated to Communism.

One of those who testified in Reed's favor was William Monroe Jr., one of Reed's students in the 1930s. Monroe was news director at a New Orleans radio station and later the monitor of "Meet the Press." Monroe considered the board's action "a thinly coated challenge of Mrs. Reed's loyalty," and he was eager to lend support to his former teacher, with whom he had kept in touch on a regular basis.[67] In his testimony before the board, Monroe recounted what he remembered of Reed's classes. As he recalled, the class often talked about labor problems, "and we would discuss the company's point of view and the man's point of view, and the students would give their own summaries of current events, for which they got material from the daily newspapers and radio." Monroe said that he had been more interested in Reed's classes than in any others he had in high school. "I always thought she was a very superior teacher and one the public schools were fortunate to have," Monroe said. The proposed transfer, he continued, "is damaging to Mrs. Reed because directly or indirectly it is a challenge to her loyalty . . . a blot on her record. From her personal point of view, it is a serious thing."[68]

Many years later, Monroe observed that some parents in 1948 did not believe that controversial issues should be discussed in the classroom, and they might well have been upset that their children were engaging in debates about politics and labor. Monroe recalled one such animated discussion about John L. Lewis and a coal miners' strike in the late 1930s. Reed was vitally interested in social issues, Monroe said, and she wanted her students exposed to controversy and aware that there was more than one side to an issue. In short, he said, she wanted her students to think for themselves. Unlike many teachers, Reed was not afraid to bring up political and social issues, even in the Cold War years, when some teachers steered clear of topics that might have caused trouble with parents and school authorities. Although Monroe could not remember Reed ever expressing her personal political opinion, he thought that "she may have given the impression of radicalism that was really Americanism. She didn't try to protect herself by keeping controversy out of her classes."[69]

The only people to testify against Reed at the 1948 hearing were three former students who had signed affidavits against her in the 1940–41 school year. One of these was Edmund Brown, who told the board, "It seemed like in every class we were always discussing isms, Communism, Socialism, Fascism, capitalism, and the students in debate form would argue back and forth as to the merits of each and the demerits." When questioned as to whether he could infer from Reed's participation in those discussions whether she was in favor of abolishing private ownership and giving the government control over everything, Brown answered in the affirmative. "That is why I signed the statement," he said.[70] Brown did not say that Reed had actually come out in favor of Communism, but he believed that "she was trying to create in the minds of the students in the class not so much that Communism was the thing, but just pressing the subject so much that you gained the impression that she favored it."[71]

Kenneth Muller told the board that Reed opposed military training at the high school, she objected to saluting the American flag, and "she spoke highly of the Communistic Movement."[72] She had also referred to the South as "an unfit place to live." As Muller recalled, "We had a little pamphlet known as 'Economic Conditions of the South,' and we had to break this down and give a lengthy speech on it and bring out just what was wrong with the South from it." Muller didn't know who had published the pamphlet and could not say whether it was Communist literature or not.[73] When asked what facts his class had discussed about the South, Muller replied, "Well, the thing is we were pretty well handicapped by a Civil War, held down in that respect. I think as a teacher she should realize that that shouldn't be harped upon. We are doing as well as we possibly can. The fact that she brings out and made us go through this little pamphlet, 'Economic Conditions of the South,' I don't see where that has any bearing on teaching children Civics or high school students Civics."[74] Apparently Muller did not think that a federal government publication such as the 1938 "Report on the Economic Conditions of the South," commissioned by President Franklin Roosevelt and written by his National Emergency Council, was appropriate reading matter for high school students. Nor, for that matter, did many other southerners.

Former Fortier student John Parham also objected to discussions about the U.S. government publication. "I believe that it was considered not quite American in its outlook," Parham recalled. "Outside of that, I think the class was well conducted. Rather unusual, you might say, in comparison with other classes. Nothing amazing about it other than the fact that Mrs. Reed seemed to hold forums more than other classes. . . . She started a discussion and she expected members of the class to carry on from there."[75]

The issue of Reed's opposition to military training at Fortier came up repeatedly during the hearing. One of her attorneys questioned the board about the relevance of that line of inquiry. "Evidently just about half of Congress opposed military training here at a time when we expect to be attacked by Russia at any minute," Reed's attorney said, "and certainly I should say that all polls indicate that nine-tenths of the mothers of this country oppose military training, so whether Mrs. Reed opposes military training or not I think is completely irrelevant." The board's lawyer disagreed, arguing that Reed should uphold the views of her institution rather than express her own opinion. "Then I think Mrs. Reed should be censured for not being loyal to Fortier rather than being disloyal to the Government or Democracy," Reed's attorney retorted.[76]

Superintendent Bourgeois testified that he was aware of Reed's past difficulties with former superintendents. Every time Reed and his predecessors had a conflict, he said, "it was the superintendent that was on trial and not Mrs. Reed." In fact, Bourgeois noted, previous superintendents became so discouraged that in the end they took no action against Reed at all. Bourgeois obviously did not want to be seen as one of the authorities who had been cowed by Reed. "Thousands of teachers have been transferred since Mrs. Reed went to Fortier," Bourgeois continued, "and the Principal has requested any number of times she be transferred. No Superintendent has dared to make that transfer!"[77]

Although Bourgeois had been careful to avoid saying that Reed was to be transferred because she advocated Communism, the board's attorney specifically made the connection, stating at the hearing that the superintendent's reason for transferring Reed was "not only her leaning towards Communism but also her failure to stress Americanism." He also cited as proof of disloyalty her refusal to sign the 1943 war work questionnaire.[78]

Reed's attorney agreed with the school board's counsel on the real intent of the proceedings. "This is a hearing, gentlemen, on whether Mrs. Reed has taught Communism," Fred Cassibry said. "Now, if this decision is contrary to Mrs. Reed, that is what she stands indicted of. Now I would say if it were an ordinary transfer, if you had some charges against Mrs. Reed that she was unruly and was a troublemaker, then it would not have the same gravity, but I say that she is practically being accused of something which our courts have held is a crime. It's libel to accuse someone of being a Communist. That is how serious it is, and I think because of the seriousness of the charges, that we should be given our opportunity to be heard."[79]

Unlike her 1943 hearing before the board, Reed herself took the stand in 1948 and testified about her teaching methods. Reed's progressive teaching techniques were far removed from the conventional methods commonly employed in high school civics classes, and it is easy to see how controversy erupted during discussions that she encouraged in her classroom. "I find that the best way to get children interested is to try to get a great deal of participation from the students," she said. She described how a class was divided into committees—a bulletin board committee in charge of displaying current events articles, an activities committee, a program committee, and a civics committee—and a chairman, a newscaster, and a secretary appointed for each class session. The class was operated according to parliamentary rules. "I sit in the back of the class, and I simply take part to keep them from going off the subject and from going far afield," Reed said. "For instance, when a child tells the news . . . if there is anything they don't mention, I have to get the floor. They have to recognize me, if there is anything I want to bring to their attention. . . . I take no part except where they have omissions." She explained that discussions were based on the topic of the day and described the scrapbooks the students kept concerning current events, noting that some of the boys skilled in drawing included their own illustrations in these books. "In every activity we try to bring out everything in the child that we can so that each child has some avenue of expression. The consequence is, I think, the children do develop a great deal, and I try as much as humanly possible to stand aside and let them discuss, and they like it." [80]

The class often talked about society's problems, Reed continued. "We try to guide them into discussions of these topics so that they will realize that they not only have privileges in this country, but they have duties and responsibilities." [81] Reed said that she tried to "enliven the class" by taking the students to the polls, the courthouse, the city council, and school board meetings. Her aim was to make civics come "alive" to her pupils and "to make civics practical at Fortier." [82]

Reed also delineated some of her past conflicts with her principal, John Conniff. Her real troubles with the principal began in 1938, she said, when he transferred her sister Roberta out of Fortier. When Reed informed Conniff that she intended to fight the transfer, he told her he did not blame her for trying to help her sister but that he intended to make the transfer permanent. "Then Mr. Conniff started on me in earnest," Reed said, "and each half year seemed to get worse." [83]

When the school board's attorney asked Reed if she had tried to influence her students regarding Henry Wallace, she replied, "Never." In answer to a board member's question about whether she belonged to any Communist-front organizations, Reed answered, "Not that I know of." [84] She also gave a short, negative response when asked if she was a Communist or a Socialist. [85] Reed had a longer answer when asked whether she believed that the American system of democracy was the best. "I wish to say," she explained, "that I don't take the position that it is a perfect system. I do not. I take the position that . . .

it is something that is alive and that is growing and that is changing, and that has tremendous problems, but I will say that I have recommended it with all of the points that we have to approach and have to correct." [86] Concluding her testimony, Reed said, "I'd like to say that one boy wrote on the questionnaire . . . 'Mrs. Reed made us feel that we were lucky to live in America.' I think that was a very nice way to put it." [87]

After listening to all of the testimony, Bourgeois, recognizing defeat when he saw it, tried to justify the hearing by waving the anti-Communist flag. "We are living in troublous times in this country," he told the board the day after the hearing. He had called the hearing, he said, because Conniff had accused Reed of having a "damaging influence on the patriotism of the student body." He pointed out that the schools had been "flagrantly accused of teaching Communism as a superior way of life" and said it had been necessary to closely investigate the charges to ensure that schoolchildren were not receiving subversive instruction. He and the board had not accused Reed of subversion, he maintained. They had simply invited Reed to discuss her case and review the available evidence. The board had made it clear all along that this was not a trial but a hearing and that Reed's rights as a teacher had been respected. Since it was obvious that no specific charges of un-Americanism could be brought against Reed, he was dropping his initial recommendation to transfer her to another subject. In conclusion, he said, he was "firmly convinced" that with the exception of Conniff's testimony that "'Mrs. Reed is antagonistic to all recognized authority' . . . the preponderance of evidence by students in Mrs. Reed's classes is definitely in her favor and definitely controverts the testimony of students made against her on the grounds of un-Americanism." [88]

The final vote was 3-1, with one board member, W. C. Fletcher, abstaining. Robert M. Haas, board president, said he agreed that Reed was innocent of these charges but that she should be transferred anyway because of all the publicity surrounding the case. Furthermore, he said, it would be better to go ahead with the plan to transfer Reed "in order to protect the children in our system and the public, and let the public of New Orleans know the School Board is doing all in its power to stamp out Communism." R. Emmet Mahoney agreed that the case against Reed had not been proved by the evidence, but because charges of un-Americanism had been made against her more than once, he still had doubts about her innocence. Because the order to transfer Reed "cannot be disassociated from the statements made against her," Mahoney stated, he would vote to retain her as a civics teacher "so it may not appear that retaliatory action had been taken against her." He voted not to transfer her, as did Louis H. Pilie and Salvadore Roccaforte.

Fletcher, who had abstained, explained that there was still "some doubt in my mind whether I heard the whole truth. We had witnesses before us who deliberately accused Mrs. Reed of teaching Communistic attitudes. On the other hand, we had many witnesses who testified to the contrary." Superintendent Bourgeois claimed that the hearing cleared the schools of charges that Communism was taught in the classrooms of New Orleans. He did warn, however, that if similar charges appeared again, he would take every action necessary to prevent "the teaching of subversive doctrines in the public schools." [89]

Reed cheerfully called the board's decision "a great victory for academic freedom in the classroom. The case was a very special illustration of democracy at work in the New Orleans public school system. It has been wonderfully educational for my boys." She realized that her method of teaching, "where I stand aside and let the students take the lead," meant that "controversies are almost certain to occur," but that she had no intention of changing her teaching techniques because of the hearing. "I am proud that I got across to my students the fact that America, even in its greatness, is no finished product wrapped up in cellophane, just to be looked at. It's a living, growing thing and so, while we have privileges, we also have duties and responsibilities. These I have always emphasized." She denied reports that she had discussed her own choice for president in her classes, and "as for the distribution of wealth, I always said jokingly that I hope I get a little of it, if that ever happens." [90]

Students and teachers who attended Reed's hearing held a range of opinions about its significance. Some saw it as part of a national "Red Hysteria . . . a politically nourished 'witch hunt.'" Others thought that the charges were part of an effort to divide the teachers' union. Still others saw the hearing as a valid attempt to eradicate Communism from the schools. [91]

After the hearing, Sarah and Roberta threw a party at their house, complete with "Victory Cake." [92] Judging from letters to the local press, the public also celebrated the board's decision; several writers described the charges as ludicrous to begin with. As Ethel Hutson, former suffrage leader and women's rights activist, wrote to the *Times-Picayune,* "If there is one teacher in the public schools of New Orleans—or in any school anywhere—who is known for independence, courage in fighting injustice and oppression, and unwillingness to allow anyone to impose on her or on anyone else, it is, and has been for close on to 40 years, Mrs. Sarah Towles Reed. She has worked and written and spoken and fought for the rights of teachers against arbitrary and unfair action, rulings, decisions of Boards and Superintendents for more than a generation." [93]

One "Observer" rejoiced that Reed had once again won a battle for all teachers, not just for herself. "Teachers may no longer cower and shrink from the intimidation of Communism as a means of whipping them into line," the writer exalted. "The battle for civil liberties and democratic freedoms must be won again and again against the periodic outcroppings of authoritarianism."[94] A fellow teacher wrote Reed personally along much the same lines, thanking her for protecting teachers' rights. "Instead of being accused of not stressing Democracy, to the contrary, I think you should be given the Congressional Medal of Honor for being one of those courageous individuals whose high democratic ideals make it possible for this great Democracy of ours to survive and progress. May there always be Sarah Reeds and more power to them!"[95] Journalist Harnett Kane told Reed that he knew that "a few people had their fingers nicely burned in the matter. One or two, I know, must feel very foolish now. Certainly any intelligent person, and any fair one, would have seen at the start how ridiculous were the accusations."[96]

The case against Sarah Reed cannot be understood outside the context of the national climate of Cold War anti-Communism. Her past conflicts with the school board, particularly her 1943 case, her work for the teachers' union, her close identification with organized labor, and her unconventional teaching methods played significant parts in the drama, as well. All available evidence points to Reed's support of Henry Wallace in the 1948 election, and at the time she was working even more closely with the black teachers' union than ever before. Any one of these elements might have been enough to upset school authorities, but a combination of all of them might well have resulted in her dismissal had she not put up such a strong defense. Neither Reed nor her union, however, were intimidated by the proceedings against her. In fact, throughout her 1948 conflict, Reed and the CTF engaged successfully in another battle with the board over teacher sabbatical leaves.

As public support for Reed in her 1948 hearing shows, liberals could still win, at least on issues of academic freedom and free speech, despite the growing conservatism of the national mood. Reed's stand on the most controversial issue of the time, however, indicates that liberals in New Orleans, as in the rest of the South, were not strong enough to effect real change. On the issue of race, liberals were cautious and largely ineffective. Although Reed had helped to organize black teachers into an AFT local and had supported their efforts to secure equal pay and better schools, she was hesitant when it came to pushing for full integration of the segregated teachers' unions. While Reed herself favored integration, she feared the effects of forcing it on other members of the white union who did not share her more liberal racial views and who would probably quit the union rather that accept a merger of the black and white locals.

Reed's attitude toward the integration issue mirrored that of many southern liberals who, even if they believed in the justness of integration, were wary of outside interference in the southern racial arrangement. Southern liberals, observed Gunnar Myrdal, were "inclined to stress the need for patience and to exalt the cautious approach, the slow change, the organic nature of social growth." But, as another commentator on the South wrote, "time was running out for Southern liberals to be evasive."[97]

10 Time Runs Out

Before the issue of integration of either schools or unions came to a head, Reed stood in the forefront of civil rights activism on behalf of schoolteachers, regularly attending meetings of both the black and the white AFT locals. Together, African American and white teachers had successfully combated the merit-responsibility issue in 1943. Subsequently, they began to cooperate even more closely on other issues of interest to both races. In 1946 teachers formed an interracial Liaison Group that met regularly every month and more often during emergency situations. The two locals merged their committees on kindergarten classes and began sharing an office and a legislative fund, setting up headquarters in the Labor Temple. When they decided to renovate the offices, teachers from both locals joined in the work.[1]

For the first time in New Orleans history, integrated groups of teachers appeared before the all-white school board to address issues of common concern, such as the board's policy against hiring married women as permanent teachers. Although the board had been forbidden since 1936 to fire a woman who married while under contract, it was not required to hire women who were already married. Both black and white women teachers resented this restriction, and in 1950 an interracial delegation convinced the Orleans Parish

School Board to overturn its policy.[2] The next year, the presidents of Locals 353 and 527 appeared together before the school board to ask for improvements to black schools.[3] Veronica Hill, president of Local 527, asked Reed to serve on a committee regarding the conversion of some white schools to black ones, and the two unions sponsored a forum on this "very touchy subject," as Hill described it. The meeting was attended by members of both unions, and panel members represented both races.[4]

The school board also made some progress in improving race relations and fostering interracial cooperation when it began organizing interracial teaching institutes in 1948 and integrated principals' meetings in the early 1950s. By 1953, however, the school administration had returned to segregated meetings and institutes. The Liaison Group objected to these setbacks, and the presidents of the two locals protested to the school board about "the racial discrimination, embarrassment and humiliation" suffered by many African American teaching candidates at the hands of the board's personnel department.[5]

In 1954 the joint executive board of the unions protested the change from integrated to segregated departmental meetings imposed by superintendent James Redmond. It encouraged him to resume holding interracial institutes, departmental meetings, and other gatherings as a means of combating prejudice and discrimination. With the Supreme Court about to rule on *Brown v. Board of Education,* the future seemed clear, and the Teachers' Federation believed that the school board ought to start getting ready for it. The superintendent, however, had no plans to prepare the teaching corps for integration. He told the union that he would go "as far and as fast as he thought he was able to," but he had no suggestions and he made no promise to develop any.[6]

Electoral politics emerged as one of the most successful areas in which the two locals cooperated. For some time, the unions had seen the importance of electing reform-minded candidates to both the school board and the city government. Politics had always played a major role in school board affairs, as the Old Regulars had regularly used board positions as patronage plums. Athough board members were elected, it was common knowledge that only candidates who had been given the nod by the Democratic machine could win. Consequently, board decisions frequently were based more on political expedience than on educational priorities. Discontent with machine control of the board grew to the point where teachers finally felt compelled to become politically involved in the selection of its members. The Teachers' Federation formed a citizens' committee in 1944 in an attempt to get at least one reform candidate elected to the board. As Reed wrote her niece, the primary motivation behind this committee was "to help us get the schools out of partisan politics. Here's hoping the Committee won't be bought out and the Federation find itself locked up for keeps in the doghouse."[7]

In a 1945 editorial, *New Orleans States* urged teachers to take a more active role in board elections. "Frankly," the paper said, "we don't see how the teachers are ever going to get decent salaries or just treatment in all other matters unless they throw their full political weight, especially their ballots, into the fight. Unless the deadheads are thrown off the pay rolls, unless the vicious practice of buying votes for the Maestri machine with little reductions in property assessments is stopped, there won't be much money to increase teacher salaries."[8]

Reed was well aware of the political prerogatives that hurt the educational system. In 1945 she pointed out that school funding had decreased because of reduced revenue from city real estate and personal property taxes, from which school funds were derived, despite significant increases in real estate and personal property values. The reason for the decrease in school funds, she said, could be found in the practice of lowering tax assessments for favored political friends and buying votes with tax reductions.[9]

In 1946 Robert Maestri's control over the Democratic machine in New Orleans ended when reform candidate deLesseps S. Morrison defeated him in the mayoral election. After their candidate's victory, the Independent Women's Organization, together with other women's groups that had played a large role in getting Morrison elected, began to focus their efforts on education. Concerned about the poor state of the public school system in New Orleans, the women backed one of their own for a position on the school board and in 1948 helped elect Jacqueline T. Leonhard, a reformer who had no ties to the Democratic machine. In 1950 the women's groups joined the two teachers' unions in backing independents Clarence Scheps, comptroller of Tulane University, and Celestine P. Besse, an engineer, in their bids for board positions.[10] Scheps had previously headed the Citizens' Committee for the Improvement of the Public Schools, which had been organized by the CTF.[11] Members of Locals 353 and 527 met jointly with the candidates at both AFL and CIO meetings, with CTF executive secretary Hasket Derby urging union members to "make an all-out effort on salaries and throw all our united strength into this School Board election." Derby reminded CTF members of the importance of this election. "Every effort is being made to discredit the constructive work of the Federation in this election campaign," he said. The incumbents, Robert Haas and R. Emmet Mahoney, "line up together in a resolute stand against change, progress and improvement in our schools."

Scheps and Besse won school board seats in the election and immediately helped push through a salary increase for all teachers.[12] The election of non-machine candidates marked a significant departure from politics-as-usual in New Orleans. When the board selected Leonhard as its president in 1950, it finally became independent of city hall politics.[13] In 1952 reform candidates Emile Wagner and Theodore Shepard won, giving the school board a total of five independent and reform-minded members.[14]

After teaching for more than forty years, Reed retired in 1951, at age sixty-nine. She confided to friends that she felt somewhat "more comfortable" about retiring because of the new makeup of the school board and the recent resignation of her old nemesis, Superintendent Bourgeois. "At last the schools of our City have had a break: We have a School Board that wants to do right things in right ways, is really interested in broad human values, and has already cleared the deck for major action. . . . Thus, now, I have hopes—high hopes for our schools."[15] She pointed out to writer Harnett Kane that, given the makeup of the new school board, "many tensions have been eased, many sore spots are healing and there is more opportunity to sit around the table and talk things out. I don't want to paint too rosy a picture because there are still problems galore."[16]

   In her perspective on the school board, Reed continued to hold some of the Progressive views from her college days. She assumed that taking politics out of the schools would overcome many of the worst problems in the educational system. Like the Progressives of the early twentieth century, latter-day liberals in New Orleans hoped that governance by disinterested experts would bring efficiency and progress to the schools. What they failed to realize was that without a political base, without allies in city or state government, the board would be unable to cope with a crisis—and a crisis was just around the corner. The board, while greatly improved from its old "machine" days, was too weak and too isolated to deal effectively with massive resistance to court-ordered school desegregation.[17]

Despite increased cooperation between the two locals and success in electing their candidates to the board, many union members were wary of real integration, and the white and black unions continued to maintain their separate identities. Veronica Hill, president of the League of Classroom Teachers, Local 527, in New Orleans, served as regional vice-president of the national AFT when the Supreme Court handed down the *Brown* decision, and the American Federation of Teachers directed all segregated locals to submit reports explaining why they had not been integrated. In 1956, as head of the AFT committee on the integration of local unions, Hill spoke at the federation's national convention. "The AFT must stand tall," Hill declaimed. "It can

no longer tolerate segregated locals." Hill received a standing ovation, the resolution in favor of integration passed, and the national convention voted to
suspend any locals that would not take steps to integrate.[18] The AFT required
all locals to be fully integrated by January 1, 1958, or lose their charters.

In Atlanta, the white local, which had no history of cooperation with its
black counterpart, decided to sever its connection with the national organization rather than integrate. After several warnings, the AFT in 1956 suspended
the New Orleans white local until it integrated its membership. Opposed to
integration, but anxious to retain its national affiliation, Local 353 sought an
extension of the national deadline for integration.

In the meantime, Local 353 submitted the issue of integration to a vote by
the paid-in-full membership of 1955–56 and 1956–57, and it prefaced this secret ballot with an explanation of both sides of the question. The Classroom
Teachers' Federation explained that it was not taking a stand on integration
per se, but was concerned, rather, with "the improvement of the welfare of
New Orleans teachers." The advantages of integrating the union, it said, lay in
keeping the union charter and thus the support of the national labor movement. The two locals might also gain a stronger bargaining position on issues
such as salaries, which were the same for both groups, if they combined their
forces.[19]

In the negative column, Local 353 pointed out, the "mores and sentiments
of the people of the South make it imperative that integration ordered by the
Supreme Court of the United States be a delayed process." Both races needed
more education if integration was to work, the Teachers' Federation stated.
"There are too many pitfalls ahead if integration is rushed into without planning and an intensified educational program set up and participated in by
both races concerned." Second, the union speculated, since the Louisiana legislature opposed integration, perhaps the Teachers' Federation should take the
same stand. Finally, Local 353 feared that supporting integration would cause
it to lose members and "weaken our organization to the point where we would
cease to function effectively."[20]

The last point was perhaps the crucial one for Reed and many of her colleagues. Regardless of how they felt about integration, many union members
realized that their organization might well fall apart under the weight of mandated integration, and they were not willing to take the risk. Better to have
a segregated union and lose national affiliation, these members felt, than to
have no union at all. Fearing that AFT ouster would undermine the collective
strength she had spent much of her adult life trying to achieve, Reed sent a
letter to all union members in New Orleans pleading for funds to send a dele-

gation to the national AFT convention in Chicago. Reed wanted to ask for an extension of the integration deadline and for more time "to give a true picture of our teacher union here in the South." The local hoped it could persuade the national that voluntary integration would occur with time but that forcing it would destroy the local. If the AFT would revoke its time limit, 353 could keep its charter and work on integration independently.[21] In fact, both the African American and the white locals sent requests to the convention for an exemption from the national deadline.[22]

The national AFT Executive Committee refused to modify its deadline. No record remains of the CTF vote of September 4, 1957, but the result was made public. Local 353 would remain segregated. On September 20, Ruby Dowling, president of the New Orleans Classroom Teachers' Federation, wrote Carl Megel, president of the American Federation of Teachers: "Circumstances beyond our control have made it necessary for Local 353 . . . to sever its long and pleasant relationship with the AFT. . . . We regret exceedingly that this drastic action has been thrust upon us and hope that you will understand the difficult position that is unfortunately ours at this time."[23]

The League of Classroom Teachers, Local 527, which agreed to accept any teacher regardless of race, became the only official AFT local in New Orleans. The old 353 continued in existence without national affiliation and merged with NOPSTA in 1968. In 1973 the dream of an integrated union finally was realized when white and African American teachers joined in the United Teachers of New Orleans. Reed continued to work with Local 527 while remaining a member of the former 353 and NOPSTA. Veronica Hill, head of 527, remained on good terms with Reed, and the two worked together on many issues, particularly those dealing with teachers' salaries. In 1967 Hill wrote Reed thanking her for her participation on a joint salary committee. "Be assured," Hill told her old friend, "that you are due and will I trust always receive the warmest appreciation for the never failing work you have always done for our group over the years."[24]

Outside of her efforts to postpone the AFT's integration deadline, Reed played no significant role in the school desegregation crisis. She seems to have stayed out of the controversy as much as possible. Her silence on the subject stands in stark contrast to her strong and vocal opinions on other subjects involving the schools. She had never had any qualms about supporting unpopular causes, even ones that jeopardized her job.

Part of the explanation for Reed's hesitant stand on union integration involves her concern about keeping the union viable, with as many members as possible. She knew that the "old diehards," as she called them, would never vote to integrate. In addition, her political and social heritage may have prevented her from becoming an ardent integrationist. As a southerner with origins in plantation country, steeped in the traditions of segregated progressivism, she may have been unable to take the leap that activism on behalf of integration would have required from someone of her age and background.

Traditionally, southern liberals conspicuously avoided the race problem. Reed had reached her political maturity during the New Deal, and in keeping with the southern liberal tradition of avoiding direct confrontation with Jim Crow laws while working for the amelioration of conditions for blacks, she and other New Dealers had tried to make segregation a concern secondary to other issues. But history had overtaken southern liberals. Segregation was the only issue that mattered in the mid-1950s South. Reed had to choose between a firm stand for integration while watching her union die and a compromise that prolonged segregation but preserved the union, albeit without national affiliation. Reed chose the latter, and as a result separated herself from the revolution exploding around her.[25]

Reed had a hard time getting used to her absence from the classroom. "To be sitting here on a Friday morning, lingering over a second cup of coffee makes me feel quite grand. I can't exactly get used to it. Somehow [I] feel like I'm cutting school," she wrote a friend. "However, I'm as smiling as the proverbial basket-of-chips. Wish that I had taken up the cigarette habit so I could blow smoke wreaths and lazily watch them disappear."[26]

Her friends and acquaintances, however, knew that Reed would not retire from her unofficial job as a teacher advocate and legislative liaison. Tulane president Rufus Harris wrote Reed that he doubted "if you will 'enjoy a well earned rest.' I am sure that you will continue to be active in improving educational standards throughout your lifetime. I know that will give you the most pleasure and I wish you every success."[27] In fact, Reed remained actively involved in union activities for twenty years after her retirement. "I suppose I'll stay harnessed and rarely hitched," Reed wrote. "It's far more normal, I think, to go ahead as usual and remain tremendously occupied."[28] When the press reported that Reed would now live in West Feliciana Parish, she wrote a colleague that the newspapers were wrong. Although, she said, "West Feliciana really possesses 'the peace of the fields and the inspiration of the hills' . . . I prefer the hurly-burly of people and the city. About all I've done is to leave the classroom. I live to work and the Federation has so much to be done."[29]

Reed's colleagues missed her. As one Fortier teacher wrote, "It doesn't seem right not to wait downstairs in the hall to hear some of your snappy comments. We were all pretty busy most of the time and probably too riled up over lots of little things to show our affection and regard for you, but you know you have a warm place in our hearts and just always will be part of the Fortier faculty." [30] Yvonne LaPrime never forgot Reed's role in helping her keep her job after she married. Congratulating Reed on her retirement, LaPrime told her that she had "read with regret that you were leaving us. . . . I shall always be grateful for your advice and words of encouragement on many different occasions. Because of these things I have a job today." [31]

Reed continued to take an active role in teacher issues, particularly those involving retirement benefits, until illness forced her to withdraw from active service to the teachers in 1972. During the years from 1924 to 1972, she did not miss a single session of the state legislature. She worked as NOPSTA's legislative chairman until her retirement from public life, and even into her nineties she served as executive secretary for the organization. In "retirement" Reed remained outspoken and active. In 1964 the New Orleans press reported that her "stern scolding" of the school board had convinced it to declare a school holiday to allow teachers to lobby for a pay raise in Baton Rouge. The holiday, Reed said, would show the governor that "there's a tiger in our tank down here." [32] The board complied, and when Reed got to Baton Rouge she was just as forceful in her argument to Governor John McKeithen. After he told the teachers that he could not support a pay hike, Reed retorted, "Governor, Can't is dead. We've buried him and been to his funeral." The teachers got their raise. [33]

After forty-five years as a teacher and nearly seventy years on the front lines of battle for teachers' rights, academic freedom, and quality education, Reed died on May 8, 1978, at the age of ninety-six. She had served as both spokeswoman and role model for teachers for more than fifty years. Because of her willingness to make her own life and politics public, Reed helped break down strictures against women taking active and vocal roles in public life. Beginning with her first battle for equal pay for women and continuing through her fights on behalf of married teachers and normal-school graduates, her efforts to increase pay and improve working conditions for all teachers were relentless. She did not hesitate to challenge those in power, whether it was her principal, the school superintendent, or the governor.

Teachers as well as others outside the profession—particularly women in community organizations and clubs—understood the importance of her work and supported her. Reed was also one of the links between the union and the outside world, keeping in touch with New Orleans leaders as well as with teachers and union members throughout the country. Indeed, for many people Reed symbolized the union as no one else could.

In her outspoken assaults on male power, Reed can be seen as one of many southern "ladies" who asserted themselves in public at a time when such behavior was looked upon by some as unladylike or worse. Reed herself recognized the humor and the truth of the ladyhood myth when she wrote a friend upon her retirement, "I trust it's not out of keeping with my years to feel as gay as the bright birds on this little Audubon print. . . . I hope it's not unladylike—so many pleasant things are!"[34]

Reed was a feminist long before the revival of the women's movement in the late 1960s. Yet her feminism was different than that of the younger generation. There is no record that Reed supported the Equal Rights Amendment, in either its first or its second incarnation. She probably would not have supported some of the younger feminists' attitudes or styles of dress. Unlike her sister Roberta, who wore slacks whenever possible, Reed maintained her ladylike dresses and always, *always* wore a hat. In some ways, she looked like the incarnation of southern ladyhood; it was her behavior that contradicted the myth. Reed never absorbed the cultural restraints of proper feminine behavior. Perhaps her temper caused her to forget what she must have known about proper decorum for a lady. A lady would not have kicked textbooks around the room with her principal watching, nor would she have lost her temper in front of the school board or made derogatory remarks about state legislators. "I'm from St. Francisville," Reed once told a reporter. "I grew up sixteen miles from an insane asylum and sixteen miles from a penitentiary, so I can handle myself with the Legislature."[35]

Reed was one of the "awakened women in the South" who had "the courage to buck the status quo."[36] She accepted the fact that her views often alienated people, but she didn't seem to care. "When a person is a fighter, she gets on the blacklist of principals," she said in her nineties. "People will say nice things about her, but she can't get ahead. They tried to promote me to principal once—I think to try to shut me up—but I'd rather be a common garden-variety-type teacher."[37] As her colleague Veronica Hill said of Reed, "The dignity of the teaching profession was something very special to Sarah. She was always in the forefront defending the worth of the teacher in public."[38]

Reed's work as a lobbyist in the state legislature was crucial to the success of bills favoring teachers. She was a familiar figure in the state capitol and a favorite of press photographers who often captured her confronting a state representative, senator, or the governor himself or observing a legislative session wearing one of her famous hats. "Everybody from the humblest employee to the governor knows Sarah, even the Greyhound bus driver whose bus Sarah so often rode, leaving at four o'clock in the morning to attend an early committee meeting in Baton Rouge," Hill told Sarah's friends who had gathered for a luncheon in her honor, even though Reed herself was too ill to attend. "Every bill introduced into the Legislature pertaining to teachers Sarah studied carefully and worked diligently for the defeat or passage, whichever was for the best interests of the teachers," Hill concluded.[39]

Reed's efforts in support of academic freedom and quality education did not go unnoticed by her students or by her colleagues. One former student wrote her after reading of her retirement, "I want you to know, Mrs. Reed, that you have always been an inspiration to me. You aroused in me my intense interest in civic affairs, government and economics. I can say this in all truthfulness — that you among all my high school teachers had more to do with the awakening of my interests in this line of study than any other teacher I ever had."[40]

Reed inspired CTF executive secretary Hasket Derby, as well. As he wrote her in 1949, "Sarah, I want you to know that I have always looked with wonder, as others have, on the work you have done for the teachers, with awe on the miracles you and Roberta have wrought against insurmountable and impossible obstacles. I have learned much from watching your brilliant intelligence and unflinching determination at work, and all tempered with such an extraordinary and shrewd sense of tactics. And I have enjoyed the comradeship immensely."[41]

Even those who strongly disagreed with her politics admired her dedication to her work. The American Legion, with whom Reed had fought over such issues as loyalty oaths, presented her, in 1955, with its Americanism Award for "service to the community and outstanding contribution in the perpetuation of the American way of life." When the Legionnaires first told her about the award, Reed said she thought "they were joking."[42]

In the years following her retirement, many organizations honored Reed with awards and certificates of appreciation. Tulane recognized the fiftieth, sixtieth, and seventieth anniversaries of her graduation from Newcomb and Tulane. Loyola gave her a citation of respect on the occasion of the fiftieth anniversary of her law degree. On her ninetieth birthday, New Orleans Mayor Moon Landrieu gave her the key to the city, and three years later a certificate of merit. Also on her ninetieth birthday, Governor John McKeithen made her an Honorary Colonel. "I'm not sure what that means," Reed commented, "But maybe I can bring the boys home from Vietnam sooner."[43]

Somehow, through all of her dealings with New Orleans and Louisiana politics, Reed remained "an incurable optimist," as she told an interviewer on her ninetieth birthday. She continued to look to the future and welcomed change.[44] In 1978 the United Teachers of New Orleans expressed appreciation for all of her work in protecting teachers' rights. At her death, the Louisiana House of Representatives sent a special resolution of condolence to her family, citing Reed's efforts to improve education in the state, noting her attendance at every session of the legislature for fifty-three years, and acknowledging the debt that students and teachers owed her for all of her work in their behalf. Reed's family, which consisted by that time of only Roberta, her niece Nora Marsh, and Nora's husband and daughter, instituted a "Good Citizen" award that they planned to confer annually on the New Orleans public high school senior who had the greatest potential to make a contribution to public life and who demonstrated characteristics of good citizenship. "Our Sarah's faith in the future and in the young people who will form it was strong and abiding. We feel that this Award is an expression of that faith and will continue the work to which she dedicated her life," the family said in announcing the award.[45] In 1988 the Orleans Parish School Board dedicated the Sarah Towles Reed High School in her honor.

Sarah Reed was buried at Ouida plantation. Roberta died in 1982 and was buried beside her. After Roberta's death, a friend of both sisters wrote their niece, "They were truly remarkable ladies, with keen intellects and so many dimensions which superseded the lives and thoughts of the vast majority of their contemporaries."[46] Reed would have appreciated the sentiment, no doubt, but she probably would have preferred a line from her obituary in the States-Item: "She won a reputation as a firebrand early in her career and never lost it."[47]

NOTES

Introduction

1. Yvonne LaPrime to STR, Aug. 2, 1951, Sarah Towles Reed Collection, Archives and Manuscripts Division, Earl K. Long Library, University of New Orleans (hereafter referred to as STR coll.).

2. Civil District Court for the Parish of Orleans, State of Louisiana, no. 249–672, Division "E," Docket 3, *Mrs. Sarah Towles Reed versus Orleans Parish School Board,* Answer, STR coll.

3. Anne Firor Scott, *The Southern Lady: From Pedestal to Politics, 1830–1930* (Chicago: University of Chicago Press, 1970), 122–23.

4. Kathryn Kish Sklar, "Hull House in the 1890s: A Community of Women Reformers," in *Unequal Sisters: A Multi-Cultural Reader in U.S. Women's History,* ed. Ellen Carol DuBois and Vickie L. Ruiz (New York: Routledge, 1990), 110–11. See also Sklar, *Florence Kelley and the Nation's Work: The Rise of Women's Political Culture, 1830–1900* (New Haven: Yale University Press, 1995).

5. Sonora Towles Marsh, *The Story of a Good Citizen: Sarah Towles Reed* (Privately published, n.d.), 4, STR coll.

I. Resisting Ladyhood

1. Minnie Ker Ringgold, *My Ancestors* (Shreveport, La.: Privately published, 1941).

2. Mary Susan Ker papers, 1785–1958, preface, Southern Historical Collection, University of North Carolina Library, Chapel Hill, N.C. (hereafter referred to as MSK papers). William Barrow Floyd, *The Barrow Family of Old Louisiana* (Lexington, Ky.: Privately published, 1963), 53–54.

3. Floyd, 48–54; Annie Ker to Sallie Ker, Jan. 30, 1873, STR coll.

4. *U.S. Manuscript Census,* 1850 and 1860.

5. *The Virginia Magazine of History and Biography,* June 1901, STR coll.; STR, notes, n.d., STR coll.

6. Joseph Karl Menn, *The Large Slaveholders of Louisiana, 1860* (New Orleans: Pelikan Publishing, 1964), 230; *Manuscript Census,* 1870.

7. John T. Towles to Mrs. Groesbeck, Oct. 20, 1867, STR coll.

8. John T. Towles to R. B. Groesbeck, March 23, 1872, STR coll.

9. William Ivy Hair, *Bourbonism and Agrarian Protest: Louisiana Politics 1877–1900* (Baton Rouge: Louisiana State University Press, 1969), 45; West Feliciana Parish notarial records, book S, p. 407.

10. Marsh, 1.

11. West Feliciana Parish notarial records, Book U., p. 3., Feb. 27, 1886.

12. Sarah Towles Reed, "Your Remembrance Has Kept Me 90 Years Young!" n.d., STR coll.

13. Marsh, 3.

14. STR, "Your Remembrance," STR coll.

15. Marsh, notes, n.d., STR coll.

16. Evans Wall to STR, n.d., STR coll.

17. Marsh, 3.

18. STR to "My darling Papa and Mamma," April 6, 1908, STR coll.

19. Ibid.

20. STR to Mary Ker, July 1898, MSK papers.

21. STR to "Chicago Dears," June 10, 1965, STR coll.

22. STR to Dr. John Ker Towles, n.d., STR coll.

23. Floyd, 52.

24. "Grandma" to Sarah, Feb. 12, 1905, STR coll.

25. Sarah Ker Towles ("Mother") to STR ("My Own Dear Child"), April 9, 1908, STR coll.

26. STR, "Your Remembrance," STR coll.

27. Rose Foster to Mary Ker, Aug. 10, 1902, MSK papers, quoted in Cita Cook, "Growing Up White, Genteel, and Female in Turn-of-the-Century Natchez: A New South Friendship Network," paper given at the Southern Historical Association meeting, Nov. 2, 1990.

28. STR to Mary Ker, Oct. 29, 1899, MSK papers. As historian Cita Cook has pointed out, and as Sarah confirms (at least at this age), most of the young women in the genteel classes who came of age between 1885 and 1915 "internalized a general air of snobbery and a respect for their parents' opinions that would keep them from developing a romantic interest in men their families would consider inappropriate" (Cook, 12).

29. STR to Mary Ker, Oct. 29, 1899, MSK papers.

30. Frank Percy to STR, March 28, 1900, STR coll.

31. Frank Percy to STR, Feb. 8, 1900, STR coll.

32. Sarah Ker Towles to Mary Ker, March 30, 1899, MSK papers.

33. Donald E. DeVore and Joseph Logsdon, *Crescent City Schools: Public Education in New Orleans, 1841–1991* (Lafayette: Center for Louisiana Studies, University of Southwestern Louisiana, 1991), 90, 102.

34. Marsh, 4.

35. STR to Mary Ker, Oct. 29, 1899, MSK papers.

36. George M. Reynolds, *Machine Politics in New Orleans, 1897–1926* (New York: Columbia University Press, 1936), 14–15.

37. Edward F. Haas, *Political Leadership in a Southern City: New Orleans in the Progressive Era, 1896–1902*, McGinty Publications, Department of History (Rustin: Louisiana Tech University, 1988), 27–36, 93. Joseph G. Dawson III, *The Louisiana Governors: From Iberville to Edwards* (Baton Rouge: Louisiana State University Press, 1990), 190.

38. STR to Mary Ker, Oct. 29, 1899, MSK papers.

39. DeVore and Logsdon, 103.

40. Ibid., 90–91; Raymond Oscar Nussbaum Jr., "Progressive Politics in New Orleans, 1896–1900" (Ph.D. diss., Tulane University, 1974), 18–19.

41. Lynn Gordon, *Gender and Higher Education in the Progressive Era* (New Haven: Yale University Press, 1990), 173.

42. Karen Kingsley, "Designing for Women: The Architecture of Newcomb College," *Louisiana History* 35 (Spring 1994): 184.

43. Newcomb Bulletin 1901–1902, *The H. Sophie Newcomb Memorial College for Women, 1901–1902* (New Orleans: Tulane University, 1902), 21, Newcomb College Archives, Tulane University, New Orleans (hereafter referred to as Newcomb Archives).

44. Barbara Miller Solomon, *In the Company of Educated Women* (New Haven: Yale University Press, 1985), 62.

45. STR, unpublished essay, n.d., STR coll.

46. "Frank" to STR, March 18, 1903, STR coll.

47. Newcomb College transcript, Newcomb Archives; Dan Towles to STR, April 2, 1903, STR coll.

48. *New Orleans Times-Picayune* clipping, n.d., STR coll.

49. Alice R. Geoffray, "Sarah Towles Reed: The Story of a Remarkable Woman," term paper, University of New Orleans, 1985, 3.

50. Gordon, 8.

51. Ibid., 95; Solomon, 95.

52. Albert to "Aunt Mamie," July 1, 1902, MSK papers.

53. Newcomb College Program, Annual Class Night 1903, STR coll.

54. Solomon, 62.

55. Gordon, 18; Solomon, 56–57. See also David Tyack and Elisabeth Hansot, *Learning Together: A History of Coeducation in American Schools* (New Haven: Yale University Press, 1990), 146–47; Shirley Marchalonis, *College Girls: A Century in Fiction* (New Brunswick, N.J.: Rutgers University Press, 1995), 30.

56. STR, Newcomb notes and papers, n.d., STR coll.

57. STR, "The Advantages and Disadvantages of Physical Culture as Illustrated by a Dialogue in the Gym Dressing-Room," Newcomb notes and papers, n.d., STR coll.

58. Scott, *The Southern Lady*, 122.

59. Scott, *Making the Invisible Woman Visible* (Urbana: University of Illinois Press, 1984), 216.

60. Scott, *The Southern Lady,* 153–56.

61. Solomon, 112.

62. Anne Firor Scott, in *The Southern Lady,* notes that Caroline Merrick, in her position as president of the WCTU, was hailed by her contemporaries as the first woman in the state to address important social issues in public (145).

63. Carmen Lindig, *The Path from the Parlor: Louisiana Women, 1879–1920* (Lafayette: Center for Louisiana Studies, University of Southwestern Louisiana, 1986), 57; Elna Green, "The Rest of the Story: Kate Gordon and the Opposition to the Nineteenth Amendment in the South," *Louisiana History* 33 (Spring 1992): 172.

64. Caroline E. Merrick, *Old Times in Dixie Land: A Southern Matron's Memories* (New York: Grafton Press, 1901), 124.

65. Ibid., 224.

66. Ibid.; Marjorie Spruill Wheeler, *New Women of the New South: The Leaders of the Woman Suffrage Movement in the Southern States* (New York: Oxford University Press, 1993), 51–52.

67. Lindig, 132.

68. Lydia E. Frotscher, clipping and scrapbook, class of 1904, Newcomb College Scrapbook Collection, Newcomb Archives, SCR-013.

69. STR, untitled manuscript, Newcomb notes and papers, n.d., STR coll.

70. Newcomb Bulletin 1901–1902, 4–5, Newcomb Archives; Pamela Tyler, *Silk Stockings and Ballot Boxes: Women and Politics in New Orleans, 1920–1965* (Athens: University of Georgia Press, 1996), 15. Sarah's enthusiasm for Newcomb remained with her throughout her life. She was for many years the chairman of her class for the alumnae association, and when she had the opportunity, she encouraged her female students to attend her alma mater. One such student wrote during her senior year to thank Sarah for pointing her in the direction of Newcomb: "This year, Miss Towles, when I thought of leaving this lovely place then you and your after-school talks over at High School kept on haunting my memory and it's been since then that I have wanted to tell you how I am thankful to you above everyone else for having encouraged me in going to Newcomb. It meant everything to me." Jeanne L. to "Dear Miss Towles," April 18, 1918, STR coll. See also Lindig, 76; Lori D. Ginzberg, *Women and the Work of Benevolence: Morality, Politics, and Class in the Nineteenth-Century United States* (New Haven: Yale University Press, 1990); Nancy A. Hewitt, *Women's Activism and Social Change, Rochester, New York, 1822–1877* (Ithaca: Cornell University Press, 1984); Karen J. Blair, *The Clubwoman as Feminist: True Womanhood Redefined, 1868–1914* (New York: Holmes and Meier, 1980); Ruth Bordin, *Women and Temperance: The Quest for Power and Liberty, 1873–1900* (Philadelphia: Temple University Press, 1981).

71. Tyler, 15.

72. Kathryn W. Kemp, "Jean and Kate Gordon: New Orleans Social Reformers, 1898–1933," *Louisiana History* 24 (Fall 1983): 390.

73. Dewey Grantham, *Southern Progressivism: The Reconciliation of Progress and Tradition* (Knoxville: University of Tennessee Press, 1983), 200.

74. Speech by STR, STR notes, n.d., STR coll.

75. Susan Ware, *Beyond Suffrage: Women in the New Deal* (Cambridge: Harvard University Press, 1981), 19–20.

76. *Newcomb Arcade* 1 (1909): 34; Katy Coyle, "Women of Sympathy and Truth: Newcomb Women and the Communities They Forged, 1887–1918," typescript, Tulane University, Dec. 4, 1992, 12; Brandt V. B. Dixon, *A Brief History of the H. Sophie Newcomb Memorial College, 1887–1919: A Personal Reminiscence* (New Orleans: Housen Printing, 1928), 136.

77. STR to Mary Ker, May 7, 1898, MSK papers.

78. Ibid.

79. Solomon, 116.

80. Ware, 19.

81. Scott, *Making the Invisible Woman Visible*, 66. As Scott reminds us, "Changes in the key values of a society or a social group rarely occur as sharp and sudden breaks with the past. . . . With broad social attitudes, the old and new often exist not only side by side, but also cut across each other."

82. *Newcomb Arcade*, June 1909, 34.

83. Scott, "Education and the Contemporary Woman," in *Making the Invisible Woman Visible*, 357.

84. Ware, 25.

85. Frank Percy to STR, March 2, 1899, STR coll.

86. Blanche Wiesen Cook, *Eleanor Roosevelt*, vol. 1, *1884–1933* (New York: Viking, 1992), 12. See also Barbara Welter, "The Cult of True Womanhood," *American Quarterly* 18 (1966): 151–74.

87. STR to friend (letter lacking address), n.d., STR coll.

88. Tulane transcript, STR coll.

89. Solomon, 127.

90. "Mamma" to "My Dear Child," Oct. 24, 1906, and Dec. 3, 1906, STR coll.; Kate to STR, March 11, 1908, STR coll.; Father to STR, Jan. 18, 1907, STR coll.; Alice Ker to Nora Marsh, July 7, 1978, STR coll. (this letter includes a biographical sketch of STR by Alice Ker Barber).

91. Martha H. Swain, "The Public Role of Southern Women," in *Sex, Race and the Role of Women in the South*, ed. Joanne V. Hawks and Sheila L. Skemp (Jackson: University Press of Mississippi, 1983), 38.

92. STR to "Sis," June 27, 1918, STR coll.

93. Ibid.

94. STR to "Dearest Uncle," ca. summer 1918, STR coll.; Marsh, 4.

95. J. K. Towles to STR ("Dear Sallie"), Dec. 10, 1912, STR coll.

96. STR to "Dearest Homefolks," Aug. 22, 1919, STR coll.

97. John Towles to parents, Easter Day 1919, STR coll.

98. Nora Marsh (Sara Reed's great niece), telephone interview with the author, Nov. 30, 1993.

99. John Towles to STR, n.d., STR coll.

100. Elkerna Reed, Plattenburg, La., to STR, New Orleans, May 7, 1909, STR coll.

101. Elkerna Reed to STR, n.d., STR coll.

102. Marjorie Roehl, "Woman Teacher Was Brave Fighter for Rights," *New Orleans Times-Picayune,* May 21, 1989. *New Orleans Item,* Aug. 26, 1921.

103. Alice Lusher to STR, Aug. 30, 1921, STR coll.

104. Nicholas Bauer to STR, Sept. 8, 1921, STR coll.; Orleans Parish School Board Collection, minutes of Sept. 9, 1921, Archives and Manuscripts Division, Earl K. Long Library, University of New Orleans (hereafter referred to as OPSB min.).

105. John Towles to STR, n.d., STR coll.

106. Sara J. Reed to Mrs. Towles, Oct. 24, 1921, STR coll.

107. Tania Messina, "Longtime Lobbyist, Sarah Reed," *New Orleans Magazine,* clipping, n.d., 30, STR coll.

108. Solomon, 131.

2. Equal Pay for Equal Work

1. S. Lawrason, Lawrason & Kilbourne, attorneys at law, St. Francisville, La., to Dan T. Towles, Nov. 4, 1920, STR coll.

2. Nora Marsh, interview with the author, Nov. 30, 1993; West Feliciana Parish notarial records, Book 29, p. 579.

3. STR to "Dearly Beloved Ones," Aug. 23, 1943, STR coll.

4. Marsh, 4. Although Reed did not write a history of the parish herself, she did make her research available to other historians, including Avery O. Craven. Craven to STR, Sept. 18, 1972, STR coll.

5. Nora Marsh, interview with author, April 30, 1996.

6. See Carroll Smith-Rosenberg, "The Female World of Love and Ritual: Relations between Women in Nineteenth-Century America," *Signs* 1 (Fall 1975): 1–29.

7. STR to "Dearly Beloved Ones," Aug. 23, 1943, STR coll.

8. Nancy F. Cott, *The Grounding of Modern Feminism* (New Haven: Yale University Press, 1987), 117.

9. Linda K. Kerber, *Women of the Republic: Intellect and Ideology in Revolutionary America* (Chapel Hill: University of North Carolina Press, 1980), 120.

10. Christine Stansell, *City of Women: Sex and Class in New York, 1789–1860* (Urbana: University of Illinois Press, 1987), 20–21. For different views on the effects of the American Revolution on the status of women, see Kerber, *Women of the Republic,* and Mary Beth Norton, *Liberty's Daughters: The Revolutionary Experience of American Women, 1750–1800* (Boston: Little and Brown, 1980).

11. Steven Hahn, *The Roots of Southern Populism: Yeoman Farmers and the Transformation of the Georgia Upcountry, 1850–1890* (New York: Oxford University Press, 1983), 253.

12. Eric Foner, *Free Soil, Free Labor, Free Men: The Ideology of the Republican Party before the Civil War* (New York: Oxford University Press, 1970), 16–17.

13. Cott, *The Grounding of Modern Feminism,* 118–19.

14. Mary A. Hill, *Charlotte Perkins Gilman: The Making of a Radical Feminist, 1860–1896* (Philadelphia: Temple University Press, 1980), 295.

15. Cott, *The Grounding of Modern Feminism,* 119.

16. Dorothy M. Brown, *Setting a Course: American Women in the 1920s* (Boston: Twayne Publishers, 1987), 79.

17. Philip S. Foner, *Women and the American Labor Movement: From World War I to the Present* (New York: Free Press, 1980), 299.

18. Brown, 85.

19. William H. Chafe, *The Paradox of Change: American Women in the Twentieth Century* (New York: Oxford University Press, 1991), 75; Stanley J. Lemons, *The Woman Citizen: Social Feminism in the 1920s* (Urbana: University of Illinois Press, 1973), 139.

20. Lemons, 140.

21. Ibid.

22. Chafe, 76.

23. Brown, 85.

24. STR, notes, n.d., STR coll.

25. Catherine Clinton, *The Other Civil War: American Women in the Nineteenth Century* (New York: Hill and Wang, 1984), 128.

26. *Faculty,* May 1936, STR coll.

27. Marsha Wedell, *Elite Women and the Reform Impulse in Memphis, 1875–1915* (Knoxville: University of Tennessee Press, 1991), 15.

28. Tyack and Hansot, 159–160.

29. Grace C. Strachan, "Equal Pay for Equal Work: An Argument in Behalf of Women Teachers," in *Woman's "True" Profession: Voices from the History of Teaching,* ed. Nancy Hoffman (Old Westbury, N.Y.: Feminist Press, 1981), 295.

30. Ibid., 300.

31. Ibid., 297.

32. Ibid., 160. See also Wayne J. Urban, *Why Teachers Organized* (Detroit: Wayne State University Press, 1982), 91–92.

33. Tyack and Hansot, 163. Rosalind Rosenberg argues that early-twentieth-century American society was plagued by a "pervasive fear of feminization. . . . As the economic change of a rapidly industrializing society brought social dislocation, Americans clung ever more tenaciously to their most basic assumptions about sexual identity and fought any changes in accepted sex-role divisions." Rosenberg, "The Academic Prism: A New View of American Women," in *Women of America: A History,* ed. Carol Ruth Berkin and Mary Beth Norton (Boston: Houghton Mifflin, 1979), 321.

34. Solomon, 128.

35. Marjorie Murphy, *Blackboard Unions: The AFT and the NEA, 1900–1980* (Ithaca: Cornell University Press, 1990), 61, 73.

36. DeVore and Logsdon, 147.

37. *New Orleans Times-Democrat,* Oct. 15, 1913, quoted in DeVore and Logsdon, 373.

38. DeVore and Logsdon, 149.

39. OPSB min., April 23, 1914.

40. OPSB min., June 27, 1919; DeVore and Logsdon, 163.

41. DeVore and Logsdon, 149.

42. Ibid., 122; Lindig, 57.

43. DeVore and Logsdon, 138.

44. Ibid., 162.

45. Tyler, 31.

46. DeVore and Logsdon, 164.

47. Nancy Cott, "Feminist Politics in the 1920s: The National Woman's Party," *Journal of American History* 71 (June 1984): 47.

48. Sara M. Evans, *Born for Liberty: A History of Women in America* (New York: Free Press, 1989), 187, 193; Glenna Matthews,*The Rise of Public Woman: Woman's Power and Woman's Place in the United States, 1630–1970* (New York: Oxford University Press, 1992), 180.

49. Evans, 187; Lemons, 63, 184.

50. Lemons, 184.

51. Bennett H. Wall, ed., *Louisiana: A History* (Arlington Heights, Ill.: Forum Press, 1984), 367.

52. Matthews, 183.

53. *New Orleans Item,* Sept. 21, 1921. Southern Conservative League, *A Brochure of the Laws of Louisiana Affecting the Rights of Women* (Shreveport, La., n.d.).

54. National Woman's Party, *Louisiana Laws Discriminating against Women* (Washington, D.C., 1922).

55. *New Orleans Times-Picayune,* Oct. 13, 1921.

56. OPSB min., April 8, 1921.

57. *New Orleans Item,* Oct. 14, 1921.

58. Ibid., Oct. 13, 1921.

59. Ibid., Oct. 15, 1921.

60. *New Orleans Times-Picayune,* Oct. 15, 1921.

61. Ibid.

62. OPSB min., Oct. 14, 1921; Sarah Reed manuscript drafts, STR coll.

63. *New Orleans Item,* Oct. 15, 1921.

64. OPSB min., Oct. 14, 1921.

65. Ibid.

66. *New Orleans Item,* Oct. 15, 1921.

67. *New Orleans Times-Picayune,* Oct. 15, 1921.

68. Ibid., Oct. 19, 1921.

69. Ibid., Oct. 23, 1921; *New Orleans Item,* Oct. 23, 1921.

70. *New Orleans Item,* Oct. 23, 1921.

71. Ibid., Oct. 26, 1921.

72. *New Orleans Times-Picayune,* Oct. 30, 1921.

73. Ibid., Nov. 6, 1921.

74. OPSB min., Feb. 2, 1922; June 11, 1922; June 23, 1922; July 11, 1922; Jan. 26, 1923; April 27, 1923.

75. OPSB Committee of the Whole Minutes, April 26, 1923, Archives and Manuscript Division, Earl K. Long Library, University of New Orleans (hereafter referred to as OPSB Committee Min.).

76. OPSB min., April 27, 1923.

77. Ibid.; *New Orleans Times-Picayune*, April 28, 1923.

78. DeVore and Logsdon, 168.

79. OPSB min., May 8, 1923.

80. OPSB min., Aug. 22, 1924.

81. OPSB Committee Min., Sept. 9, 1924.

82. OPSB min., Sept. 12, 1924.

83. OPSB min., Nov. 25, 1924.

84. OPSB Committee Min., Nov. 25, 1924.

85. OPSB Committee Min., Jan. 9, 1925.

86. OPSB min., March 13, 1925.

3. "I Belong in the Ranks"

1. Papers of the executive board of NOPSTA, 1925–26, STR coll.

2. Incorporation papers of NOPSTA, Jan. 11, 1933, STR coll.; *Quartee*, Feb. 1931, STR coll.

3. Murphy, 61. For a discussion of the Atlanta union, see Joseph W. Newman, "Mary C. Barker and the Atlanta Teachers' Union," in *Southern Workers and Their Unions, 1880–1975: Selected Papers, The Second Southern Labor History Conference, 1978,* ed. Merl E. Reed, Leslie S. Hough, and Gary M. Fink (Westport, Conn.: Greenwood Press, 1981), 60–79.

4. OPSB min., Feb. 12, 1926.

5. Brief by W. Catesby Jones, attorney at law, New Orleans, March 31, 1926, STR coll.

6. OPSB Committee Min., April 7, 1925.

7. DeVore and Logsdon, 168.

8. STR, notes, n.d., STR coll.

9. OPSB min., Feb. 12, 1926.

10. DeVore and Logsdon, 162.

11. OPSB min., Feb. 12, 1926; STR, notes, n.d., STR coll.

12. *New Orleans Times-Picayune*, Feb. 13, 1926.

13. Ibid., March 7, 1926.

14. STR, notes, n.d., STR coll.

15. *New Orleans Times-Picayune*, March 7, 1926.

16. Ibid., March 9, 1926.

17. Brief by W. Catesby Jones, attorney at law, New Orleans, March 31, 1926, STR coll.

18. Publicity committee of NOPSTA, Oct. 20, 1926, STR coll.

19. *New Orleans Times-Picayune,* March 7, 1926; publicity committee of NOPSTA, Oct. 20, 1926, STR coll.

20. OPSB Committee Min., April 6, 1926.

21. *New Orleans Times-Picayune,* May 25, 1926.

22. OPSB min., Sept. 10, 1926.

23. Mary Maher, chairman of the subcommittee Public School Alliance, to Friends of Public Schools, Oct. 22, 1926, OPSB general files, Archives and Manuscript Division, Earl K. Long Library, University of New Orleans.

24. *New Orleans Item-Tribune,* Oct. 17, 1926; Amy H. Hinrichs to Augustine Aurianne, president of NOPSTA, Oct. 28, 1926, STR coll.

25. *New Orleans Times-Picayune,* Oct. 28, 1926.

26. STR, notes, n.d., STR coll.

27. STR, notes, n.d., STR coll.

28. Broadside, 1926, STR coll.

29. NOPSTA treasurer's report, Nov. 23, 1926, STR coll.

30. Augustine Aurianne to NOPSTA Fellow Members, Feb. 25, 1927, STR coll.

31. James Fortier to Amy Hinrichs, Sept. 13, 1927, STR coll.

32. STR to NOPSTA, March 25, 1927, STR coll.

33. OPSB min., Feb. 11, 1927.

34. OPSB min., April 8, 1927.

35. OPSB min., May 13, 1927.

36. STR, *New Orleans Teacher,* Nov. 1928, STR coll.

37. *New Orleans Teacher,* Nov. 1928, STR coll.; Annual Report of the President for the Term of Office Feb. 1927–Nov. 1928, NOPSTA, STR coll.

38. Emma Pritchard Cooley to STR ("My Dear Mrs. Reed"), July 21, 1927, STR coll.

39. STR to Griffith, Oct. 8, 1927, STR coll. The play was indeed the thing when the NOPSTA Dramatic Club put on a production of a light-hearted skit about the salary fight. "The Frightful Four," written by Reed, starred Reed, NOPSTA president Amy Hinrichs, and other members of the association. In the play, "Redman" Reed, one of the frightful four, acts as the American Indians' spokesman before the Oracle (the school board), to solicit help for an Indian child named Little Salary Schedule, who has suffered for many years from various cuts. "Oh, I can't stand any more cuts!" Little Salary moans. "In '24 I lost a hand; in '25 a leg; this year I'll lose my whole right arm; and if I'm a good child I'm promised another cut next year, and next year, and next year. *(Weeps).* Oh, when will it stop! Where will it stop!" Finally, Little Salary is adopted by Amendment 8. When an Indian tells Amendment 8 that a newspaper has called her a pig because she just squeaked through, she replies, "Well, the little animal that squeaks through the gate brings home the bacon—the bacon of 10 months' pay." See STR, "The Frightful Four," New Orleans Public School Teachers' Association Program and Reception, Athenaeum, April 22, year unknown, STR coll.; STR notes, n.d., STR coll.

40. *New Orleans Teachers,* Nov. 1928, STR coll.: Annual Report of the President for the Term of Office Feb. 1927–Nov. 1928, NOPSTA, STR coll.

41. OPSB min., Sept. 10, 1926.

42. High School Teachers' Association to OPSB, Dec. 9, 1927, STR coll.; OPSB min., Dec. 9, 1927.

43. STR drafts, n.d., STR coll.

44. OPSB min., Dec. 9, 1927.

45. Mary L. Kolb, corresponding secretary, N.O. High School Association, to Fellow Members, n.d., STR coll.

46. OPSB min., June 20, 1928.

47. OPSB min., July 6, 1928; text of Act 110, STR coll.

48. *New Orleans Teacher,* February 1929, STR coll.

49. Amy Hinrichs to STR, May 31, 1928, STR coll.

50. STR to "My Dear Colleagues," June 5, 1928, STR coll.

51. Notation on letter from Amy Hinrichs to A. J. Tete, May 31, 1928, STR coll.

52. OPSB min., Feb. 8, 1929; opinion of Attorney General Saint given to OPSB, Sept. 12, 1928, OPSB general files.

53. STR, drafts, n.d., STR coll.

54. STR, drafts, n.d., STR coll; OPSB min., Aug. 10, 1928.

55. OPSB min., Sept. 6, 1929; Statement of the Position of the OPSB Relative to Act no. 110 of 1928, STR coll.

56. Reed, notes and drafts, n.d., STR coll.

57. *Quartee,* May-June, 1932, p. 43, STR coll.

58. *Quartee,* April 1932, STR coll.

59. STR, notes, n.d., STR coll.

60. NOPSTA flier, n.d., STR coll.

61. *New Orleans Teacher,* Feb. 1929, STR coll.; *Quartee,* April 1932, p. 38, STR coll.

62. *New Orleans Times-Picayune,* Sept. 7, 1929.

63. NOPSTA broadside, n.d., STR coll.

64. OPSB min., May 14, 1930.

65. *New Orleans Times-Picayune,* May 15, 1930, p. 3.

66. Editorial, *Quartee,* April 1932, p. 38, STR coll.; STR, "Rime and Reason of Act 110," *Quartee,* May-June 1932, p. 41, STR coll.

67. *New Orleans Teacher,* Nov. 1928, STR coll.

68. OPSB min., June 14, 1929.

4. Depression Years

1. Theo Hotard, farewell speech, Dec. 8, 1944, STR coll.

2. Betty Field, "The Politics of the New Deal in Louisiana, 1933–1939" (Ph.D. diss., Tulane University, 1979), 52.

3. Douglas L. Smith, *The New Deal in the Urban South* (Baton Rouge: Louisiana State University Press, 1988), 22, 25.

4. *Quartee,* Jan. 1932, STR coll.

5. *Quartee,* March 1932, STR coll.

6. Ibid. See Tyack et al., *Public Schools in Hard Times,* chapter 3, for other educators' protests against reductions in school funding and expenditures during the Depression.

7. *Quartee,* April 1932.

8. Roman Heleniak, "Local Reaction to the Great Depression in New Orleans, 1929–1933," *Louisiana History* 10 (Fall 1969): 303; OPSB min., Aug. 12, 1932.

9. OPSB min., Aug. 12, 1932.

10. A. J. Tete, secretary, OPSB, to STR, Sept. 1, 1932, STR coll.

11. J. K. Byrne and Co., certified public accountant, to the New Orleans Public School Teachers Association, Sept. 13, 1932, STR coll.

12. *New Orleans Item,* June 15, 1933, and March 28, 1933; *New Orleans Times-Picayune,* May 13, 1933.

13. OPSB min., May 12, 1933.

14. Murphy, 134.

15. Ibid., 136. See also Tyack et al., *Public Schools in Hard Times.*

16. Murphy, 136; Tyack et al., *Public Schools in Hard Times,* 39.

17. Smith, 23.

18. Anne to STR and Roberta, Dec. 4, 1932, STR coll.

19. OPSB min., Sept. 2, 1933.

20. OPSB min., Oct. 13, 1933.

21. Schoolmasters Club, 1933–35, Sept. 19, 1933, OPSB Box 147, Archives and Manuscripts Division, Earl K. Long Library, University of New Orleans (hereafter referred to as Schoolmasters Club).

22. Schoolmasters Club, Sept. 18, 1934; April 2, 1935; April 9, 1938; April 11, 1939; April 2, 1940; May 19, 1941.

23. OPSB min., Aug. 23, 1934.

24. OPSB min., Sept. 14, 1934.

25. *New Orleans Item,* Oct. 12, 1934.

26. OPSB min., Oct. 10, 1935; March 13, 1936; April 14, 1936; July 10, 1936; March 12, 1937.

27. OPSB min., Oct. 11, 1935; *New Orleans Morning Tribune,* Oct. 12, 1935.

28. Michael Provosty, city attorney, to A. J. Tete, secretary, OPSB, June 27, 1931, OPSB general files.

29. OPSB min., Oct. 9, 1931.

30. *Quartee,* Nov. 1931.

31. Ibid.

32. Emery C. Lively, "The Corps Must Protect Itself," *Quartee,* May–June 1932.

33. A. P. Harvey, Central Trades and Labor Council of New Orleans, to Miss Allie Mann, Atlanta, Ga., April 29, 1934, STR coll.

34. William Edward Eaton, *The American Federation of Teachers, 1916–1961: A History of the Movement* (Carbondale: Southern Illinois University Press, 1975), 68.

35. Allie Mann, vice-president, American Federation of Teachers, to STR ("My dear Mrs. Reed"), May 5, 1934, STR coll.

36. Murphy, 4.

37. Paula O'Conor, "Grade-School Teachers Become Labor Leaders: Margaret Haley, Florence Rood, and Mary Barker of the AFT," *Labor's Heritage* (Fall 1995): 8.

38. Margaret Haley, "Why Teachers Should Organize: Address to the National Education Association," in *Woman's "True" Profession: Voices from the History of Teaching,* ed. Nancy Hoffman (New York: Feminist Press, 1981), 293–94.

39. Murphy, 73.

40. Ibid., 61.

41. Patricia A. Schmuck, "Women School Employees in the United States," in *Women Educators: Employees of Schools in Western Countries,* ed. Patricia A. Schmuck (Albany: State University of New York Press, 1987), 162; Barbara J. Harris, *Beyond Her Sphere: Women and the Professions in American History* (Westport, Conn.: Greenwood Press, 1978), 142.

42. *New Orleans Item,* Aug. 28, 1948.

43. Murphy, 67–68.

44. Bernard A. Cook and James R. Watson, *Louisiana Labor: From Slavery to "Right-to-Work"* (Lanham, Md.: University Press of America, 1985), 200, 205.

45. Alan Dawley, *Struggles for Justice: Social Responsibility and the Liberal State* (Cambridge: Harvard University Press, Belknap Press, 1991), 372.

46. Ibid., 372–73.

47. Cook and Watson, 204.

48. Flynt, "The New Deal and Southern Labor," in *The New Deal and the South,* ed. James C. Cobb and Michael Namorato, 66.

49. Richard H. Pells, *Radical Visions and American Dreams: Culture and Social Thought in the Depression Years* (Middletown, Conn.: Wesleyan University Press, 1973), 232.

50. New Orleans Classroom Teachers' Federation, Local 353, American Federation of Teachers 1937–38 Year Book, STR coll.

51. Newman, "Mary C. Barker and the Atlanta Teachers' Union," 70.

52. Eaton, 171.

53. American Federation of Teachers, Monthly Reports to the Secretary-Treasurer, Sept. 1935–June 1956, AFT Archives, Archives of Labor and Urban Affairs, Walter P. Reuther Library, Wayne State University, Detroit, Michigan. In December 1935 the CTF had 26 members. The figure rose dramatically in 1947 to 225, declining again to 182 in June of 1956. Its largest membership was 425, achieved in July of 1953.

54. OPSB min., March 10, 1944.

55. Michael K. Honey, *Southern Labor and Black Civil Rights: Organizing Memphis Workers* (Urbana: University of Illinois Press, 1993), 76.

56. Flier from Roberta Towles, chairman, Organization Committee, to the teachers of New Orleans, n.d., STR coll.

57. Constitution and By-Laws of the New Orleans Classroom Teachers' Federation,

Local 353, AFT, effective Aug. 1, 1938, STR coll.; Edith Rosepha Ambrose, "Sarah Towles Reed and the Origins of Teacher Unions in New Orleans," M.A. thesis, University of New Orleans, 1991, 44.

58. STR notes, n.d., STR coll.

59. Guy Clifford Mitchell, "Growth of State Control of Public Education in Louisiana" (Ph.D. diss., University of Michigan, 1942), 394–95; T. Harry Williams, *Huey Long* (New York: Knopf, 1969), 359, 897; *New Orleans Times-Picayune*, May 15, 1936.

60. Mitchell, 410.

61. Michael Kurtz and Morgan D. Peoples, *Earl K. Long: The Saga of Uncle Earl and Louisiana Politics* (Baton Rouge: Louisiana State University Press, 1990), 83.

62. *New Orleans Times-Picayune*, June 9, 1936.

63. Mitchell, 405.

64. *New Orleans Times-Picayune*, June 19, 1936; *Faculty*, June 1936, STR coll.; Mitchell, 411.

65. *Baton Rouge Morning Advocate*, June 27, 1936.

66. Myrtle H. Rey, President's Annual Report, NOPSTA, 1936, STR coll.

67. *Faculty*, June 1936, STR coll.

68. Naomi to STR ("Dear Sarah"), July 11, 1936, STR coll.

69. Legislative letter, May 30, 1938, STR coll.

70. Circular no. 792 by state Department of Education of Louisiana to parish superintendents and members of parish school boards, March 24, 1937, OPSB general files, Box 32.

71. Myrtle H. Rey, president, CTF, to All Labor Bodies, May 26, 1938, STR coll.

72. Statement to the press from CTF, n.d., STR coll.

73. Manfred Willmer, executive secretary, to Major James E. Crown, editor, *New Orleans States,* Jan. 24, 1938, STR coll.

74. Manfred Willmer to Governor Richard W. Leche, Jan. 31, 1938, STR coll.

75. Resolutions, Louisiana State Federation of Labor Convention, April 6, 1938, STR coll.

76. Manfred Willmer to Irvin R. Kuenzli, secretary-treasurer, American Federation of Teachers, Chicago, Feb. 4, 1938, STR coll.

77. Manfred Willmer to Robert L. Soule, secretary, Central Trades and Labor Council, March 31, 1938, STR coll.; L. W. Ferguson to Manfred Willmer, Feb. 10, 1938, STR coll.

78. Statement to the press from CTF, n.d., STR coll.

79. Myrtle H. Rey, President's Annual Report, NOPSTA, 1936, STR coll.

80. Vivian Bourgeois to STR ("Dear Mrs. Reed"), Oct. 2, 1936, STR coll.

81. *NOPSTA News,* March 1937, STR coll.

82. OPSB min., May 14, 1937; *New Orleans Times-Picayune*, May 15, 1937.

83. *New Orleans Times-Picayune*, May 18, 1937.

84. Ibid., May 23, 1937; *New Orleans Item,* May 23, 1937.

85. Ibid.

86. OPSB min., June 11, 1937; Aug. 13, 1937.

87. *NOPSTA News,* March 1937, STR coll.

88. New Orleans Classroom Teachers' Federation, Local 353, 1937–38 Yearbook, STR coll.; Mitchell, 467; *New Orleans Times-Picayune,* March 1, 1938.

89. *New Orleans Times-Picayune,* Aug. 18, 1937.

90. Ibid., Aug. 10, 1940.

91. Ibid.

92. Louis G. Riecke, STR et al., to Board of Liquidation, Sept. 3, 1940, STR coll.

93. *New Orleans Item,* Aug. 29, 1940

94. *New Orleans Times-Picayune,* Aug. 30, 1940.

95. Ibid., Sept. 10, 1940.

96. *New Orleans Item,* Sept. 10, 1940.

97. OPSB min., Sept. 14, 1940.

98. *New Orleans Times-Picayune,* Sept. 28, 1940.

99. Schoolmasters Club, Executive Meeting Records, Sept. 17, 1940.

100. *New Orleans Item,* June 1, 1941.

101. Hale Boggs to STR, June 4, 1941, STR coll.

102. *New Orleans Item,* June 1, 1941.

103. STR to "Dearest Dears," Dec. 25, 1944, STR coll.

5. Women's Issues

1. Henry B. Curtis, assistant city attorney, to OPSB, June 26, 1929, OPSB general files, Box 6; "Rules and Regulations of OPSB and of the New Orleans Public Schools, 1930," OPSB general files, Box 1.

2. Claudia Goldin, *Understanding the Gender Gap: An Economic History of American Women* (New York: Oxford University Press, 1990), 161.

3. Ibid., 170.

4. Ibid., 171.

5. Ware, 79; Alice Kessler-Harris, *Out to Work: A History of Wage-Earning Women in the United States* (New York: Oxford University Press, 1982), 263. There were other discriminatory policies in New Deal agencies and programs, particularly in the wages paid women in the CWA and the WPA. Lower wages for women were also incorporated into some NRA codes.

6. Goldin, 166; Philip Foner, 298.

7. Chafe, 116.

8. *New Orleans Times-Picayune,* July 31, 1933.

9. Phillip Foner, 298; Chafe, 116.

10. Chafe, 116.

11. Goldin, 162.

12. Chafe, 116.

13. Lemons, 231.

14. Frances R. Donovan, *The Schoolma'am* (New York: Frederick A. Stokes, 1938; reprint, Arno Press, 1974), 61 (page references are to reprint edition).

15. OPSB min., Dec. 23, 1921.

16. OPSB min, Sept. 22, 1922.

17. Henry B. Curtis, assistant city attorney, to OPSB, June 26, 1929, OPSB general files, Box 6.

18. Ruling by Peyton R. Sandoz, assistant attorney general, State of Louisiana Department of Education, Baton Rouge, circular no. 2685, to parish superintendents and presidents of parish school boards, Nov. 1, 1929, OPSB general files, Box 18.

19. A. J. Tete, secretary, OPSB, to T. H. Harris, state superintendent of education, Nov. 13, 1929, OPSB general files, Box 18.

20. T. H. Harris, state superintendent of education, State of Louisiana, to A. J. Tete, secretary, OPSB, Nov. 15, 1929, OPSB general files, Box 18. It is important to note that Orleans Parish was usually exempt from such rulings.

21. "Are Married Women Better Teachers?" *Quartee,* Nov. 1932, STR coll.

22. Letter from Paul Judge, Nov. 12, 1932, in *Quartee,* Dec. 1932, STR coll.

23. Letter from Helen Furness, Nov. 9, 1932, in *Quartee,* Dec. 1932, STR coll.

24. Marjorie Roehl, "Schoolmarm image downed when 4 win battle to marry," *New Orleans Times-Picayune,* May 16, 1987.

25. Gladys Castel de Ben, Yvonne Crespo LaPrime, Nellie Pearce Cupit, and Martha Wegert Comeaux to OPSB, OPSB general files, Box 18.

26. STR, notes, n.d., Yvonne LaPrime papers, OPSB-147, Box 2, Archives and Manuscript Division, Earl K. Long Library, University of New Orleans (hereafter referred to as LaPrime papers).

27. Edward Rightor to Mrs. Bernard LaPrime, Oct. 2, 1936, OPSB general files, Box 2.

28. Roehl, "Schoolmarm image," *New Orleans Times-Picayune,* May 17, 1987.

29. Lessley P. Gardinor, second assistant attorney general, to Hon. A. J. Tete, secretary, OPSB, Oct. 7, 1936, OPSB general files, Box 18.

30. Roehl, "Schoolmarm image," *New Orleans Times-Picayune,* May 17, 1987.

31. LaPrime papers, Box 2; OPSB min., March 12, 1937.

32. State of Louisiana, Civil District Court for the Parish of Orleans, *State of Louisiana ex rel. Mrs. Annabelle Robertson Miester v. Orleans Parish School Board,* OPSB general files.

33. Secretary, OPSB, to Edward M. Robert, city attorney, OPSB general files, Box 18.

34. *NOPSTA News,* March 1937, STR coll. In two other cases regarding the married teachers' law, the women were not as fortunate as Miester. Anna Calamari and Evelyn M. McMurray also married in the summer of 1936, but they had officially resigned from their jobs, as was the custom at the time, and then, after the ruling in favor of married teachers, had attempted to regain their positions. The state supreme court, to whom the two women appealed after losing their suits in lower courts, ruled that they had waited too long to ask for reinstatement and were not, therefore, entitled

to their former positions. In the Calamari case, the school had had to hire another teacher following her resignation since, the school board argued, "The public school must remain open. This important function cannot be made to depend on the whim of a teacher in choosing the time she will legally assert her rights." Calamari and McMurray's attorney unsuccessfully argued that the school board had illegally kept the married teacher rule "long after it was made illegal by the 1934 statute, and it was not until midwinter of 1936 that the Board finally yielded to the law. In the meantime, the illegal rule had trapped the relators. They were out of their life work by the illegal acts of the defendants." LaPrime papers, Box 2; OPSB min., March 12, 1937.

35. Alma Repak, President, Student Body, Margaret C. Hanson Normal School, Class of 1936, to OPSB, Sept. 2, 1936, OPSB general files, Box 18.

36. Information in regard to married teachers up to and including Jan. 1, 1940, OPSB general files, Box 18.

37. *New Orleans Item,* March 12, 1942.

38. Mrs. Howard R. Lively, corresponding secretary of New Orleans Council of Parent-Teacher Associations, to OPSB, Nov. 21, 1946, OPSB general files, Box 20; OPSB to Mrs. Howard R. Lively, March 14, 1947, OPSB general files, Box 20.

39. Lionel J. Bourgeois, Superintendent, to Mr. Earnest C. Ball, Superintendent, Memphis City Schools, Dec. 7, 1948, OPSB general files, Box 32.

40. Mrs. Howard Lively to OPSB, March 28, 1947, OPSB general files, Box 20.

41. Mrs. C. W. Chachare Jr., President, New Orleans Council of PTA, to Robert Haas, School Board Office, Jan. 30, 1950, OPSB general files, Box 20; Julianne R. Haspel, Legislation Chairman, National Council for Jewish Women, to OPSB, Feb. 2, 1950, OPSB general files, Box 20.

42. Goldin, 163.

43. STR, notes, n.d., STR coll.

44. OPSB min., Sept. 10, 1937.

45. Manfred Willmer to CTF school representatives, Nov. 28, 1937, STR coll.; Myrtle H. Rey, president, CTF, to Governor Richard W. Leche, Chairman, State Budget Committee, Sept. 10, 1938 (see salary schedule), STR coll.

46. Myrtle Rey, president, CTF, to Governor Richard W. Leche, Sept. 10, 1938, STR coll.

47. OPSB min., Nov. 12, 1937.

48. OPSB min., Dec. 10, 1937.

49. Ibid.

50. High School Association to OPSB, OPSB general files, Box 20; Rose M. Porretto, President, New Orleans High School Association, to "Fellow High School Teachers," Nov. 16, 1942, STR coll. The High School Association, a self-proclaimed conservative organization dedicated to salary increases for degree teachers, is not to be confused with the High School Teachers' Association.

51. Manfred Willmer to Dr. Alonzo G. Grace, April 25, 1938, STR coll.

52. CTF Yearbook, 1938, STR coll.

53. Myrtle H. Rey, President, CTF, to Governor Richard W. Leche, Sept. 10, 1938, STR coll.

54. OPSB min., Jan. 14, 1938; Feb. 11, 1938; April 8, 1938; May 13, 1938; Sept. 9, 1938; Oct. 17, 1938; Aug. 8, 1941; March 13, 1942; April 10, 1942; June 12, 1942.

55. OPSB min., Feb. 11, 1938.

56. OPSB min., Oct. 14, 1938.

57. Essay, n.d., no author, STR coll.

58. STR, notes, n.d., STR coll.

59. OPSB min., March 13, 1942; April 10, 1942.

60. Lionel J. Bourgeois, Assistant Superintendent, Orleans Parish Public School System, to the President and Members of the Louisiana State Senate and to the Speaker and Members of the Louisiana State House of Representatives, June 22, 1942, STR coll.; A. J. Tete, Superintendent, OPSB, and Lionel J. Bourgeois, Assistant Superintendent, OPSB, to the President and Members of the Louisiana State Senate, n.d., STR coll.

61. Flier, "The New Orleans Classroom Teachers Federation Urges You to Support and Vote for HB 498," n.d., STR coll.

62. *New Orleans Times-Picayune,* June 24, 1942.

63. Ibid., June 26, 1942.

64. Martin Ten Hoor, chairman, Educational Committee, New Orleans Association of Commerce, to Hon. Jacob S. Landry, Chairman, Committee on Education–Senate, July 1, 1942, STR coll.

65. STR, notes, n.d., STR coll.

66. OPSB min., Oct. 15, 1942.

67. *New Orleans Times-Picayune,* Oct. 18, 1942.

68. Mitchell, chapter 10.

69. Haas, chapter 1; Alan Brinkley, *Voices of Protest: Huey Long, Father Coughlin and the Great Depression* (New York: Vintage, 1983), 68–69.

70. Cook and Watson, 212.

71. STR, notes, n.d., STR coll.

6. Segregation and Subterfuge

1. *New Yorker,* Sept. 6, 1993, p. 31; Adam Fairclough, *Race and Democracy: The Civil Rights Struggle in Louisiana, 1915–1972* (Athens: University of Georgia Press, 1995), x.

2. Alonzo Hamby, *Beyond the New Deal: Harry S. Truman and American Liberalism* (New York: Columbia University Press, 1973), 8.

3. Fairclough, 44.

4. Ibid., 51.

5. Ibid.

6. In fact, Roberta Towles was the first woman elected to the West Feliciana Police Jury. She served on the jury from 1932 until 1956, when she declined to run for reelection.

7. H. C. Nixon to A. L. Wirin, American Civil Liberties Union, August 27, 1937, Lee papers, Box 2, folder 19.

8. Statements by Irene Scott, Reuben Cole, and Willie D. Scott, notarized by Herman Midlo, notary public, July 2, 1937, Lee papers.

9. George A. Dreyfous and M. Swearingen, "Report to the Executive Committee of the LLPCR on Investigations in West Feliciana Parish" (hereafter referred to as Dreyfous and Swearingen Report), Oct. 17, 1937, Harold N. Lee papers, Box 1, folder 4, Howard-Tilton Library, Tulane University (hereafter referred to as Lee papers).

10. Dreyfous and Swearingen Report; H. C. Nixon to A. L. Wirin, American Civil Liberties Union, August 27, 1937, Lee papers, Box 1, folder 5; Fairclough 51–53.

11. Veronica Hill, interview by author, April 1, 1996, Gretna, La.

12. *New Orleans Item,* Sept. 1, 1937; Hill, interview by author; OPSB Committee Min., Aug. 31, 1937. A slightly different version of this incident appeared in the *New Orleans Times-Picayune,* Sept. 1, 1937.

13. *New Orleans Times-Picayune,* Sept. 1, 1937.

14. George B. Tindall, *The Emergence of the New South, 1913–1945* (Baton Rouge: Louisiana State University Press, 1967).

15. Veronica Hill, interview by Al Kennedy, videotape, June 23, 1994.

16. Eaton, 62; Record Book and Minutes of the New Orleans Federation of Classroom Teachers, AFT Local 527 (hereafter referred to as AFT Local 527 min.), Sept. 9, 1937, Box 7, William H. Davis Sr. Collection, Archives and Manuscripts Division, Earl K. Long Library, University of New Orleans (hereafter referred to as Davis coll.).

17. AFT Local 527 min., Sept. 23, 1937, Davis coll.

18. Ibid., Oct. 8, 1937.

19. Ibid., Sept. 23, 1937.

20. Fairclough, 63.

21. Manfred Willmer to Irvin R. Kuengli, Feb. 4, 1938, interview by author, April 1, 1996, Gretna, La.

22. Willmer to Kuengli, Feb. 4, 1938, STR coll.; Fairclough, 6.

23. Fairclough, 37; DeVore and Logsdon, 197–98.

24. Fairclough, 23.

25. Resolution of the New Orleans Council of Parents and Teachers for an Impartial Study of the New Orleans School System, STR coll.

26. Willmer to Kuengli, Feb. 4, 1938, STR coll.

27. DeVore and Logsdon, 170–71.

28. Ibid., 175–76.

29. The Citizen's Planning Committee for Public Education in New Orleans, *Tomorrow's Citizens: Summary Report on the New Orleans Study and Program of Public Education,* 1940, STR coll.

30. Ibid.

31. Dewey W. Grantham, *The South in Modern America: A Region at Odds* (New York: Harper Perennial, 1994), 165.

32. Linda Reed, *Simple Decency & Common Sense: The Southern Conference Movement, 1938–1963* (Bloomington: Indiana University Press, 1991), xx.

33. Gunnar Myrdal, *An American Dilemma: The Negro Problem and Modern Democracy* (New York: Harper & Row, 1944), 49, quoted in Tindall, 636.

34. Reed, 20; OPSB Report to the President and Members, December 9, 1938, STR coll.

35. *New Orleans Times-Picayune*, Nov. 24, 1938.

36. Pamela Jean Turner, "Civil Rights and Anti-Communism in New Orleans, 1946–1965" (M.A. thesis, University of New Orleans, 1981), 5.

37. *New Orleans Times-Picayune*, Nov. 24, 1938.

38. Salmond, 155.

39. Tindall, 637; Grantham, *The South in Modern America*, 164.

40. Patricia Sullivan, *Days of Hope: Race and Democracy in the New Deal Era* (Chapel Hill: University of North Carolina Press, 1996), 105.

41. Dewey W. Grantham, *The Life and Death of the Solid South: A Political History* (Lexington: University Press of Kentucky, 1988), 11.

42. Morton Sosna, *In Search of the Silent South: Southern Liberals and the Race Issue* (New York: Columbia University Press, 1977), 63.

43. Eaton, 69; Lawrence A. Cremin, *American Education: The Metropolitan Experience, 1876–1980* (New York: Harper & Row, 1988), 199.

44. Tindall, 563–564; Liva Baker, *The Second Battle of New Orleans: The Hundred-Year Struggle to Integrate the Schools* (New York: HarperCollins, 1996), 57–59; See also Mark V. Tushnet, *The NAACP's Legal Strategy against Segregated Education, 1925–1950* (Chapel Hill: University of North Carolina Press, 1987).

45. *The Voice of the New Orleans League of Classroom Teachers, Local 527*, Alexander Pierre Tureaud papers, Amistad Research Center, Tulane University, New Orleans; Hill, interview by author.

46. Baker, 56.

47. DeVore and Logsdon, 210; OPSB min., May 9, 1941; *New Orleans Times-Picayune*, May 10, 1941.

48. *New Orleans Times-Picayune*, May 10, 1941; *New Orleans Item*, May 10, 1941; Baker, 57.

49. *The Voice*, Tureaud papers.

50. *New Orleans Item*, June 1, 1941.

51. Baker, 62.

52. *New Orleans Times-Picayune*, June 20, 1941.

53. Baker, 63.

54. Raphael Cassimere Jr., "Equalizing Teachers' Pay in Louisiana, *Integrated Education* 15 (July-August 1977), 6.

55. A. P. Tureaud to Thurgood Marshall, July 22, 1942, Tureaud papers.

56. Thurgood Marshall to A. P. Tureaud, June 19, 1942, Tureaud papers.

57. Ibid., July 6, 1942.

58. *New Orleans Times-Picayune,* Aug. 20, 1942; *New Orleans States,* Sept. 2, 1942; OPSB min., Sept. 11, 1942; Tushnet, 98; Judgment by U.S. District Court, Eastern District of Louisiana, Judge Wayne G. Borah, in re *McKelpin vs. OPSB and A. J. Tete, Superintendent of Schools.*

59. Louisiana Teachers Association, Baton Rouge, May 13, 1943, STR coll.; Baker, 63.

60. D. E. Byrd, president, NAACP, to Hon. Sam H. Jones, Governor of Louisiana, June 14, 1943, STR coll.

61. Special Bulletin of the Public School Council on Education, July 1943, STR coll., Box 22; "Principles Governing Salary Schedule based on Education, Experience, Merit and Responsibility, State Board of Education, June 7, 1943, STR coll.; *New Orleans Times-Picayune,* June 6, 1943.

62. Author unknown, to "Diva of Public Education!" (STR), Nov. 28, 1944, STR coll.

63. Milton R. Konvitz, assistant special counsel to the NAACP, to A. P. Tureaud, June 15, 1943, Tureaud papers.

64. *New Orleans Item,* June 17, 1943.

65. *New Orleans Times-Picayune,* June 30, 1943.

66. Wayne J. Urban, "Old Wine, Old Bottles?: Merit Pay and Organized Teachers," in *Merit, Money and Teachers' Careers: Studies on Merit Pay and Career Ladders for Teachers,* ed. Henry Johnson (Lanham, Md.: University Press of America, 1985), 25–26.

67. *New Orleans Times-Picayune,* July 1, 1943.

68. E. R. Hester, President, LTA, to Superintendent J. E. Pitcher and Dean E.B., August 17, 1943, Rufus C. Harris papers, Howard-Tilton Library, Tulane University, New Orleans; State Board of Education, *Teachers Merit and Responsibility Resolution, 1943,* Harris papers.

69. Leon M. Wallace, president, Colored Business and Civic Association, Baton Rouge, to A. P. Tureaud, June 30, 1943, Tureaud papers, Box 8, folder 16.

70. *Baton Rouge Advocate,* July 1, 1943; *New Orleans Item,* July 1, 1943; *New Orleans Times-Picayune,* July 1, 1943.

71. *New Orleans Item,* July 2, 1943.

72. *New Orleans Item,* July 3, 1943; *New Orleans States,* July 1, 1943; Flier, "Teachers Protest Resolution," Roosevelt Hotel, July 2, 1943, STR coll.; *New Orleans Times-Picayune,* Aug. 3, 1943.

73. *New Orleans Item,* July 17, 1943.

74. *New Orleans Item,* editorial, Aug. 24, 1943.

75. STR to "Dearly Beloved Ones," Aug. 23, 1943, STR coll.

7. Challenging Authority

1. H. C. Nixon, "Liberalism in the South," *NOPSTA News,* Jan. 1937, p. 2, STR coll.

2. David Caute, *The Great Fear: The Anti-Communist Purge under Truman and Eisenhower* (New York: Simon and Schuster, 1978), 403.

3. Murphy, 96.

4. Ellen Schrecker, *No Ivory Tower: McCarthyism and the Universities* (New York: Oxford University Press, 1986), 52; Caute, 403.

5. Murphy, 97; Eaton, 27.

6. Murphy, 97.

7. American Civil Liberties Union of New York City, "Special Oaths of Loyalty for School Teachers: Memorandum of Fact and Arguments against Those Laws with Particular Reference to New York State," November 1934, Lee papers, Box 1, folder 1.

8. Irving Bernstein, *The Lean Years: A History of the American Worker, 1920–1933* (New York: Houghton Mifflin, 1960), 426–27.

9. Robert Cohen, *When the Old Left Was Young: Student Radicals and America's First Mass Student Movement, 1929–1941* (New York: Oxford University Press, 1993), 301.

10. Caute, 88–89.

11. Ibid., 349.

12. Ibid., 138.

13. Ibid.

14. Tyack et al., *Public Schools in Hard Times,* 63.

15. Schrecker, 68.

16. Tyack et al., *Public Schools in Hard Times,* 64.

17. Murphy, 179.

18. Caute, 404.

19. Schrecker, 68–69; Caute, 404.

20. Murphy, 137.

21. Communist Platform for New Orleans City Election, ca. 1934, STR coll.

22. OPSB min., May 1, May 11, 1934.

23. OPSB min., May 11, 1934.

24. OPSB min., May 11, 1934; *New Orleans Times-Picayune,* May 12, 1934.

25. *Quartee,* May-June, 1934.

26. *New Orleans Item,* Oct. 16, 1936.

27. *New Orleans Times-Picayune,* May 12, 1934.

28. *New Orleans Times-Picayune,* May 4, 1934.

29. Coalition of Patriotic Societies, Inc., to "Dear Fellow Citizens," April 1, 1937, Lee papers, Box 1, folder 3.

30. *Faculty,* publication of New Orleans Schoolmasters Club, May 1936.

31. Ibid., June 1936.

32. Myrtle H. Rey, President's Report, NOPSTA, 1936, STR coll.

33. *NOPSTA News,* May 1936, STR coll.

34. *New Orleans Times-Picayune,* June 15, 1936.

35. Schoolmasters Club min., Nov. 10, 1936.

36. *New Orleans Item,* Oct. 1, 1936.

37. New Orleans Classroom Teachers' Federation, Local 353, ATF, 1937–1938 Year Book, STR coll.

38. Unsigned letter to Hon. Frank J. Stich, May 16, 1938, Lee papers.

39. Harold Lee to James M. Britchly, Feb. 27, 1939, Lee papers, Box 1, folder 13; Harold Lee to "The Members of the League," July 9, 1938, Lee papers.

40. OPSB min., March 8, 1938.

41. Cohen, 77.

42. Alvin E. Johnson Jr. to STR, Sept. 17, 1935, STR coll.

43. Harvey Klehr, *The Heyday of American Communism: The Depression Decade* (New York: Basic Books, 1984), 275.

44. Ibid., 248.

45. David Lee Wells, "The ILWU in New Orleans: CIO Radicalism in the Crescent City, 1937–1957" (M.A. thesis, University of New Orleans, 1979), 7; Cook and Watson, 225–26.

46. William V. Moore, "Civil Liberties in Louisiana: The Louisiana League for the Preservation of Constitutional Justice," *Louisiana History* 31 (Winter 1990): 69; Turner, 7–8.

47. Unsigned, to the Members of the League, July 9, 1938, Lee papers.

48. Tindall, 527.

49. Moore, 59.

50. F. Ray Marshall, *Labor in the South* (Cambridge: Harvard University Press, 1967), 207; Cook and Watson, 227–28.

51. Cook and Watson, 228; *New Orleans States,* July 13, 1938.

52. Turner, 8.

53. *St. Louis Post-Dispatch,* Nov. 22, 1936, STR coll.

54. Moore, 62.

55. Ibid., 61.

56. *St. Louis Post-Dispatch,* Nov. 22, 1936, STR coll.

57. Ibid.

58. OPSB min., June 12, 1936; *New Orleans Times-Picayune,* June 13, 1936.

59. OPSB min., June 17, 1936.

60. OPSB min., Sept. 13, 1940.

61. *St. Francisville Democrat,* June 12, 1980.

62. *New Orleans Times-Picayune,* May 13, 1950.

63. Author unknown, memorandum relative to the transfer of Miss Roberta Towles, 3216 Upperline St., History Teacher, from Alcee Fortier High School, 5624 Freret St., New Orleans, to Charles J. Colton School, 2300 St. Claude St., New Orleans, n.d., STR coll.

64. Ibid.

65. OPSB min., Feb. 14, 1938; *New Orleans Times-Picayune,* Feb. 15, 1938; *New Orleans States,* Feb. 15, 1938.

66. Manfred Willmer, executive secretary, *New Orleans Classroom Teachers' Federation News Bulletin,* Feb. 18, 1938, STR coll.

67. *New Orleans Times-Picayune,* Feb. 16, 1938.

68. *New Orleans Item-Tribune,* March 3, 1938.

69. Eaton, 74. See also the discussion of Columbia Teachers College and progressive education in Tyack et al., *Public Schools in Hard Times,* 18–27, and Lawrence A. Cremin, *The Transformation of the School: Progressivism in American Education, 1876–1957* (New York: Knopf, 1961).

70. John R. Conniff, Principal, Alcee Fortier School, to August J. Tete, Superintendent, OPSB, Feb. 21, 1944, STR coll.

71. Tyack et al., *Public Schools in Hard Times,* 65.

72. Richard H. Pells, *Radical Visions and American Dreams: Culture and Social Thought in the Depression Years* (Middletown, Conn.: Wesleyan University Press, 1973), 118–21.

73. *Faculty,* June 1936.

74. Diane Ravitch, *The Troubled Crusade: American Education, 1945–1980* (New York: Basic Books, 1983), 105.

75. Ibid., 167.

76. Manfred Willmer to William Green, President, AFL, Washington, D.C., April 8, 1938, STR coll.

77. OPSB min., March 11, 1938.

78. OPSB min., May 13, 1938.

79. Willmer notes, n.d., STR coll.

80. Manfred Willmer, executive secretary, to Dr. Alonzo Grace, Aug. 3, 1938, STR coll.

81. Ibid.

82. J. R. Conniff to the students and faculty of Fortier High School, March 2, 1938, STR coll.

83. Willmer to Grace, Aug. 3, 1938, STR coll.

84. Ibid.

85. NOCTF to Henry Schaumburg, president, OPSB, May 13, 1938, STR coll.

86. Petition to OPSB, n.d., STR coll.; Robert L. Soule, secretary of the Central Trades and Labor Council, to Superintendent Nicholas Bauer, March 17, 1938, STR coll.

87. 1938 resolution passed by the 22nd Annual Convention of the American Federation of Teachers, Cedar Point, Ohio, Aug. 15–19, 1938, STR coll.

88. Arnold Shukotoff, Chairman, AFT, to Nicholas Bauer, Superintendent, Oct. 19, 1938, STR coll.

89. Opinions of the Attorney General, 15th Compilation and Supplements of School Laws, Aug. 26, 1938, OPSB general files.

90. NOCTF, Local 353, AFT, 1937–1938 Year Book, 121–82, STR coll.

91. Jacqueline Leonhard, interview by the author, May 30, 1996.

92. Schoolmasters' Club, April 10, 1938; May 3, 1938.

93. *Faculty,* Feb. 1937, p. 6.

94. *New Orleans Times-Picayune,* Nov. 2, 1943.

95. *New Orleans Times-Picayune,* Nov. 16, 1943.

96. T. H. Harris, State Superintendent, State Dept. of Education of Louisiana, Baton Rouge, Circular no. 961 to Parish Superintendents, Jan. 2, 1938, OPSB general files; *Baton Rouge Morning Advocate,* Feb. 1, 1938.

97. *New Orleans Times-Picayune,* Feb. 7, 1938.

98. Schrecker, 74–75.

99. Schrecker, 76; *New Orleans Item-Tribune,* November 10, 1940.

100. *New Orleans Item,* July 4, 1941.

101. Murphy, 170; *New York Sun,* Dec. 14, 1948; Caute, 432.

102. Mary Grossman to STR, Jan. 19, 1943, STR coll.; Executive Committee, Local 353, to Executive Council, AFT, Chicago, n.d. (draft of letter), STR coll.; Dale Zysman, Vice-president, Teachers Union of the City of New York, Local 5, AFT, to STR, Feb. 7, 1941, STR coll.; Eaton, 120. New York's Rapp-Coudert committee did not believe the local's protestations of innocence. When it concluded its long investigation in 1942, it denounced Local 5, now affiliated with the CIO, as "a Communist-dominated organization which has consistently followed the party line through all its twisting and turning." Although the Teachers Union continued to deny the committee's charges, a House Committee on Education and Labor agreed in 1948 that the Teachers Union was controlled by Communists.

103. *Tribune,* June 18, 1940.

104. *New Orleans Item,* January 10, 1941.

105. *New Orleans States,* July 22, 1940.

106. *New Orleans Times-Picayune,* Aug. 3, 1940.

107. Ibid., Sept. 5, 1940.

108. Kurtz and Peoples, 8.

109. *New Orleans Times-Picayune,* August 10, 1940.

110. OPSB min., Jan. 10, 1941.

111. OPSB Committee min., Sept. 24, 1940.

112. Eduard C. Lindeman, Chairman, Committee on Academic Freedom of the American Civil Liberties Union, to Henry C. Schaumburg, President, OPSB, Nov. 1, 1940, OPSB general files, Box 1.

113. *New Orleans Item,* Nov. 19, 1940.

114. Petition to the Hon. Members of the OPSB, Jan. 10, 1941, OPSB General files.

115. *New Orleans Item,* Jan. 10, 1941.

116. Ibid.

117. *New Orleans Item-Tribune,* Jan. 11, 1941.

118. *New Orleans Item,* Jan. 11, 1941.

119. Ibid.; *New Orleans Times-Picayune,* Jan. 12, 1941.

120. *NOPSTA News,* Jan. 1941; OPSB min., Jan. 10, 1941; Address of Harold Lee, n.d., OPSB general files, Box 1.

121. Louisiana League for the Preservation of Constitutional Rights, Statement in regard to the passage of the amended School Board Rule, Lee papers, Box 4, folder 1.

122. *NOPSTA News,* Jan. 1941; OPSB min., Jan. 10, 1941; *New Orleans Item-Tribune,* Jan. 11, 1941.

123. OPSB min., Jan. 10, 1941.

124. *New Orleans Times-Picayune,* Jan. 11, 1941.

125. Ibid.; Louisiana League for the Preservation of Constitutional Rights, Statement in regard to the passage of the amended School Board rule, Lee papers, Box 4, folder 1.

8. The Teachers' Federation on Trial

1. OPSB, Hearing in the Matter of the Alleged Failure of Mrs. Sarah Towles Reed, Teacher at the Fortier High School, to Adequately Stress Americanism in Her Civics Classes, 1948 transcript, p. 57, STR coll. (hereafter referred to as OPSB hearing on alleged un-Americanism).

2. OPSB Committee Min., March 11, 1941.

3. Ibid.

4. Ibid.

5. OPSB Committee Min., April 8, 1941.

6. STR to Nicholas Bauer, Superintendent, March 29, 1941, STR coll.

7. STR to President and Members of OPSB, April 21, 1941, STR coll.

8. OPSB min., March 13, 1942.

9. OPSB min., Jan. 8, 1943.

10. *New Orleans States,* Jan. 9, 1943.

11. OPSB Committee Min., Feb. 9, 1943.

12. STR to "Dearly Beloved Ones," Aug. 23, 1943, STR coll.

13. STR notes, n.d., STR coll.

14. Ibid.

15. *New Orleans Item,* Feb. 12, 1943.

16. *New Orleans Times-Picayune,* Feb. 15, 1943.

17. Civil District Court, Parish of Orleans, State of Louisiana, *State Ex. Rel. Mrs. Sarah Towles Reed v. OPSB,* Petition for Writ of Mandamus, STR coll.; *New Orleans Item,* Feb. 18, 1943; *New Orleans Times-Picayune,* Feb. 25, 1943.

18. OPSB min., Feb. 23, 1943; A. J. Tete, Superintendent, OPSB, to STR, Feb. 24, 1943, STR coll.

19. *New Orleans Item,* March 13, 1943; *State Ex. Rel. Mrs. Sarah Towles Reed v. Orleans Parish School Board,* March 1943, 248–889, OPSB general files.

20. STR notes, n.d., STR coll.

21. *New Orleans Times-Picayune,* Feb. 26, 1943.

22. *New Orleans Item,* March 9, 1943; *New Orleans Times-Picayune,* March 10, 1943.

23. *New Orleans Item,* March 13, 1943.

24. OPSB Committee Min., March 9, 1943; April 8, 1943.

25. AFT Local 527 min., March 4, 1943, Davis coll.

26. Irene Owens, President, CTF, Local 353, to President and Members, Central Trades and Labor Council, New Orleans, March 12, 1943, STR coll.

27. *New Orleans Item,* March 18, 1943.

28. *New Orleans States,* March 17, 1943.

29. OPSB min., Oct. 8, 1943.

30. *New Orleans Item,* March 17, 1943.

31. *New Orleans Item,* March 18, 1943.

32. STR to "Dearly Beloved Ones," Aug. 23, 1943, STR coll.

33. *New Orleans States,* March 30, 1943.

34. Gladys Peck to STR, Oct. 9, 1944, STR coll.

35. *New Orleans States,* March 19, 1943.

36. Jennie Roch, secretary, OPSB, to STR, March 19, 1943, STR coll.

37. *New Orleans States,* April 8, 1943.

38. *New Orleans Item,* April 1, 1943; *New Orleans Times-Picayune,* April 1, 1943.

39. *New Orleans Item,* March 19, 1943.

40. Ibid.

41. *New Orleans Times-Picayune,* May 2, 1944.

42. Petition, Fortier High School faculty, to L. H. Gosserand and Paul Habans, representing Mrs. Sarah Reed, April 27, 1944, STR coll.

43. Petition, Fortier High School students, May 3, 1944, STR coll.

44. Ibid.

45. *New Orleans Times-Picayune,* May 4, 1944.

46. *New Orleans States,* May 5, 1944.

47. *New Orleans Item,* May 3, 1944.

48. *New Orleans Times-Picayune,* May 6, 1944.

49. Extracts from Annual Report of the Principal of Alcee Fortier High School, STR coll.; Civil District Court, *Reed v. OPSB,* Answer, STR coll.

50. *New Orleans Times-Picayune,* May 4, 1944.

51. OPSB Committee Min., April 8, 1941.

52. Martin Kombar, Affidavit, Dec. 30, 1940, STR coll.; Civil District Court, *Reed v. OPSB,* Answer, STR coll.

53. Robert E. Brown, Affidavit, Dec. 30, 1940, STR coll.; Civil District Court, *Reed v. OPSB,* Answer, STR coll.

54. Edmund Brown, Affidavit, Dec. 30, 1940, STR coll.; Civil District Court, *Reed v. OPSB,* Answer, STR coll.

55. William von Phul Trufant, Affidavit, Jan. 18, 1941, STR coll.

56. John Parran and Kenneth Muller, Affidavits, Jan. 25, 1941, STR coll.; Extracts from Annual Report of the Principal of Alcee Fortier High School, STR coll.; Civil District Court, *Reed v. OPSB,* Answer, STR coll.

57. *New Orleans Times-Picayune,* July 12, 1944; *New Orleans Item,* July 12, 1944.

58. Civil District Court, Parish of Orleans, State of Louisiana, no. 249–672, Division "E," docket 3, *Mrs. Sarah Towles Reed v. OPSB,* Answer, STR coll. (hereafter referred to as Civil District Court, *Reed v. OPSB*).

59. *New Orleans Times-Picayune,* May 3, 1944.

60. Robert E. Brown, Affidavit, Dec. 30, 1940, STR coll.

61. "Citizen's Planning Committee for Public Education in New Orleans," n.d., STR coll.

62. STR, notes, n.d., STR coll.

63. STR, scrapbooks, n.d., STR coll.

64. STR, notes, n.d., STR coll.

65. Marsh, 6.

66. OPSB min., Dec. 13, 1935.

67. Ida B. Little, Superintendent, Alexander Milne Home School for Destitute Orphan Girls, to STR, Fortier High School, Nov. 24, 1944, STR coll.

68. Robert C. Biever, Camp Wheeler, Ga., to STR ("Dear Mrs. Reed"), May 21, 1943, STR coll.

69. Perry Willis, Office of the Commander, Amphibious Forces, U.S. Pacific Fleet, Okinawa, to STR, May 5, 1945, STR coll.; Guy Sparks Jr., Oxford, Ala., to STR, Sept. 17, 1945, STR coll.

70. Although there is no evidence in her collected papers to indicate when she became acquainted with progressive education, her discussions about her classroom show clearly her familiarity with the pedagogy outlined in progressive journals, especially the *Social Frontier.* For an in-depth study of progressive education, see Cremin, *The Transformation of the School.* See Larry Cuban, *How Teachers Taught: Constancy and Change in American Classrooms, 1890–1980* (New York: Longman, 1984), for an analysis of teaching practices in rural and urban schools. He summarizes his findings from the period 1890–1940 on pp. 126–38.

71. Blanche Wiesen Cook, 403–5. Both Roosevelt and Reed clearly were influenced by John Dewey, who stressed the link between democracy and education. In *Schools of Tomorrow,* Dewey wrote, "The conventional type of education which trains children to obedience and docility . . . is suited to an autocratic society. . . . If we train our children to take orders, to do things simply because they are told to, and fail to give them confidence to act and think for themselves, we are putting an almost insurmountable obstacle in the way of overcoming the present defects of our system and of establishing the truth of democratic ideals." John Dewey and Evelyn Dewey, *Schools of Tomorrow* (New York: E. P. Dutton, 1915), 303–4. Reed's approach to her classroom also closely resembles that of progressive educator Marietta Johnson, founder of the School of Organic Education in Fairhope, Ala., which opened in 1907 and which

Dewey wrote about in *Schools of Tomorrow*. See Paul Gaston, *Women of Fair Hope* (Athens: University of Georgia Press, 1984).

72. *New Orleans Times-Picayune,* April 11, 1945.

73. Court of Appeals, Parish of Orleans, State of Louisiana, *Mrs. Sarah Towles Reed, Plaintiff-Appellant vs. OPSB, Defendant-Appellee,* no. 18,202, STR coll.

74. *New Orleans Times-Picayune,* May 1, 1945.

75. Appeal from the Civil District Court for the Parish of Orleans, Division "E," Hon. Frank Stitch, Judge, STR coll.

76. *Federation Bulletin,* April-May, 1945, STR coll.

77. John Conniff to A. J. Tete, Superintendent, OPSB, Oct. 27, 1943, STR coll.

9. Cold War Politics

1. Ellen Schrecker, *The Age of McCarthyism: A Brief History with Documents* (Boston: St. Martin's Press, Bedford Books, 1994), 87–88.

2. Arthur Miller, "Why I Wrote *The Crucible,*" *New Yorker,* Oct. 21 and 28, 1996, 159.

3. Lionel J. Bourgeois, Assistant Superintendent, Instruction, OPSB, to STR, Alcee Fortier High School, May 24, 1948, STR coll.

4. Lionel J. Bourgeois to STR, May 3, 1945, STR coll.

5. *New Orleans Item,* Dec. 3, 1945.

6. Robert Griffith, *The Politics of Fear: Joseph R. McCarthy and the Senate* (Lexington: University Press of Kentucky, 1970), 11.

7. Hamby, 137.

8. Ibid.

9. Richard H. Pells, *The Liberal Mind in a Conservative Age: American Intellectuals in the 1940s and 1950s* (New York: Harper and Row, 1985) 266–67; McCullough, 551–52; Schrecker, *No Ivory Tower,* 5.

10. Howard Zinn, *Postwar America: 1945–1971* (Indianapolis: Bobbs-Merrill, 1973), 157.

11. Pells, *The Liberal Mind,* 267; Caute, 27–28.

12. Caute, 56.

13. Burns, 232.

14. Schrecker, *No Ivory Tower,* 6.

15. Pete Daniel, *Standing at the Crossroads: Southern Life in the Twentieth Century* (New York: Hill and Wang, 1986), 155; Grantham, *The South in Modern America,* 199.

16. Lionel J. Bourgeois to STR, Dec. 8, 1947, STR coll.

17. Grantham, *The South in Modern America,* 156.

18. Tindall, 633.

19. Numan V. Bartley, *The New South, 1945–1980* (Baton Rouge: Louisiana State University Press, 1995), 190–91.

20. Turner, 20.

21. Ibid., 20–21; Bartley, 189.

22. Tyler, 111.

23. Turner, 12.

24. Ibid., 22.

25. Ivor A. Trapolin, Chairman, Greater New Orleans Bureau, to STR, June 27, 1947, STR coll.

26. Honey, *Southern Labor,* 230.

27. Turner, 2.

28. Egerton, 10.

29. Editor of the *Militant Truth,* quoted in Bartley, 41.

30. Michael Honey, "Industrial Unionism and Racial Justice in Memphis," in *Organized Labor in the Twentieth-Century South,* ed. Robert H. Zieger (Knoxville: University of Tennessee Press, 1991), 147.

31. Evans, 244.

32. *New Orleans Item,* Nov. 1, 1946.

33. Gwendolyn Samuelson, Secretary, Civil Rights Defense Committee, to STR ("My Dear Friend"), n.d., STR coll.

34. *New Orleans Item,* Nov. 8, 1946.

35. Samuelson to STR, n.d., STR coll.

36. Pells, *The Liberal Mind,* 71.

37. Ibid.

38. Lionel S. Lewis, *Cold War on Campus: A Study of the Politics of Organizational Control* (New Brunswick, N.J.: Transaction Books, 1988), 49.

39. David G. McCullough, *Truman* (New York: Simon and Schuster, 1992), 667; Honey, *Southern Labor,* 250.

40. *New Orleans Times-Picayune,* July 25, 1948.

41. *New Orleans Times-Picayune,* July 26, 1948.

42. Grantham, *The Life and Death of the Solid South,* 123–24.

43. Numan V. Bartley, "The Southern Conference and the Shaping of Post-World War II Southern Politics," in *Developing Dixie: Modernization in a Traditional Society,* ed. Winfred B. Moore Jr., Joseph F. Tripp, and Lyon G. Tyler Jr. (Westport, Conn.: Greenwood Press, 1988), 193.

44. *New Orleans Times-Picayune,* Feb. 8, 1949.

45. Ibid., April 18, 1948.

46. Charles H. McCormick, *This Nest of Vipers: McCarthyism and Higher Education in the Mundel Affair, 1951–52* (Urbana: University of Illinois Press, 1989), 42.

47. *New York Times,* Oct. 21, 1948.

48. *New York Sun,* Nov. 6, 1948.

49. *New Orleans States,* May 6, 1948.

50. *New Orleans Item,* June 23, 1948; *New Orleans States,* June 22, 1948.

51. *New Orleans Times-Picayune,* June 23, 1948; *New Orleans Item,* June 23, 1948.

52. *New Orleans States,* June 18, 1948.

53. Ibid.

54. Ibid.

55. Bourgeois to STR, May 24, 1948, STR coll.

56. Edwin W. Eley, Acting Superintendent, to STR, July 23, 1948, STR coll.

57. STR to Bourgeois, July 30, 1948, STR coll.

58. Bourgeois to STR, Aug. 2, 1948, STR coll.

59. Ibid. Mistakenly, the board seems to have thought that Reed, to avoid the inevitable publicity, would accept the transfer or resign rather than face, as the superintendent put it, public "humiliation." This happened elsewhere, as Ellen Schrecker has noted, when in the post–World War II Red Scare, many teachers were quietly "let go" without a public investigation, in an attempt to avoid controversy and embarrassment for both the teachers and the schools (*No Ivory Tower,* 241).

60. *Federation Review,* Sept. 1951, p. 4.

61. P. J. Thompson Sr., Acting secretary, Central Trades and Labor Council, to Bourgeois, July 27, 1948, OPSB general files.

62. Lionel J. Bourgeois, superintendent, to the president and members of the OPSB, Aug. 9, 1948, OPSB general files.

63. Ibid.

64. *New Orleans Item,* Aug. 27, 1948.

65. Ibid.

66. OPSB hearing on alleged un-Americanism, p. 57, STR coll.

67. Monroe to Dean Vernon X. Miller, Loyola University Law School, July 31, 1948, STR coll.

68. OPSB hearing on alleged un-Americanism, p. 13, STR coll.

69. Bill Monroe, telephone interview with the author, Nov. 28, 1990.

70. OPSB hearing on alleged un-Americanism, p. 56, STR coll.

71. Ibid., 60.

72. Ibid., 68.

73. Ibid., 69.

74. OPSB hearing on alleged un-Americanism, 78.

75. Ibid., 112.

76. Ibid., 113.

77. Ibid., 41.

78. OPSB hearing on alleged un-Americanism, 95.

79. Ibid., 86.

80. Ibid., 156.

81. Ibid., 157.

82. Ibid., 159.

83. OPSB hearing on alleged un-Americanism, 180–81.

84. Ibid., 162.

85. Ibid., 164.

86. Ibid., 165.

87. Ibid.

88. OPSB min., Aug. 27, 1948; Lionel J. Bourgeois to President and Members of OPSB, Aug. 27, 1948, OPSB general files, Box 2.

89. OPSB min., Aug. 27, 1948.

90. *New Orleans Item,* Aug. 28, 1948.

91. Ibid.

92. *New Orleans Times-Picayune,* Aug. 28, 1948.

93. Ibid., Sept. 5, 1948.

94. Ibid.

95. Nancy DiMartino to STR, Aug. 31, 1948, STR coll.

96. Harnett Kane to STR, Aug. 29, 1948, STR coll.

97. Gunnar Myrdal, *An American Dilemma,* 466–73, quoted in Dan T. Carter, *Scottsboro: A Tragedy of the American South* (Baton Rouge: Louisiana State University Press, 1979), 117; Sosna, 163, and chapter 8.

10. Time Runs Out

1. Edith Rosepha Ambrose, "Sarah Towles Reed: Teacher and Activist," *Louisiana History* 37 (Winter 1996): 57–58.

2. Jonie Griffin, "'We believe that servility breeds servility . . .': The Classroom Teachers' Federation and Human Rights in New Orleans, 1925–1958," paper presented at the Southern Historical Association Meeting, Atlanta, November 1991, 11; Samson P. Bordelon, "The New Orleans Public Schools under the Superintendency of Lionel John Bourgeois," (Ph.D. diss., University of Southern Mississippi, 1996) 49.

3. Griffin, 11; OPSB min., Feb. 1951.

4. Veronica Hill, President, Local 527, to STR, Jan. 22, 1952, STR coll.

5. Veronica Hill, President, Local 527, and Irene Owens, President, CTF, to Clarence Scheps, President, OPSB, March 27, 1953, OPSB general files, Box 16; Veronica Hill to Selma Herr, Tulane University, May 7, 1953, OPSB general files; Hasket Derby to Carl Megel, President, AFT, June 1, 1954, STR coll.; Veronica B. Hill, Report on Joint Action of Locals 353 and 527, n.d., AFT Archives.

6. Derby to Megel, June 1, 1954, STR coll.

7. STR to "Dearest Dears," Dec. 25, 1944, STR coll.

8. *New Orleans States,* May 26, 1945.

9. Ibid.

10. Tyler, 163.

11. Bordelon, 233.

12. Veronica B. Hill, Report on Joint Action of Locals 353 and 527, n.d., AFT Archives; *Federation Review,* Sept. 1951, STR coll.; Hasket Derby to "School Representative," Sept. 29, 1950, STR coll.; Hasket Derby to "Federation Members," Oct. 26, 1950, STR coll.

13. Haas, *deLesseps S. Morrison,* 170.

14. Tyler, 165.

15. STR to Mr. Henson, August 24, 1951, STR coll.

16. STR to Harnett T. Kane, Aug. 24, 1951, STR coll.

17. Robert H. Wiebe, *The Search for Order, 1877–1920* (New York: Hill and Wang, 1967), 170; Morton Inger, *Politics and Reality in an American City: The New Orleans School Crisis of 1960* (New York: Center for Urban Education, 1969), 27.

18. Veronica Hill, interview with the author, April 1, 1996.

19. Eaton, 159–60; Murphy, 198–99; Meeting of Executive Board, Local 353, June 19, 1957, STR coll.

20. Meeting of Executive Board, Local 353, June 19, 1957, STR coll.

21. STR to Members of CTF, asking for donations to attend AFT convention in order to ask for extension of deadline, July 29, 1957, STR coll.

22. Meeting of Executive Board, Local 353, June 19, 1957, STR coll.

23. NOCTF ballot, Sept. 26, 1956, STR coll.; Griffin, 16; Ruby Dowling to Carl Megel, President, AFT, Sept. 20, 1957, AFT Archives.

24. Murphy, 198–99; STR to "Dear Member," July 29, 1957, STR coll.; Veronica Hill to STR, Jan. 18, 1957, STR coll.

25. Sosna, 165–66.

26. STR to Florence, Sept. 6, 1951, STR coll.

27. Rufus C. Harris to "Dear Mrs. Reed," August 6, 1951, STR coll.

28. STR to Lana ———— (illegible), Sept. 27, 1951, STR coll.

29. STR, Weyanoke, to "Fair-Maiden, Many Thanks!" Sept. 7, 1951, STR coll.

30. Josie to STR, n.d., STR coll.

31. Yvonne LaPrime to STR, Aug. 2, 1951, STR coll.

32. *New Orleans Times-Picayune,* Nov. 10, 1964.

33. *Baton Rouge State-Times,* Nov. 16, 1964; *New Orleans States-Item,* Dec. 1, 1964.

34. STR to "Fair-Maiden," Sept. 7, 1951, STR coll.

35. *New Orleans States-Item,* May 10, 1978.

36. Salmond, 157.

37. *New Orleans States-Item,* March 10, 1972.

38. Veronica Hill, Speech written for luncheon in honor of STR, n.d., STR coll.

39. Ibid.

40. Kent Courtney to STR, Aug. 9, 1951, STR coll.

41. Hasket Derby to STR, Sept. 29, 1949, STR coll.

42. *New Orleans Item,* April 22, 1951.

43. *New Orleans States-Item,* March 10, 1972.

44. STR to Alec Gifford, Channel 8, n.d. (near ninetieth birthday), STR coll.; *New Orleans States-Item,* March 10, 1972.

45. Publicity notice, n.d., STR coll.

46. William Barrow Floyd to Nora, July 2, 1982, STR coll.

47. *New Orleans States-Item,* May 10, 1978.

SELECTED BIBLIOGRAPHY

Papers and Archival Collections

American Federation of Teachers Archives. Archives of Labor and Urban Affairs. Walter P. Reuther Library, Wayne State University, Detroit.

Davis, William H., Sr. Collection (AFT Local 527). Archives and Manuscripts Division. Earl K. Long Library, University of New Orleans.

Harris, Rufus C. Papers. Howard-Tilton Library, Tulane University, New Orleans.

Ker, Mary Susan. Papers, 1785–1958. Southern Historical Collection. University of North Carolina, Chapel Hill.

LaPrime, Yvonne. Papers. Orleans Parish School Board Collection. Box 147. Archives and Manuscripts Division. Earl K. Long Library, University of New Orleans.

Lee, Harold N. Papers. Howard-Tilton Library, Tulane University, New Orleans.

Newcomb Archives. Newcomb College Center for Research on Women. Tulane University, New Orleans.

Orleans Parish School Board Collection. Archives and Manuscripts Division. Earl K. Long Library, University of New Orleans.

Reed, Sarah Towles. Papers. Archives and Manuscripts Division. Earl K. Long Library, University of New Orleans.

Schoolmasters Club, 1933–1935. Orleans Parish School Board Collection. Box 147. Archives and Manuscripts Division. Earl K. Long Library, University of New Orleans.

Tureaud, Alexander Pierre. Amistad Research Center. Tulane University, New Orleans.

Other Works

Alpern, Sara, Joyce Antler, Elisabeth Israels Parry, and Ingrid Winther Scobie, eds. *The Challenge of Feminist Biography: Writing the Lives of Modern American Women.* Urbana: University of Illinois Press, 1992.

Ambrose, Edith Rosepha. "Sarah Towles Reed and the Origins of Teacher Unions in New Orleans." M.A. thesis, University of New Orleans, 1991.

———. "Sarah Towles Reed: Teacher and Activist." *Louisiana History* 37 (Winter 1996): 31–60.

Baker, Liva. *The Second Battle of New Orleans: The Hundred-Year Struggle to Integrate the Schools.* New York: HarperCollins, 1996.

Bartley, Numan V. "The Southern Conference and the Shaping of Post – World War II Southern Politics." In *Developing Dixie: Modernization in a Traditional Society,* ed. Winfred B. Moore Jr., Joseph F. Tripp, and Lyon G. Tyler Jr., 179–97. Westport, Conn.: Greenwood Press, 1988.

Berkin, Carol Ruth. "Not Separate, Not Equal." In *Women in America,* ed. Carol R. Berkin and Mary Beth Norton. Boston: Houghton Mifflin, 1979.

Bernstein, Irving. *The Lean Years: A History of the American Worker, 1920–1933.* New York: Houghton Mifflin, 1960.

Blair, Karen J. *The Clubwoman as Feminist: True Womanhood Redefined, 1868–1914.* New York: Holmes and Meier, 1980.

Bordelon, Samson Paul. "The New Orleans Public Schools under the Superintendency of Lionel John Bourgeois." Ph.D. diss., University of Southern Mississippi, 1966.

Bordin, Ruth. *Women and Temperance: The Quest for Power and Liberty, 1873–1900.* Philadelphia: Temple University Press, 1981.

Brightman, Carol. *Writing Dangerously: Mary McCarthy and Her World.* New York: Clarkson Potter, 1992.

Brinkley, Alan. *Voices of Protest: Huey Long, Father Coughlin and the Great Depression.* New York: Vintage, 1983.

Brown, Dorothy M. *Setting a Course: American Women in the 1920s.* Boston: Twayne Publishers, 1987.

Burns, James MacGregor. *The Crosswinds of Freedom: From Roosevelt to Reagan— America in the Last Half Century.* New York: Vintage, 1990.

Bystydzienski, Jill. "Women's Participation in Teachers' Unions in England and the United States." In *Women Educators: Employees of Schools in Western Countries,* ed. Patricia A. Schmuck, 151–72, Albany: State University of New York Press, 1987.

Carpenter, Gerald. "Public Opinion in the New Orleans Street Railway Strike of 1929–1930," In *Essays in Southern Labor History: Selected Papers, Southern Labor History Conference, 1976,* ed. Gary M. Fink and Merl E. Reed, 189–207. Westport, Conn.: Greenwood Press, 1977.

Carter, Dan T. *Scottsboro: A Tragedy of the American South.* Baton Rouge: Louisiana State University Press, 1979.

Caute, David. *The Great Fear: The Anti-Communist Purge under Truman and Eisenhower.* New York: Simon and Schuster, 1978.

———. *The Fellow-Travellers: A Postscript to the Enlightenment.* New York: Macmillan, 1973.

Chafe, William H. *The Paradox of Change: American Women in the 20th Century.* New York: Oxford University Press, 1991.

Clinton, Catherine. *The Other Civil War: American Women in the Nineteenth Century.* New York: Hill and Wang, 1984.

Cobb, James C., and Michael V. Namorato. *The New Deal and the South.* Jackson: University Press of Mississippi, 1984.

Cohen, Robert. *When the Old Left Was Young: Student Radicals and America's First Mass Student Movement, 1929–1941.* New York: Oxford University Press, 1993.

Conway, Jill Kathryn. *The First Generation of American Women Graduates.* New York: Garland Publishing, 1987.

Cook, Bernard A., and James R. Watson. *Louisiana Labor: From Slavery to "Right-To-Work."* Lanham, Md.: University Press of America, 1985.

Cook, Blanche Wiesen. *Eleanor Roosevelt: Volume One, 1884–1933.* New York: Viking, 1992.

Cook, Cita. "Growing Up White, Genteel, and Female in Turn-of-the-Century Natchez: A New South Friendship Network." Paper presented at the Southern Historical Association meeting, November 2, 1990.

Cott, Nancy F. *The Grounding of Modern Feminism.* New Haven: Yale University Press, 1987.

———. "Feminist Politics in the 1920s: The National Woman's Party," *Journal of American History* 71 (June 1984): 443–68.

Coyle, Katy. "Women of Sympathy and Truth: Newcomb Women and the Communities They Forged, 1887–1918." Typescript, Tulane University, December 4, 1992.

Cremin, Lawrence A. *American Education: The Metropolitan Experience, 1876–1980.* New York: Harper & Row, 1988.

———. *The Transformation of the School: Progressivism in American Education, 1876–1957.* New York: Knopf, 1961.

Cuban, Larry. *How Teachers Taught: Constancy and Change in American Classrooms, 1890–1980.* New York: Longman, 1984.

Daniel, Pete. *Standing at the Crossroads: Southern Life in the Twentieth Century.* New York: Hill and Wang, 1986.

Dawley, Alan. *Struggles for Justice: Social Responsibility and the Liberal State.* Cambridge: Harvard University, Belknap Press, 1991.

Dawson, Joseph G. III. *The Louisiana Governors: From Iberville to Edwards.* Baton Rouge: Louisiana State University Press, 1990.

DeVore, Donald E., and Joseph Logsdon. *Crescent City Schools: Public Education in New Orleans, 1841–1991.* Lafayette: Center for Louisiana Studies, University of Southwestern Louisiana, 1991.

Dewey, John, and Evelyn Dewey. *Schools of Tomorrow.* New York: E. P. Dutton, 1915.

Dixon, Brandt V. B. *A Brief History of the H. Sophie Newcomb Memorial College, 1887–1919: A Personal Reminiscence.* New Orleans: Housen Printing, 1928.

Donovan, Frances R. *The Schoolma'am.* New York: Frederick A. Stokes, 1938. Reprint, Arno Press, 1974.

Eaton, William Edward. *The American Federation of Teachers, 1916–1961: A History of the Movement.* Carbondale: Southern Illinois University Press, 1975.

Egerton, John. *Speak Now against the Day: The Generation before the Civil Rights Movement in the South.* New York: Knopf, 1994.

Evans, Sara M. *Born for Liberty: A History of Women in America.* New York: Free Press, 1989.

Fairclough, Adam. *Race and Democracy: The Civil Rights Struggle in Louisiana, 1915–1972.* Athens: University of Georgia Press, 1995.

Field, Betty. "The Politics of the New Deal in Louisiana, 1933–1939." Ph.D. diss., Tulane University, 1973.

Floyd, William Barrow. *The Barrow Family of Old Louisiana.* Lexington, Ky.: Privately published, 1963.

Flynt, Wayne. "The New Deal and Southern Labor." In *The New Deal and the South,* ed. James C. Cobb and Michael Namorato, 63–96. Jackson: University Press of Mississippi, 1984.

Foner, Eric. *Free Soil, Free Labor, Free Men: The Ideology of the Republican Party before the Civil War,* New York: Oxford University Press, 1970.

Foner, Philip S. *Women and the American Labor Movement: From World War I to the Present.* New York: Free Press, 1980.

Friedman, Jean E. *The Enclosed Garden: Women and Community in the Evangelical South, 1830–1900.* Chapel Hill: University of North Carolina Press, 1985.

Gaston, Paul M. *Women of Fair Hope.* Athens: University of Georgia Press, 1984.

Gilley, B. H. "Kate Gordon and Louisiana Woman Suffrage." *Louisiana History* 24 (Summer 1983): 289–306.

Ginzberg, Lori D. *Women and the Work of Benevolence: Morality, Politics, and Class in the Nineteenth-Century United States.* New Haven: Yale University Press, 1990.

Goldfield, David R. *Black, White, and Southern: Race Relations and Southern Culture, 1940 to the Present.* Baton Rouge: Louisiana State University Press, 1990.

Goldin, Claudia. *Understanding the Gender Gap: An Economic History of American Women.* New York: Oxford University Press, 1990.

Gordon, Lynn. *Gender and Higher Education in the Progressive Era.* New Haven: Yale University Press, 1990.

Grantham, Dewey W. *The Life and Death of the Solid South: A Political History.* Lexington: University Press of Kentucky, 1988.

———. *Southern Progressivism: The Reconciliation of Progress and Tradition.* Knoxville: University of Tennessee Press, 1983.

———. *The South in Modern America: A Region at Odds.* New York: HarperPerennial, 1995.

Green, Elna. "The Rest of the Story: Kate Gordon and the Opposition to the Nineteenth Amendment in the South. *Louisiana History* 33 (Spring 1992): 171–89.

Griffin, Jonie. "'We believe that servility breeds servility . . .': The Classroom Teachers' Federation and Human Rights in New Orleans, 1928–1958," paper presented at Southern Historical Association meeting, Atlanta, November 1991.

Griffith, Robert. *The Politics of Fear: Joseph R. McCarthy and the Senate.* Lexington: University Press of Kentucky, 1970.

Haas, Edward F. *deLesseps S. Morrison and the Image of Reform: New Orleans Politics, 1946–1961.* Baton Rouge: Louisiana State University Press, 1974.

———. "The Illusion of Reform: DeLesseps S. Morrison and New Orleans Politics, 1946–1961." Ph.D. diss., University of Maryland, 1972.

————. "New Orleans on the Half-Shell: The Maestri Era, 1936–1946." *Louisiana History* 13 (Summer 1972): 283–310.

————. *Political Leadership in a Southern City: New Orleans in the Progressive Era, 1896–1902.* Rustin: McGinty Publications, Department of History, Louisiana Tech University, 1988.

Hahn, Steven. *The Roots of Southern Populism: Yeoman Farmers and the Transformation of the Georgia Upcountry.* New York: Oxford University Press, 1983.

Hair, William Ivy. *Bourbonism and Agrarian Protest: Louisiana Politics 1877–1900.* Baton Rouge: Louisiana State University Press, 1969.

————. *The Kingfish and His Realm: The Life and Times of Huey P. Long.* Baton Rouge: Louisiana State University Press, 1991.

Haley, Margaret. "Why Teachers Should Organize: Address to the National Education Association." In *Woman's "True" Profession: Voices from the History of Teaching,* ed. Nancy Hoffman, 289–295. New York: Feminist Press, 1981.

Hall, Jacquelyn Dowd. "Disorderly Women: Gender and Labor Militancy in the Appalachian South." In *Unequal Sisters: A Multi-Cultural Reader in U.S. Women's History,* ed. Ellen Carol DuBois and Vicki L. Ruiz, 298–321. New York: Routledge, 1990.

————. *Revolt against Chivalry: Jessie Daniel Ames and the Women's Campaign Against Lynching.* New York: Columbia University Press, 1979.

Hamby, Alonzo. *Beyond the New Deal: Harry S. Truman and American Liberalism.* New York: Columbia University Press, 1973.

Harris, Barbara J. *Beyond Her Sphere: Women and the Professions in American History.* Westport: Greenwood Press, 1978.

Heleniak, Roman. "Local Reaction to the Great Depression in New Orleans, 1929–1933," *Louisiana History* 10 (Fall 1969): 289–306.

Hewitt, Nancy A. *Women's Activism and Social Change: Rochester, New York, 1822–1872.* Ithaca: Cornell University Press, 1984.

Hill, Mary A. *Charlotte Perkins Gilman: The Making of a Radical Feminist, 1860–1896.* Philadelphia: Temple University Press, 1980.

Hoffman, Nancy. *Women's "True" Profession: Voices from the History of Teaching.* Old Westbury, N.Y.: Feminist Press, 1981.

Honey, Michael K. "Industrial Unionism and Racial Justice in Memphis." In *Organized Labor in the Twentieth-Century South,* ed. Robert H. Zieger, 135–57. Knoxville: University of Tennessee Press, 1991.

————. *Southern Labor and Black Civil Rights: Organizing Memphis Workers.* Urbana: University of Illinois Press, 1993.

Inger, Morton. *Politics and Reality in an American City: The New Orleans School Crisis of 1960.* New York: Center for Urban Education, 1969.

Kemp, Kathryn W. "Jean and Kate Gordon: New Orleans Social Reformers, 1898–1933," *Louisiana History* 24 (Fall 1983): 389–401.

Kerber, Linda K. *Women of the Republic: Intellect and Ideology in Revolutionary America.* Chapel Hill: University of North Carolina Press, 1980.

Kessler-Harris, Alice. *Out to Work: A History of Wage-Earning Women in the United States.* New York: Oxford University Press, 1982.

Klehr, Harvey. *The Heyday of American Communism: The Depression Decade.* New York: Basic Books, 1984.

Kurtz, Michael, and Morgan D. Peoples. *Earl K. Long: The Saga of Uncle Earl and Louisiana Politics.* Baton Rouge: Louisiana State University Press, 1990.

Lebsock, Suzanne. *The Free Women of Petersburg: Status and Culture in a Southern Town, 1784–1860.* New York: W. W. Norton, 1984.

Lemons, J. Stanley. *The Woman Citizen: Social Feminism in the 1920s.* Urbana: University of Illinois Press, 1973.

Lewis, Lionel S. *Cold War on Campus: A Study of the Politics of Organizational Control.* New Brunswick, N.J.: Transaction Books, 1988.

Lindig, Carmen. *The Path from the Parlor: Louisiana Women, 1879–1920.* Lafayette: Center for Louisiana Studies, University of Southwestern Louisiana, 1986.

McCormick, Charles H. *This Nest of Vipers: McCarthyism and Higher Education in the Mundel Affair, 1951–52.* Urbana: University of Illinois Press, 1989.

McCullough, David G. *Truman.* New York: Simon and Schuster, 1992.

Maney, Patrick J. *The Roosevelt Presence: A Biography of Franklin Delano Roosevelt.* New York: Twayne, 1992.

Marsh, Sonora Towles. *The Story of a Good Citizen: Sarah Towles Reed.* New Orleans: Privately published, n.d.

Marshall, F. Ray. *Labor in the South.* Cambridge: Harvard University Press, 1967.

Martin, Theodora Penny. *The Sound of Our Own Voices: Women's Study Clubs, 1860–1910.* Boston: Beacon Press, 1987.

Matthews, Glenna. *The Rise of Public Woman: Woman's Power and Woman's Place in the United States, 1630–1970.* New York: Oxford University Press, 1992.

Mendenhall, Marjorie Stratford. "Southern Women of a 'Lost Generation,'" In *Unheard Voices: The First Historians of Southern Women,* ed. Anne Firor Scott, 92–110. Charlottesville: University of Virginia Press, 1993.

Menn, Joseph Karl. *The Large Slaveholders of Louisiana, 1860.* New Orleans: Pelikan Publishing, 1964.

Merrick, Caroline E. *Old Times in Dixie Land: A Southern Matron's Memories.* New York: Grafton Press, 1901.

Milkman, Ruth. "Women's Work and the Economic Crisis: Some Lessons from the Great Depression," In *A Heritage of Her Own: Toward a New Social History of American Women,* ed. Nancy F. Cott and Elizabeth H. Pleck, 507–541. New York: Simon and Schuster, 1979.

Miller, Arthur. "Why I Wrote *The Crucible.*" *New Yorker* (October 21 and 28, 1996): 158–164.

Mitchell, Guy Clifford. "Growth of State Control of Public Education in Louisiana." Ph.D. diss., University of Michigan, 1942.

Moore, William V. "Civil Liberties in Louisiana: The Louisiana League for the Preservation of Constitutional Rights." *Louisiana History* 31 (Winter 1990): 59–81.

Murphy, Marjorie. *Blackboard Unions: The AFT and the NEA, 1900–1980.* Ithaca: Cornell University Press, 1990.

Navasky, Victor S. *Naming Names.* New York: Viking Press, 1980.

Newman, Joseph W. "Mary C. Barker and the Atlanta Teachers' Union." In *Southern Workers and Their Unions, 1880–1975: Selected Papers, The Second Southern Labor History Conference, 1978,* ed. Merl E. Reed, Leslie S. Hough, and Gary M. Fink, 61–79. Westport, Conn.: Greenwood Press, 1981.

Noble, David W. *The Progressive Mind, 1890–1917.* Minneapolis: Burgess Publishing, 1981.

Norton, Mary Beth. *Liberty's Daughters: The Revolutionary Experience of American Women, 1750–1800.* Boston: Little-Brown, 1980.

Nussbaum, Raymond Oscar Jr. "Progressive Politics in New Orleans, 1896–1900." Ph.D. diss., Tulane University, 1974.

Pells, Richard H. *The Liberal Mind in a Conservative Age: American Intellectuals in the 1940s and 1950s.* New York: Harper and Row, 1985.

——. *Radical Visions and American Dreams: Culture and Social Thought in the Depression Years.* Middletown, Conn.: Wesleyan University Press, 1973.

Ravitch, Diane. *The Troubled Crusade: American Education, 1945–1980.* New York: Basic Books, 1983.

Reed, Linda. *Simple Decency & Common Sense: The Southern Conference Movement, 1938–1963.* Bloomington: Indiana University Press, 1991.

Reid, Robert L., ed. *Battleground: The Autobiography of Margaret A. Haley.* Urbana: University of Illinois Press, 1982.

Reynolds, George M. *Machine Politics in New Orleans, 1897–1926.* New York: Columbia University Press, 1936.

Ringgold, Minnie Ker. *My Ancestors.* Shreveport, La.: Privately published, 1941.

Rosenberg, Rosalind. "The Academic Prism: A New View of American Women." In *Women of America: A History,* ed. Carol Ruth Berkin and Mary Beth Norton. Boston: Houghton Mifflin, 1979.

——. *Beyond Separate Spheres: Intellectual Roots of Modern Feminism.* New Haven: Yale University Press, 1982.

Ryan, Mary P. *Women in Public: Between Banners and Ballots, 1825–1880.* Baltimore: Johns Hopkins Press, 1990.

Salmond, John A. *Miss Lucy of the CIO: The Life and Times of Lucy Randolph Mason, 1882–1959.* Athens: University of Georgia Press, 1988.

Schmuck, Patricia A. "Women School Employees in the United States." In *Women Educators: Employees of Schools in Western Countries,* ed. Patricia A. Schmuck, 75–97. Albany: State University of New York Press, 1987.

Schott, Matthew James. "John M. Parker of Louisiana and the Varieties of American Progressivism." Ph.D. diss., Vanderbilt University, 1969.

Schrecker, Ellen. *The Age Of McCarthyism: A Brief History with Documents.* Boston: St. Martin's Press, Bedford Books, 1994.

———. *No Ivory Tower: McCarthyism and the Universities.* New York: Oxford University Press, 1986.

Scott, Anne Firor. *Making the Invisible Woman Visible.* Urbana: University of Illinois Press, 1984.

———. *The Southern Lady: From Pedestal to Politics 1830–1930.* Chicago: University of Chicago Press, 1970.

Selcraig, James. *The Red Scare in the Midwest, 1945–1955: A State and Local Study.* Ann Arbor: UMI Research Press, 1982.

Sklar, Kathryn Kish. *Florence Kelley and the Nation's Work: The Rise of Women's Political Culture, 1830–1900.* New Haven: Yale University Press, 1995.

———. "Hull House in the 1880s: A Community of Women Reformers." In *Unequal Sisters: A Multi-Cultural Reader in U.S. Women's History,* ed. Ellen Carol DuBois and Vickie L. Ruiz, 109–122. New York: Routledge, 1990.

Smith, Douglas L. *The New Deal in the Urban South.* Baton Rouge: Louisiana State University Press, 1988.

Smith-Rosenberg, Carroll. *Disorderly Conduct: Visions of Gender in Victorian America.* New York: Knopf, 1985.

———. "The Female World of Love and Ritual: Relations between Women in Nineteenth-Century America." *Signs* 1 (Fall 1975): 1–29.

Solomon, Barbara Miller. *In the Company of Educated Women.* New Haven: Yale University Press, 1985.

Sosna, Morton. *In Search of the Silent South: Southern Liberals and the Race Issue.* New York: Columbia University Press, 1977.

Stansell, Christine. *City of Women: Sex and Class in New York, 1789–1860.* Urbana: University of Illinois Press, 1987.

Strachan, Grace C. "Equal Pay for Equal Work: An Argument in Behalf of Women Teachers." In *Woman's True Profession: Voices from the History of Teaching,* ed. Nancy Hoffman, 295–300. New York: Feminist Press, 1981.

Sullivan, Patricia. *Days of Hope: Race and Democracy in the New Deal Era.* Chapel Hill: University of North Carolina Press, 1996.

Swain, Martha A. "The Public Role of Southern Women." In *Sex, Race, and the Role of Women in the South,* ed. Joanne V. Hawks and Sheila L. Skemp, 37–58. Jackson: University Press of Mississippi, 1983.

Tindall, George B. *The Emergence of the New South, 1913–1945.* Baton Rouge: Louisiana State University Press, 1967.

Turner, Pamela Jean. "Civil Rights and Anti-Communism in New Orleans, 1946–1965." M.A. thesis, University of New Orleans, 1981.

Tushnet, Mark V. *The NAACP's Legal Strategy Against Segregated Education, 1925–1950.* Chapel Hill: University of North Carolina Press, 1987.

Tyack, David, and Elisabeth Hansot. *Learning Together: A History of Coeducation in American Schools.* New Haven: Yale University Press, 1990.

Tyack, David, Robert Lowe, and Elisabeth Hansot. *Public Schools in Hard Times: The Great Depression and Recent Years.* Cambridge: Harvard University Press, 1984.

Tyler, Pamela. *Silk Stockings and Ballot Boxes: Women and Politics in New Orleans, 1920–1963.* Athens: University of Georgia Press, 1996.

Urban, Wayne J. "Old Wine, New Bottles? Merit Pay and Organized Teachers." In *Merit, Money and Teachers' Careers: Studies in Merit Pay and Career Ladders for Teachers,* ed. Henry C. Johnson Jr., 25–38, Lanham, Md.: University Press of America, 1985.

———. *Why Teachers Organized.* Detroit: Wayne State University Press, 1982.

Wall, Bennett H., ed. *Louisiana: A History.* Arlington Heights: Forum Press, 1984.

Ware, Susan. *Beyond Suffrage: Women in the New Deal.* Cambridge: Harvard University Press, 1981.

Wedell, Marsha. *Elite Women and the Reform Impulse in Memphis, 1875–1915.* Knoxville: University of Tennessee Press, 1991.

Wells, David Lee. "The ILWU in New Orleans: CIO Radicalism in the Crescent City, 1937–1957." M.A. thesis, University of New Orleans, 1979.

Wheeler, Marjorie Spruill. *New Women of the New South: The Leaders of the Woman Suffrage Movement in the Southern States.* New York: Oxford University Press, 1993.

Wiebe, Robert H. *The Search for Order, 1877–1920.* New York: Hill and Wang, 1967.

Williams, T. Harry. *Huey Long.* New York: Knopf, 1969.

Woloch, Nancy. *Women and the American Experience.* New York: Knopf, 1984.

Zinn, Howard. *Postwar America: 1945–1971.* Indianapolis: Bobbs-Merrill, 1973.

INDEX